Praying for Sheetrock

Praying for Sheetrock

A Work of Nonfiction

Melissa Fay Greene

Addison-Wesley Publishing Company, Inc.

*Reading, Massachusetts Menlo Park, California New York
Don Mills, Ontario Wokingham, England Amsterdam Bonn
Sydney Singapore Tokyo Madrid San Juan
Paris Seoul Milan Mexico City Taipei*

Grateful acknowledgment is made to Silver Jingle Music for permission to reprint previously published excerpts from "The Saga of the Great Sapelo Bust," by Vic Waters. Copyright © 1978 by Vic Waters. All rights reserved. Used by permission.

Library of Congress Cataloging-in-Publication Data

Greene, Melissa Fay.
Praying for sheetrock: a work of nonfiction /
by Melissa Fay Greene.
p. cm.
ISBN 0-201-55048-2
1. McIntosh County (Ga.)—Social conditions. 2. McIntosh County (Ga.)—Politics and government. 3. Corruption (in politics)—Georgia—McIntosh County—History—20th century. 4. McIntosh County (Ga.)—Race relations. 5. Criminal justice, Administration of—Georgia—McIntosh County—History—20th century. 6. Police corruption—Georgia—McIntosh County—History—20th century. 7. Poppell, Thomas Hardwick. 8. Sheriffs—Georgia—McIntosh County—Biography. I. Title.
HN79.G42M354 1991
306'.09758'737—dc20 91-547
CIP

Jacket design © 1991 by Paula Scher
Jacket photograph © 1991 by John Guider
Text design by Janis Owens
Set in 11-point Fairfield Medium by DEKR Corporation, Woburn MA

1 2 3 4 5 6 7 8 9-MA-9594939291

First printing, August 1991

To my mother, Rosalyn Pollock Greene

To my husband's mother and father,
Ruth and Howard Samuel

To my father of blessed memory, Gerald A. Greene

Contents

Part Three

Author's Note

"Glacial epochs are great things, but they are vague, vague," wrote Mark Twain. And so it is with historical epochs.

After the fact, historians may look back upon a season when a thousand lives, a hundred thousand lives, moved in unison; but in the beginning there are really only individuals, acting in isolation and uncertainty, out of necessity or idealism, unaware they are living through an epoch.

McIntosh County, on the flowery coast of Georgia—small, isolated, lovely—experienced the same grand historical tremors and transformations as the rest of America in recent years as long-entrenched authority began to yield to the democratic demands of social and political outsiders.

But in McIntosh, "entrenched authority" was not numberless white men, generals, captains of industry, and vast hierarchies of elected and appointed officials: it was one white man, Sheriff Tom Poppell. And the demands of social outsiders and political newcomers were not expressed by hundreds of eloquent leaders rising from the churches and universities, nor by hundreds of thousands of protesters in the streets: the new demands were worded by one stammering, uneducated, local black man, Thurnell Alston, a disabled boilermaker, standing in front of a hundred quiet country people.

The official history of the civil rights movement is told like a litany at times, as if well-anticipated goals were achieved in a series of distinct and strategic skirmishes: Montgomery, Little Rock, Greensboro, Albany. But it happened in McIntosh County, too. Whether you see the place as a footnote or as the front lines, it happened here, too.

In order to see how it happened—how old Southern political traditions faded into modern times; how the U.S. Constitution eradicated local county customs; how people faced the issues of the day not by race alone, but according to their inner moral compasses—one must drop down to the level of the sidewalks, kitchens, and backyards. What were people saying? Who was saying what? How did their own histories, biases, and perceptions inspire them? And why did an epoch of social change play differently here than in New York or Detroit, Atlanta or Memphis, or in the small county up the road?

This is a chronicle of large and important things happening in a very little place. It is about the end of the good old boy era and the rise of civil rights, and what that famous epoch looked like, sounded like, smelled like, and felt like in a Georgia backwater in the 1970s.

McIntosh County is pretty country and it's got some nice people, but it's the most different place I've ever been to in my life.

—Harry Coursey, GBI Special Agent, Savannah

Prologue

1

June 1971

Two trucks collided on the crisscrossed highways in the small hours of the morning when the mist was thick. The protesting squeal of metal against metal and smashing glass silenced whatever small noises were afoot in the dark county at that hour, the little noises of munching and grunting that arose from the great salt marsh nearby. At seventy miles per hour, the two semitrailers suddenly had found themselves in the coastal lowlands; the black-tops of the rural state routes were slick; and the truck headlights merely illumined the fog from within as if sheets of satin were draped across the road.

The trucks exploded into each other without braking. After that blast of sound and its fallout of hollow chrome pieces dropping onto the road and rolling away, the quietness of the rural county flowed back in, and the muddy sucking and rustling noises arose again from the marsh. The cabs of the big trucks began to burn, pouring their own heavy smoke into the fog.

The McIntosh County Volunteer Fire Department truck arrived first, unfurling a long red scarf of sound on the country roads behind it. It was the night's second accident. The young firemen drenched the burning cabs, while the county ambulance veered into place and departed with the truck drivers. East of Highway 17, the country itself ran out, softening into marsh on its way to the sea.

The county sheriff, awakened by a phone call for the second time that night, stood alone on the highway in the fog and directed cars with a flashlight around the circle of spilled oil and shivered glass. For fifty years before the construction of modern Interstate 95, on the east coast, old U.S. 17 through McIntosh County was the northerners' main route to Florida. Traffic, even in the middle of the night, was fast and constant.

Soon the sun came out of the ocean, the mist dried up, and shrieks of long-necked birds flew back and forth across the breezy morning marshes. The sheriff, a thin, blue-eyed, silver-haired man of fifty, rolled up his sleeves, removed his sunglasses from their case, wiped them with a handkerchief, blotted his face and neck, and prepared for the daylong siege of the white heat of June along Georgia's subtropical coast.

The High Sheriff, Thomas Hardwick Poppell, was five foot nine and 150 pounds, a slender and nattily dressed man in this coastal population of fishermen and lumberjacks. He was a self-made man and was going to die rich. He cursed like a sailor. "He was a little old dried-up fella," said a former state trooper. "He wasn't your typical south Georgia sheriff. He didn't have the pot belly and all that people think of when they think of a south Georgia sheriff. He never dressed the part. He would have on things like white loafers with a pair of bell-bottom slacks during the years when those things were in, a nice-looking pair of bell-bottom slacks. He'd have on an Izod shirt, maybe a white belt. He was a sharp dresser. And of course that hair was just as white as it could be."

"The sheriff could walk in and sit down anywhere in the county," said one local man, "even if it was your own table and it was suppertime."

And others said, "You weren't scared when you saw him coming, but you could feel the power."

Sheriff Tom Poppell, born in McIntosh County in 1921, was

in the midst of a thirty-one-year reign. He had inherited the office from his father, old, cranky, tobacco-chewing Sheriff Ad Poppell, who died in 1948. The sheriff's eighty-year-old mother, Janey Poppell, was the county jailer, lived on the top floor of the city jail, and cooked for the prisoners. The sheriff's sister, Maude Poppell Haggard, was the county clerk, and his brother, A. S. "Junior" Poppell, was clerk of superior court. Sheriff Tom Poppell was to be reelected to office every term until his own death, completing the longest-running sheriff's dynasty in the history of Georgia, and after he died the county commission would try to make his *wife* sheriff.

"If he hadn't died, Tom'd *still* be sheriff," many people said in the 1990s. And others remarked, "Yeah, and he died unindicted."

With daylight Sheriff Poppell knew, and the firefighters knew, and the deputies knew, and the people in the cabins in the surrounding woods knew—and if the truck drivers had realized their trucks had crashed in McIntosh County, Georgia (431 miles of swamp, marsh, and forest: population 7,000) *they* would have known—that it was nearing time for a little redistribution of wealth. It was one of the things for which Tom Poppell was famous across the South. It was one of the things that invariably put the sheriff in an excellent mood.

In midmorning the local black population began to gather at the crash site. They parked their cars down the road near the sheriff's jeep and walked north along the highway, shielding their faces against the spray of steam and ash stirred up by the firefighters. The people chatted as they came. Women wore shoulder bags and immense flowered dresses; men in sleeveless undershirts and beaten old fedoras led small children by the hand. The wreck had occurred at the crossroads called Eulonia in the deeply wooded north end of the county. This had been the dark, rich territory of the black people since the end of the Civil War, when William Tecumseh Sherman himself had waved a pistol at the district and given it to the newly freed slaves. Thus, it was a black crowd which assembled that day. Had the crash occurred fifteen miles to the south, closer to the majority-white county seat of Darien, a white crowd would have gathered.

"Good morning, Sheriff!" called the black women in their musical voices, and he, on the road, unsmilingly raised one hand at a slant to return the greeting.

One of the two wrecked trucks had overturned and spilled its cargo onto the highway, and it was around this unidentified heap of goods that the people congregated. The sheriff watched in the distance as a few black men stopped to straighten out and tear open the tumbled-out cartons and learn what he himself had discovered in the dark that morning: the truck had been transporting shoes. The country people sedately divided up the shoe cartons and opened them with a pop-pop-pop of pulled-apart staples, then passed around the fresh shoe boxes. They hummed with pleasure at the beautiful new shoes—red leather, black leather, green leather—lying two-by-two in tissue paper wrappings. The people stacked the purloined shoe boxes in their arms and walked carefully along the highway back to their cars. They drove home to their cabins and house trailers deep in the pine woods, and sat on benches under the trees, calling for the grandchildren to come try some on, and pointing their toes this way and that.

All day long under a sky like white coals the High Sheriff stood spread-legged on the highway, directing traffic; the road crews swept and shoveled; and hundreds of local families quietly harvested shoes. Some called out, "Thank you, sir!" as they left, and others caught the sheriff's eye and nodded or touched a finger to their hats; and Poppell turned his glittering sunglasses and sunburnt face in their direction, his thin lips a straight white line, and as before raised and dropped one hand in response.

"It was the spirit of fleecing the Yankees that was tolerated by even the law-abiding citizens, I suppose," said Woody Hunter, dean of the Emory University Law School and a former resident of McIntosh. "Tom Poppell was Billy the Kid. He was Robin Hood."

"It wasn't like the sheriff encouraged it," said a former volunteer fireman, a white native of McIntosh who had helped to fight the blazing shoe truck twenty years earlier and had watched the people come for their shoes. "We had the postwar South, the poorest-of-the-poor South right here in McIntosh County. It was the dirt-poor type of people swarmed the place like ants, and Tom wasn't about to stop anybody from getting a pair of shoes."

"The sheriff knew people can't walk a damn straight line," said Archie Davis, owner of a restaurant called Archie's, in Darien. "He wasn't a chain-gang recruiter. You're talking about a time when people had no money. Every one of us, if we'd look back, we'd change things—we'd like a clean slate. I don't know how to say it other than he was a regular person. If someone's house burned, he'd be the first one there to help him.

"He had a lot of charisma. He was the kind of guy you might fight him politically, but when it was over and you were in trouble, he was the first one to help you. You build a base with that—I'm talking local people, 95 percent born and bred here. He didn't walk on water, he was just good people. If you weren't careful, he'd be your best friend."

"He would handle everything just as cool and brilliant, just country brilliance is all I know how to describe it," said a Darien lawyer. "Amazing what he could get done with a couple of phone calls. Now the court system is full of all sorts of little junk, but back then the sheriff was judge, jury, and monarch. He'd help a young man out of trouble the first time. But then a lot of people he flat run out of the county because they wouldn't abide by his law. We lived under Poppell's Law, I guess you'd say. He just wrote his own law."

In 1971, Tom Poppell was a dinosaur, the last of his kind. Statewide observers called him "the last of the old-time political bosses in Georgia." Georgia State Troopers, Georgia Bureau of Investigation agents, FBI agents, DEA agents, and U.S. Customs agents up and down the southern coast all agreed with the words of a Brunswick police detective: "The only crime that *existed* in McIntosh County was Tom Poppell's. He was the last of the great old-time High Sheriffs."

2

The shoe truck was not the first wrecked or sabotaged truck on Highway 17 to be looted under the supervision of the McIntosh County Sheriff's Department, nor was it the last truck or even the best, but it was a fine truck and is fondly remembered.

It *was* the first crash site attended by a local black man named Thurnell Alston, who trudged among the others that day and filched a few shoes. He was a boilermaker living with his wife and children in a narrow cinder-block house ten yards from U.S. 17. He was a tall, thin, chain-smoking black man with bushy, blue-black hair; a long, rather sorrowful face; slate-black skin; and elegant, long hands. He had lived in McIntosh County all his life, and was related by blood or marriage to probably a third of the black community there.

Before the decade was out, Thurnell Alston was advanced by the black community to challenge the rule of Sheriff Poppell. But on that summer day in 1971, with politics the last thing on his mind, Thurnell idly drifted alongside his neighbors north on U.S. 17 to the overturned truck and rummaged through the boxes. "Sure I got shoes, we all got shoes," he said. "Word just got out there was a truck wrecked in our area. People coming by with shoes. Guys had boxes of shoes all in the woods: 'Come get you a pair of shoes!'

"'Where you get them from?'

"'Man, they got a whole truckload down there!'"

"There was always some truck wrecking down there," he said. "The people around McIntosh get all the benefits from it. All our lives, people always saying, 'Hey, the sheriff give this to me!' These people haven't been nowhere else. The sheriff just really had them hoodwinked. They're just ignorant to what's going on. When there's somebody the sheriff wants elected, you know, you see him and his mother riding around. And these older black people say, 'There go Miss Janey! There go the sheriff! How you doing, Miss Janey? How you doing, Sheriff?' And all this is for votes. The people here were just happy with nothing. It was a plantation mentality. The sheriff was running this county just like an old plantation."

McIntosh County citizens remember fondly not only the shoe truck but trucks full of canned goods, fresh produce and meats, building materials and tools, cookies and cakes, candy and guns, and once, fur stoles and fur coats. All of the cargoes disappeared, and the trucking companies were compelled to report "total loss" to their insurance carriers. "Anything trucks be carrying from Miami to New York, from New York to Miami," said Thurnell Alston, "whatever it was, whatever of value was in those trucks during those times, that's probably in McIntosh County right now today."

Years after the movement for civil equality between the races began to transform the rest of the South, news of it barely had filtered into McIntosh County. In 1971 McIntosh County was a majority-black county with virtually 100 percent black voter registration. Yet the residents had never elected a black person to the mayor's office, the county commission, the city council, or the school board; had never seen a black person appointed to any governing board or selected for grand jury or trial jury service; had not elected a black to state government since the end of Reconstruction; and had not seen any black person hired by any local employer above the level of unskilled laborer, maid, or cook. The black residents saw their children bussed past the white school to an all-black school furnished with used supplies and outdated textbooks.

At the time of the shoe truck in 1971, the black community of McIntosh County was blind and deaf to issues of civil equality, equal employment, and local corruption. On the day of the shoe truck, the people were still years away from balking at Sheriff Poppell's authority. On that day their minds were otherwise occupied. On that day the people had new shoes to try on.

Part One

You can't learn anything riding down 1-95 with the Yankees. You've got to go the old way, 17, what **we** *call the old way.*

—Sonny Seiler, Savannah attorney

One

The Old Way

1

U.S. 17 was an old blacktop two-lane running down the Georgia coast at sea level, never straying far from the edge of the continent.

In Savannah it was a dirty liquor street swelling at dusk with honking cars double-parked outside the package stores. Pawnshops closed for the night, dropping latticed chains over their windows, and bail bondsmen opened for business: shirtsleeved men half-seated on desktops waited with crossed arms for the black rotary-dial phones to start ringing. On their walls hung hand-printed signs like, "It's always SPRINGtime at Bulldog Bonding."

Further south, on the outskirts of Savannah, the old highway was lined by mobile home dealerships. Further south still, people *lived* in the mobile homes, set back from the road with chickens and rusty swingsets in the yards, and the nearby businesses were auto junkyards. Further south, used merchandise was sold out of abandoned barns the people called "flea markets." Miss Nellie's Hidden Treasures displayed, at roadside, Mexican vases, shoe boxes of old vacuum cleaner attachments, gold-framed paintings of bullfights or of Elvis on black velvet, dilapidated playpens, and cast-iron black-faced jockeys in their simpering crouch.

In Liberty County and Chatman County, commerce dwindled to the occasional peach or Vidalia onion stand. In midsummer, corn filled the fields and laundered sheets and overalls stiffened on clotheslines outside the sharecropper shacks. One last bit of trade before the road rolled south into the deep country was Mama Harris, Palm Reader. Then Highway 17 dove into the great dark pine forests of McIntosh County.

Wild turkeys, foxes, quail, and deer crunched across a pine needle floor for a hundred miles. Woodpeckers darted among the upper branches like small red arrows in the green light. The old highway lay peacefully abandoned, soft and yellow as a footbridge baking in the summer heat while box turtles scraped across it. Vultures stood on it in a circle like gaunt old card players: tall, cackling cronies with bony shoulders, divvying up the pot.

Occasionally a brontosaurlike lumber truck erupted from a side road, spraying gravel, belching smoke, and brainlessly sashaying down the center line. It drove the felled slash pine north to the port and to the pulp and paper mills of Savannah—Union Camp was the largest paper mill in the world—or south to the turpentine and paper plants of Brunswick. In both cities a sulfurous haze, the industrial rotten-egg odor of jobs, clouded the in-town neighborhoods; but in McIntosh County, where the forests grew, the water tasted like cold stones and the air was clean and piney.

Gradually, to the east, the forest broke open, then disappeared, replaced by vast soft acres of salt marsh. Four hundred thousand acres of marsh stretched between the dry land and the barrier islands of McIntosh County—at some places, a mile wide; at others, ten miles wide. The primeval home of every shy and ticklish, tentacle-waving form of sea life and mud life, the coastal Georgia salt marsh is one of Earth's rare moist and sunny places where life loves to experiment. Because it is flushed out twice daily by the systole of saltwater tide and diastole of alluvial tide, the marsh looks new, as if still wet from creation.

The wetland has been claimed in various epochs by prehistoric Indians, Spanish missionaries, Blackbeard the pirate, French and English explorers, Sir Francis Drake, slaveholders and slaves,

Confederates and Yankees, the victorious General Sherman, freed slaves, and unreconstructed Rebels. Citizens at the edge of the dry land have addressed one another as Monsignor, Excellency, Governor, General, Mistress, Master, Nigger. Furies inspiring men to violence have occurred at the marsh's edge, while in its midst the frogs simply continued to blow their round bass notes. Mastodons once claimed the coast, too, and gigantic pigs and ground sloths the size of elephants; and they all have gone.

Once or twice a century, men stood up on their hind legs beside the swamp and waved their arms—the crown of the evolution of the shy tentacled sea creatures—and swelled with the thought of their own self-importance. A shouted word flew for miles, out to sea, and a gunshot echoed farther than that. The men who raised their voices, flashed their whips, fired their muskets or their revolvers, and imposed their own sense of order on their neighbors found it remarkably easy to do so. Just after the shout or the gunshot, there was silence; then the clicking of the fiddler crabs began again, and the people in their houses scraped their dishes clean and buttoned up their children and chopped wood into logs in their backyard and fed their dogs. So the strong men raised their voices again, fired their weapons, and again, rising to fill the vacuum of silence were not voices of protest or discontent but the sound of clicking, scraping, chopping. Thus, through minor heroics, brashness, and noise on one side, everyday life on the other, local heroes and strongmen arose.

In modern times Sheriff Poppell was the neighborhood headman who exerted his will and shaped the county, and the people acquiesced as people do when they are not, themselves, hungry for power and when they are permitted to make a nice living far from the rumpus. With Poppell as sheriff, McIntosh County was not the sleepy backwater it ought to have been, nor Darien the homey one-horse town it richly deserved to be. Darien—population 1,800—consisted in 1971 of a few public office buildings, a few All-U-Can-Eat catfish restaurants, the county courthouse, a library, some hardware stores, an eighteenth-century British fort, a car wash, and a wide, hot main street—U.S. 17. But the place was jumping. Expensive cars with unsavory drivers roared through town, jeweled rings sparkled on men's hands as they cracked open their boiled crabs at lunch; gunfire rang out; and one sensed, in sheds off the road, the late-night shuffle of fifty-dollar bills. From the late 1940s through the late 1970s, McIntosh County was a mini–Las Vegas, a mini–Atlantic City, a southern Hong Kong or Bangkok where white men came looking for, and found, women, gambling, liquor, drugs, guns, sanctuary from the law, and boats available for smuggling.

Next door to these fearsome enterprises, just down the road from them, a straight-thinking, churchgoing white community attended to its civic needs in Darien; and a watchful, churchgoing black community made do in nameless hamlets in the pine woods. Sheriff Poppell amiably kept the peace between the black and white communities and between the law-abiding world and the criminals. From his illegal businesses and the looting of trucks, he tossed the occasional bonus to the law-abiding Darien whites and rural blacks. For most of this century, there was a strange racial calm in the county, consisting in part of good manners, in part of intimidation, and in part because the Sheriff cared less about the colors black and white than he did about the color green, and the sound it made shuffled, dealt out and redealt, folded and pocketed beside the wrecked trucks and inside the local truckstop, prostitution houses, clip joints, and warehouse sheds after hours.

Half the population of McIntosh was white and most of the whites lived in Darien. They lived in soft blue, pale green, or yellow wooden houses, with birdbaths and day lilies in the yard. The aluminum of their screen doors was cut in the shape of marsh birds and tall grasses. "People grew up together on these dirt streets fishing and hunting," said Archie Davis. "This was just small-town America. Four or five kids come playing down the street; the grownups knew all of them, knew their daddies."

Emily Varnedoe, a white woman of ninety, had lived in a little house beside the salt marsh most of her life. In the silences after a raised voice or a gunshot flew over the county—as strong men took over McIntosh and steered it this way rather than that—it was such as Emily Varnedoe who shrugged and continued to stir the greens in the saucepan, to repot the geraniums, to tuck in the child, and to settle herself under an afghan in front of the TV, knowing nothing of bullies and race and shoot-em-ups.

She lived quietly and cheerfully, hands crossed in her lap, looking through her windows across the yellow grass sloping toward the water. As she grew old, Emily mused more and more often on one or two things, an old fact and a recent fact, and it consumed a good deal of her day—seated in a chair, clinging to its arms with all her might—just to consider and reconsider these one or two things, not analyze them in their different aspects or wish they had been done differently; no, just bring them to the forefront of thought and make sure that the facts of each case were still arranged correctly.

Mrs. Varnedoe's son, Jesse, went to North Georgia College where he met his wife, Glenda. This was one of the facts of Emily's life which ceaselessly occupied her thoughts. "He went to North Georgia College, he and his wife, but they both told us they would never marry until they graduated," she said. "And so they both graduated before they married. They live in Tampa now. He sells insurance and she worked in the insurance office, and then she left and now she is working in a real estate office. And she says there are forty people working in that office and that's a lot! But they waited to marry, don't you know, until after they could graduate."

When Mrs. Varnedoe finished a statement her jaws moved for a moment more, thoughtfully and silently, and then she looked at you to see what you made of it, offering, in case there had been any misunderstanding: "I sent him. I paid for him to go to North Georgia College. He went there and finished up there, he and the girl he married. And he said they would not marry until they both graduated." A framed photograph of the crewcut college boy leaned backward on the mother's small television, and one would have thought the happy twin events, graduation and marriage (they didn't marry until after they graduated) had just taken place, but Jesse (North Georgia College, 1957) was fifty-four.

Emily Varnedoe's face was like a cream-colored, stained velvet bag, with a drawstring at the pursed lips. Her lips pushed out even in repose, as if to show that this was a garrulous woman who had learned to be silent—had learned that no one out there was available to listen to all her opinions.

"It's quiet over here except for the hummingbird season," she said. What great stillness is possible in a life when a person is distracted from her thoughts by hummingbirds in the yard! Does she lean forward and pound on the glass: "Hey, pipe down out there fellas!"? She sat, lips pursed, hands folded, looking toward the marsh, waiting for the hummingbirds.

There were white people in Darien who knew from which antebellum plantation family they were descended and black people who knew the location of the plantations that had owned their great-grandparents; there were close and long-time connections between the two communities unlike anything in the North. All political discourse and confrontations in McIntosh County would take place between acquaintances: when angry groups of blacks and whites faced each other, everyone would know everyone else's names and addresses, and know their mamas.

Because the whites got to McIntosh first, or "first" in relation to the McIntosh blacks, history itself was laid claim to, as if it were acreage of good bottom land. There were native Americans all along the tangled coast in the sixteenth century when the wooden sailing ships first appeared, but the Europeans killed or converted the local tribes and pushed their way into town long before sending for the Africans.

Permanent settlement first was established along the Altamaha River in 1736 by a troop of Scottish Highland warriors who built a British outpost against the Spaniards in Florida. A second embarkation from Scotland landed in 1742. The name *McIntosh* derived from the leading clan of pioneers.

The colonial history is treasured in Darien. The history of the conquest and settlement of McIntosh is as full of nobility, strife, malaria, starvation, alligators, true love, and Indian wars as any student of history could wish. History, in fact, is what Darien has the way other communities have rich topsoil or a wealth of hidden talent or fine high school athletics. Coastal people understand history personally, the way religious people do, the way ancient people did. They own history in a way lost to most Americans except in a generic, national sort of way, because the rest of us move around so much, intermarry, adopt new local loyalties, and blur the simple narrative line.

Hundreds of direct descendants of the early Scottish settlers of McIntosh still live on the very tracts of land given their families by King George II at the first embarkation in 1736 or at the second in 1742. "We've always known where we were from," said Gay Jacobs, a strong and pretty, black-eyed and amiable liberal Democrat who lived at the waterfront and ran a shrimp business. "I mean this is still part of the original land grant that my—I don't know what, how many greats back—was given. I think my family has always felt a certain responsibility to do right. About politics, about racial issues, to do right and to be right."

The Direct Descendants, as they are actually known, periodically hold reunions at the public library or in one another's homes. They wear corsages and name tags, sip punch, and listen to edifying lectures by speakers dispatched from the Savannah Historical Society. One-hundred-eighty descendants of the two McIntosh clans who landed in 1736 and founded Darien still are living. "One-hundred-eighty if no one was born or died in the last three weeks," piped up Lillian Schaitberger, a sixty-nine-year-old descendant of Donald McIntosh. She is both the treasurer of the Lower Altamaha Historical Society and the person responsible for periodically updating the list of the true and living Direct Descendants from the *first,* not the second, embarkation. "I have had people to get upset," said Schaitberger: "'If you're *going* to do it, why not do *everybody*?' one woman told me. She was a descendant, you see, of the *second* landing in 1742. I told her, 'If you'd read the booklet closely, you'd have seen it listed the descendants of the first landing only.'"

It *was* a fine and difficult thing the Highland settlers did, living alert and armed against a Spanish enemy mounted on heavy horses (wearing feathers, high boots, and sashes in military gaiety) who charged up the coast toward the Scottish cornfields and cabins, their muskets leveled and the hooves of the horses smashing along the surf. It required physical courage for the Scots to remain on the land, to hoe, to plant, to carry water, to bear children, to believe in the community while, in the distance, there were horses.

It is quite another thing to survive into modern times when a new definition of community is required, to admit that within your town there are households that define themselves—that *you* define—as outsider, alien. Does Darien belong to the Direct Descendants alone (even generously counting the descendants of the second embarkation as bona fide DDs)? Does it belong to the Direct Descendants and their kind (for some had great-great-grandfathers planting fields in Virginia and the Carolinas, after all)? Or does it belong to more people—to more kinds of people—than that? To ask this question requires a moral courage.

But the Direct Descendants and their fellow white citizens prefer to muse on an older and clearer time, a time of wood forts and musketry, of tall ships and cannons, of kilts and bagpipes, of enemies fleeing pell-mell out of the marsh. Contrary to stereotype, they are not nostalgic for the plantation era, though Darien was one of the jewels in the crown of the Confederacy and its planters among the richest and most refined gentlemen in the world. They do not honor slavery or mourn its passing. They honor the time *before* slavery, before Africans touched foot on the land beside the Altamaha River. They wish the question had never come up.

Two

Off the Road and Far From Money

1

Half the population of McIntosh was black, and most of the blacks inhabited the semitamed land between the shoreline of salt marsh and the fringes of the great southern pine forests. They still lived in slave or sharecropper shacks—"made out of wood and wind," the people said—or in trailers on dirt roads that disappeared into the pine woods or in simple cinder-block houses, like Thurnell Alston's, facing U.S. 17.

The historic black community of McIntosh lived in a sort of pale outside a century of American progress and success. They survived by raising vegetables and keeping chickens and pigs, by working menial jobs in Darien, and by fishing the network of tidewater rivers and blackwater swamps. They lived without plumbing, telephones, hot water, paved roads, electricity, gas heat, or air conditioning into the 1970s. Their tiny hamlets (Darien was the county's only town) offered no goods and services other than a nailed-together church, a rundown laundromat, a juke joint, a beautician working out of her side porch, a palm reader, and maybe a "shine house."

The white people owned and managed all the businesses in Darien—all the restaurants, motels, antique stores, grocery and hardware stores, and docks, as well as nearly all the boats and all but one gas station. And they filled every elected, appointed, salaried, and professional office and position. (Sheriff Tom Poppell, however, for reasons of his own, had employed black deputies since the forties.)

By daylight, during work hours, black people traveled south on U.S. 17 into Darien: they swept sidewalks, mopped floors, mowed lawns, diapered babies, cooked home meals, cooked restaurant meals, cooked school cafeteria lunches, cleaned motel rooms, pumped gas, raised children, washed and ironed clothing, collected garbage, caught and processed seafood, cut pulpwood, taught black children, and prepared black dead for burial. At the end of the day in a soft migration like birds lifting off a lawn at dusk, they drove or walked home to their distant wooded lots.

"You know there was fear," said Sammie Pinkney, a local black man and friend of Thurnell Alston. "You can't get a dog to go up against a tiger. Nineteen-forties, -fifties, and -sixties, it was nothing for them to take a man out and beat him half to death. Or beat him *to* death. Or hang him. And nothing was ever said."

In 1971 the epic of the civil rights movement was still a fabulous tale about distant places to the black people of McIntosh. The small black community followed the career of Martin Luther King, Jr., but no one among them had ever met him or seen him in person. An elderly black couple, Danny and Belle Thorpe, recalled feeling fearful when King and his civil rights movement began stirring things up: "We hear the people telling about it and all," the old couple said, "and we didn't know how things was coming out. Far away it seemed, not like something happening here. And he never have come here. He come there to Atlanta and as far south as South Carolina but never have come here." And then King was assassinated and was mourned by scarlet-robed rural church choirs swaying and weeping and clapping in unison on their wood podiums. In mourning him from their great distance, the black people of McIntosh helped to bury him. A funeral was a thing they understood; dissent was something they did not.

In the era of the shoe truck, the faces of Martin Luther King, Jr., John F. Kennedy, and Robert F. Kennedy adorned the cardboard fans that waved like marsh grasses in the stifling clapboard churches in the summer heat; on the flip side of the fans were portraits of Jesus. In their homes, the black people nailed pen-and-ink drawings of King and the Kennedys to their walls, usually flanking a large framed painting of the Last Supper. Ministers preached about "Martin, Robert, and John," who might as well have been the thirteenth, fourteenth, and fifteenth Apostles, respectively. They were martyrs, saints. Martin Luther King might have delivered the "I Have a Dream" speech dressed in flowing white robes, so hallowed and remote did his life appear to McIntosh County. The people felt about Montgomery and Selma roughly the way they felt about Mount Sinai and Gethsemane. The stories of heroes were stirring, but it seemed unlikely that such miracles would occur again, much less locally.

The black community of McIntosh was so isolated that, like a few others on America's southern coast, its language was distinctive and was called Gullah, a unique blend of eighteenth-century English, Scottish, and African tongues with modern Black English. The old people in particular spoke this rich brogue. Because the people lived far from any city, and because the old people and the middle-aged people had grown up without television and had as their chief form of entertainment the bombastic and vividly euphemistic preachings of the local home-schooled ministers, their speech was full of original and biblical-sounding constructions.

A Georgia peach, a real Georgia peach, a backyard great-grandmother's-orchard peach, is as thickly furred as a sweater, and so fluent and sweet that once you bite through the flannel, it brings tears to your eyes. The voices of the coastal people were like half-wild and lovely local peaches, compared to the bald, dry, homogeneous peaches displayed at a slant in the national chain supermarkets.

"Come in! Come in! Let's have some gossip and slander!" cried an old man living near the sea, whenever a passerby roamed within sight of his porch. "I believe these young ladies of today might clothe themselves more modestly," he said. "Of course, I am getting on and it has been many years since I was conversant with the wherewithal and nomenclature of the female."

For most of this century the McIntosh County black people lived much as they had since emancipation. They relied on the Lord, the sheriff, and the neighbors. "In Grandfather's day," said Henry Curry, a gentle and elegant man in his nineties, the patriarch of the black community and a church deacon, "they didn't have the education, but here what 'tis: If you had any trouble, your trouble is my trouble. Someone get down sick, it be a crowd to that house twenty-four hours, bring food and stay there, look to the welfare of that individual. A few of them work the river, but the majority live off that farm. If I get a little bit back and yours is ahead, you come over and help me bring mine on up. If you didn't have a place to live, you could sleep out there in the woods." Curry remembered the assassination of President McKinley from his boyhood because a black man had caught the killer and the people had felt proud.

"Back then," he said in a deep, slow, rich, and patient voice, "Tuesday night, be a crowd to the church. Thursday night, sexton ring that bell, be a crowd to the church. Sunday morning, be a crowd. Those folks had something to thank the Lord for. Back then, not fancy, one person could live off a dollar and a half a week. You could get sugar for six cents a pound, bacon for five cents, grits you get a big sack, nine cents a sack. All the way from one end of the year to another, you could kill four or five hogs, get bacon year-round, three or four them big cans of lard. Rice, when time to harvest rice, had to move the old rice out of the way. You could get on fine. Folks was happy, didn't cost so much to live."

"We were raised not to mix," said Belle Thorpe in 1990, a grandmotherly, bewigged, perfumed, and powdered church woman who lived in the part of the black county called Crescent.

"As a boy, I felt that as a race we should stay in our place," said Danny Thorpe, her husband, an elderly shrimp fisherman and deacon of his church, a once tall and loose-limbed man.

The two delicate beige-skinned elderly people moved slowly and gingerly, fearful of falling, through the crowded rooms of their tiny, hot house, with its exterior siding of roof shingles and its hard, cool dirt yard where clumps of wildflowers bloomed. Belle had a high, whiny voice and a way of saying yes when she meant no, dragging the word out, as in, "Well, Yeeeeessss," her voice dipping down and back up, describing a large U of sound. She fussed with her appearance for many hours before leaving the house, adjusting the smooth black wig, the lacy blouse, the satin slip, the broad expanse of elastic-waisted flowered skirt, hoping, by her pleasing and modest appearance, not to give offense, not to presume.

He had a long, misshapen, grizzled, and unshaved head, a low soft voice, and a demeanor as humble as his wife's. Kindly, sweetly, gently, and in great poverty, they had lived together for fifty years.

"I don't see much difference in him," said Belle Thorpe. "He was always industrious. He was a deacon and I was singing in the choir. He just say, well, he wanted a Christian woman, so we just fell in love. So we always be thinking one thing."

"She hasn't done much changing either," said the deacon. "She always was nice looking, I'll say that to her face. Behind her back I'll say it too: she was always nice looking. And that's my reason, I guess, I fell in love with her."

Glancing shyly at each other, he frowned and she laughed, and then they looked straight ahead again. They looked like a black version of Grant Wood's *American Gothic.*

They both had obeyed their early instructions about race and had taken care throughout their lives not to forget their place in the world, the place that had been drilled into them in earliest childhood. No memory remained of a time when they were anything to the world other than colored. With Deacon Thorpe the natural liveliness of childhood had been drained away under the attrition of somber warnings and replaced with a humility and submission that promoted survival but undermined good judgment. His one secret rebellion—and he may surely be forgiven it—is his refusal to consider that his forebears must have been slaves. "Both of us born and raised in the county," said Danny of himself and his wife. "Parents and grandparents born in Darien, all of them. No they wasn't any slaves. They weren't slaves. I'm quite confident they come in since slaves."

"We always did get along, you know, with the white race," said Mrs. Thorpe, "because we thought each race should stay, you know, where they are."

"We didn't mix at that time," said Deacon Thorpe.

"My sister was a cook to Archie Davis Cafeteria," she said. "And if I go there and want anything, she couldn't hand it through the front door, see. You have to go around to the back. Things is different now. We *all* could go there and sit to the table together now and eat together. I've eaten at Archie's. And any cafeteria around here you can go right on in there and sit there. My grandson took us to the Ramada Inn last Thursday night. He came down from New York and he say, 'I'm going to take you all out to dinner!' and took us over to the Ramada Inn in Brunswick. And we had the nicest food and the waitress was white and she was just as nice as she could be. Now see, one time you couldn't go in there. And now all the whites and all of us is all sitting around. If you carry yourself in a nice way, then the whites, they won't mind mixing with you because they see that you are trying to be somebody. You go in these places and act just as intelligent as the whites."

"Racism is pretty much gone out of my life," said Deacon Thorpe. "I get along with them so good and so forth. God make us both, both races, and I feel I'm just as good as the other man. It was broken down and we started mixing. We sit right in there and eat together and everything. I don't find no fault with the other race. But of course I feel that I'm black and I ought to stay with my black race. Because if I didn't, I then get beside myself and I be mixing with the white folks, and maybe I separate from my wife and go marry some of them. I don't want to do that. No."

The two of them sat musing, shyly and still in love. Mrs. Thorpe sat smiling and Deacon Thorpe frowning at the prospect of his abandoning her to go live the high life with marriageable white women. That was, of course, the Great White Fear, and they were not going to start questioning it now. Still, the deacon, a religious man in his high-eighties, in fragile health, . . . nevertheless, he would watch himself.

2

There is a moment in Autumn when the leaves still curling on the trees and the leaves which have fallen are in equilibrium: dry gold pools spreading under gold-crested oaks. Then the yards and the forest floor seem to mirror the treetops, as if all the trunks rose out of ankle-deep water on which a palette of red-gold leaves reflected. Then the old women in the county bang down their windows and bend to twist the keys of their space heaters; the tall wood rooms fill with the woolly heat; and the old women get back in bed, groaning. The old men draw on long-sleeve flannel shirts, one on top of another, and let their whiskers coarsen. They eat nearly-burnt toast over a paper towel on the kitchen table, and drink a glass of tap water. The wives, after a time, get up, knot their robes, and shuffle into the kitchen, smelling of Mentholatum.

"You eat?"

"Yep."

"Well lemme cook." The old wives swing iron skillets up onto the gas burners, and bacon hisses in the heat.

The flawless autumn sky is lit from below by the fiery treetops. The trees could be snapping candle flames, the ground a bright tablecloth, and the sky a blue porcelain platter. If the Messiah were to arrive today, this cloudless, radiant county would be magnificent enough to receive Him. It is quiet. From the pine woods comes the high, continuous growl of a buzz saw, and on the dirt roads crows pace and argue. If the Messiah did arrive today, the old black people of McIntosh would be the *least* astonished group in America. They might send a young person to go look, and those with telephones might call their daughters, but the rest would remain in their upholstered rockers near their space heaters with their quilts across their laps, finish their coffee and their Bible chapters, and wait to be called upon Personally.

Then there would be ancient cookies in dusty tins extracted from high closet shelves, and teacups trembling on a proffered tray, and lamps carried up front from the bedrooms and plugged in, and a dozen more amenities until the Guest has had a moment to look around and have a sip of tea. Then there would come the complaints: "Did y'all have to cause my Raymond to lose that job back in '81? You know he was fixing to change his habits, and he never did make good after that"—the big women aproned, standing, hands on hips; the men shushing them, embarrassed, but swinging around to hear the reply nonetheless. "Excuse me, Lord, but my old Buick only had eighty thousand miles on it. You couldn't have given me another year out of it?"

The old people of McIntosh County have lived on close, practical, and well-understood terms with God all their lives, a matter of some seventy, eighty, or ninety years. If a messenger of God were to appear on their porch one morning, there'd be no awkwardness of address, no groping for greetings of sufficient splendor, no fumbling for religious rituals last exercised in childhood, and no exaggerated prostration either: "Gertie?! Angel of the Lord's here!"

The old people understand that God may work in subtle, or even inscrutable ways, but they expect justice in exchange for a lifetime's devotion. And they wouldn't mind, at least occasionally, actual manifestations of the divine will. God's presence, gently moving over McIntosh County, summoned by the old people's prayers, tends to deliver. There has been a just and gritty exchange of good deeds and rewards, and of strayings from the path of righteousness and punishments. What the people sow, in due time they are likely to reap. If they pay attention, the world glitters with God's lessons all around them. And when, in the 1970s, the white people invoked history, the black people, packing their churches, called out to God.

For most of this century, the patriarch of the black community was Henry Curry, a shrimp fisherman and the deacon of a church, the son of a former slave. He died in 1989 at the age of 101. Henry Curry spent his adult life on the water, contemplating the life of McIntosh County from a distance, from east of it. He loved the water. A handful of black men a generation before him had owned their own boats, but not his father, born a slave, who farmed all his life and died in a rotten cabin, nor all his cousins, brothers, and neighbors, who dredged crop after meager crop from the ground. He was, in his last decade, a thin, powdery black-skinned man with a long, narrow skull and blue rheumy eyes. He spoke in a deep, slow, rich voice, a voice that survived with all its resonance and integrity long after the elderly man had begun to cave in around it. All the moral courage and clarity of the proud man poured into his voice at the end, like dark wine from a crystal beaker into a crystal wine glass.

Curry lived with his wife in a tiny, immaculate, sealed-up house, in four rooms so still that the softly falling sun motes in the dining room seemed to *ping*! when they touched the polished table. He sat in an armchair by the front window of the white wooden house, facing the white sand road that connected U.S. 17 to the water. His long fingers wiggled in his lap as he stared straight ahead. He knit fishing nets: a loose-weave net for sale to outsiders, but for his friends, the tight-weave poor man's net "that'll snare every living thing."

"This place here belongs to my wife," said the old man, married since 1912. "Anyplace where she's contented, I'm contented, and when she gets discontented, I'm discontented too. We met in June 1912. We were married in December 1912. That were intended from the Beginning. But I believe that we don't know folks, we're acquainted with them. There's always something in an individual you ain't never going to know. Look at Samson and *his* wife. If he'd a-known her, think he'd have let that trap catch him? I been with her sixty-six years and I still don't know her feelings underneath. We're *acquainted* with one another. We know one another to an *extent*. That's my belief about it."

Occasionally the full-grown adopted sons of the Currys visited. These three bulky men, the natural sons of Mrs. Curry's niece, seemed to duck when they entered the front door and to squeeze themselves through the doorways between the rooms. When they pounded along the vinyl runner from the front door to the kitchen, all the china and glassware in the prim wooden cabinets began to chime and vibrate. And after the kindhearted men had screwed back on the missing knob on the stove or tightened a loose switch plate, they jiggled the change and car keys in their pockets, shouted a few words of parting, and slammed the door. Then the two shy, dry, sweet old people seemed to chime and vibrate themselves, as they tremblingly found their own paths on the vinyl runner and pedaled slowly along it back to their armchairs.

"Back in my folks' time, it was slaves," said Deacon Curry. "My father were born in 1848. There were three sisters of him that had good experience of slave time. A slave couldn't go anywhere lessen he had a permit and the three of them lived seven mile apart. They run away. The white men caught them and whipped them back. But I never did hear my father speak of it. After he became a man, he was independent. He was working for himself. That all he ever did. He wasn't subject to nobody. After he become a man, I'm quite confident he wasn't subject to nobody."

Henry had been raised to sharecrop. As a young man, he studied the families standing ankle deep in fields adjoining his: tied up in rainbows of kerchiefs, bandannas, and aprons, faces and eyes numbed by dust, they sent even the smallest children stomping between the rows to scare birds, and they tied aprons with pockets around the slightly bigger children and taught them to pick cotton. Sometimes a remark or a joke traveled from field to field, inspiring a moment of upright posture and laughter; sometimes an old woman, bent over, wailed out an old slave song they all knew—beginning a line or two in, having sung to that point in her mind—and they'd all pick it up, a sort of minor-key moaning, the hoes falling in unison. To Curry, the young man, they all stood desolately midstream in a slow, flat, brown river they'd never get across.

His generation was the first freeborn generation. Still, he knew what it was to wake and learn that a neighbor had been surprised coming home late and alone the night before, and lynched. He knew hunger. He knew the suffocation of field labor. He distrusted the land because no matter how sincerely the people tapped at its surface, it never enriched them. He drowned himself in work. He whipped his hands through the cotton plants until his palms shone, and he knelt, harvesting potatoes or peas, until standing up at day's end dizzied him. As soon as he was able, he ran from that work. Not that farming itself demeaned the people, but the economics of the sharecropping arrangement was humiliating, keeping the people virtually bound to the land and to the land's owner. And when he went to sea and faced a vast, bright solitude, blue sky and cold water, he thanked God with such a shock of gratitude and grief that he never got over it. He took to worshipping God inwardly all the time, seeing God's work everywhere, now that His servant was seaborne and upright and paid no man rent.

"I had a man once, working with me from Sapelo Island," he said. "We were working for R. J. Reynolds [the white tobacco millionaire], and I was supposed to pick up my man down at the riverfront at night. Well, Reynolds said I couldn't go down to his dock at night. With all he had, and me being a poor man, I couldn't go to his dock at night. 'Stay away from my dock!' he says. With all he got. Now the dock is right there and *he* gone. *Been* gone. We don't carry nothing. The Bible strictly tell us: There's nothing we bring in and nothing we going to carry. Live happy while we're here, these one or two years; it don't take long for a lifetime to pass.

"If you had every dollar that's in Georgia, you'd have a pile of money! Would you fare any better than you is now? No, because tonight you can go home and lay down and sleep and be contented.

If you had all that money you couldn't sleep, worrying to death, 'This one's going to grab it,' or 'That one's going to grab it!' I say, sleep well and leave it.

"What I want is to live in a state of contentment, two or three meal a day, place to sleep, got my freedom. What more I want? My something-to-eat or my clothing might not be as fine as the other man's, but it taking care of my wants."

At the coast, the continental forest breaks open. Beyond the rain of pine needles, the sky whitens and the horizon streams mistily among clouds and water and marsh. A network of streams floods the marsh. Fishermen are easily stranded here, tricked by the watery landscape that suddenly grows shallow, mud rising under the vines swimming beneath the surface. Today buoys mark the green maze, but Henry Curry knew the devious paths of the waterways and outlasted the others.

Skipping at nightfall across the intracoastal river, Curry steered sometimes toward the famous mansions that glowed orange in the dusk like jack-o-lanterns behind their white picket fences, then he wheeled around toward the chrome-and-purple moonlit ocean and, in a fine temper, shook more and more curly shrimp from his net onto the ice in the hold.

The deep voice:

"The riverwork is lovely. Yeah. Yeah. I loved the work when I first start. I had two or three different methods. I try one, then I try another. I catch shrimp, oysters, mullet. I learn that the southeast wind is no good for fishing. But you take a west wind and a northeast wind, you catch more under those wind than you do under any other. The shrimp work up underneath those wind. He has as much sense as I or you—of course, his is a fish sense, ours is a human. If the wind from the southeast, he work up underneath this side. I don't know why he shifts, but he knows.

Sometimes he move over, and the next day the wind shift. He know when it's coming, that shrimp.

"I work the river from '12 to '56, South Carolina to Fernandina, no one place regular. I the only man living that caught the first shrimp in Georgia in 1913. Be out one day or two, depending how they was running. If a net is four feet long, it'll cover an eight-feet space; a six-feet net will cover a twelve-feet space, and everything in there you can catch him, if that net is working. Before I started on the river, I was making a dollar and a half a day. You didn't get no wage. But on the *river* doing shrimp fishing, you could make fifty or seventy-five dollars. Back yonder we have boats with 25, 35, and 40 powers pulling one net. Now they have 300, 400, 500 horsepowers, some pulling four nets. I believe they intend to empty that ocean.

"But, oh, that coast look lovely. We don't get too over-far from it. Once in a while we get a little over three mile. Think about it all the time, that it look the way it used to be.

"Ever since I were large enough to know," he said, "maybe 1902, we had black captains. You get out there, regardless of where you go, you see someone you know and a bunch of them will unite together. At night three or four boats tie up together, have dinner, get some experience from the other, what's the best to do. I didn't do too much of that, but once in a while I did. We played five-up or poker sometimes till twelve o'clock. Had electric lights on the boat, battery. Good deal of the boats had radios. That riverwork is lovely."

Gay Jacobs, a Direct Descendant and the jovial owner of a dock and shrimp business, grew up admiring the ancient black captains like Curry and Danny Thorpe and Wilbur Wiley. "I've learned that there is all types of education," she said. "The old-timers forecast the weather. They'll say, 'The shrimp have red legs, we're going to have a northeaster now, maybe two or three day blow of wind,' or, 'The legs getting clear now,' or 'The shrimps were off so-and-so, at such-and-such a point on the beach.'

"Wilbur Wiley worked on one of my uncle's shrimp boats some twenty-five years," she said. "His mind was like a nautical chart. He had to compensate for not being able to read or write; he couldn't read the charts, he didn't even know about the markers. He had memorized the landscape, the landmarks, the submerged trees. When our oldest son wanted to learn how to fish, Wilbur took him out. The man was an Einstein, a Ph.D. of the water. He could tell you within two inches where every single thing was under the water—rocks or anchors or wrecked boats, things the nets catch on—over thirty miles of marsh and ocean.

"Several years ago," said Gay, "a boat was taken out there to sink an artificial reef for sports fishermen offshore. They had this guy, Doctor Something-or-other from the University of Georgia, leading the expedition, and all these politicians. It was the first artificial reef they placed out there, all this publicity. Well, the doctor got deathly ill, didn't know where on earth he was. He couldn't tell how to get back to that dock. Well, they began to panic, how to get back, and media people aboard, but the one good thing they had on their fancy boat with all its equipment was a poor old black captain, and he, of course, was in his element. He knew where he was. He didn't say a word, just brought them in, when all the marsh looked alike to everyone else. Even to me, and I've lived here all my life, it all starts to look the same, but he brought them in, never said a word, just took over the wheel."

Elegant, peaceful man. Deacon Curry was more calm and watchful at the end of his life than ever before, though he had always been calm and watchful. He witnessed the manifestations of God's work, the poverty of lost men hoarding yachts and money, and the richness of the black people who trekked, singing, across fields to church on Sunday, or used to. Heavenly logic glittered in him.

"I do not preach," he said. "If I were to go to any of these stores round here and forge a note, the law going to punish me, ain't they? Now if the law going to punish for forgery, what will the *Lord* do if I go out there and say the Lord sent me to preach and he didn't send me? We have so many people out there of both race preaching and don't have a church. Would you hire me and ain't got some work for me to do? Well, if the Lord going to call me to preach, he going to give me some place *to* preach."

Nevertheless, younger men like Thurnell Alston and Sammie Pinkney visited Curry to ask his advice because he was a deacon and an intellectual man. They sat politely in his airless living room, refrained from smoking, and tried to state their questions loudly. They hoped for specific answers, for recommendations, but all the young men swam before Henry's failing eyes, and the only certain thing (with the years of his life in unchronological eddies around him) was that a young robed prophet had wandered Israel and had placed lessons before the people like platters at a feast, and that he served himself still from those teachings:

"We going to leave from here one day, every one of us, white and black and we ain't coming back. We going to get paid according to our work. There a little crab place to Darien. Say I hadn't worked there any, think if I go there Saturday morning they going to pay me? Say, 'What's your name?'

"'Henry Curry.'

"'What *you* coming for?'

"Same way when we go yonder to that payroll. If we done the work He bid us to do, then come ye blessings, herald the King of Patience and the Foundation of the World. And if I didn't, He tell me, 'Depart in curses!' and yonder I be gone and be lost forever. He say, 'So as ye done to the least of my brethren, ye did it unto Me.'"

Darien was a fishing village. A navy-blue tidewater river with white fringes slid under a low paved bridge in the center of town. Seagulls stood on telephone posts on Main Street. And there was salt in the air, and fresh shrimp in icy bins on truck beds. There were corners in which Darien looked like the town Pollyanna lived in: a happy, windblown, clean, white-clapboard, oak-shaded, work-ethic kind of town.

But within the structure of this salty blue-and-white fishing village moved the other race, humbly mopping, wiping, vacuuming, taking their leave at the end of day with a mumbled 'I'm going now.'

When messages from the outside world began to leak into McIntosh County about riots and civil disobedience and racial confrontations, white Darien shuddered. And when images appeared on television of bitter mobs of blacks torching their own ghettos and smashing windows, of contorted-faced mobs of whites barely restrained by police lines and hurling rocks, and—strangest of all, hardest to decipher—of lines of blacks and whites singing and marching together with linked arms, Darien wilfully sank deeper into its own ladylike foliage of magnolia and tupelo and wisteria, and maintained a sweet-as-honey, slow-as-molasses pace of life, wishing the outer world would go away.

And blacks in their distant cabins shut their doors and windows and located, through static, on their radios and televisions, the voices and images of Martin Luther King, Jr., Malcolm X, and Bobby Seale. In Leningrad and Moscow in the same years, Jews and intellectuals drove far into the country to escape the censor's blackout of the airwaves over the city. They parked in starry fields in the small hours of the morning and captured fragments, falling from the night sky, of the Voice of America, on black-market radios. Just this exotic and incredible and forbidden did the voices of the civil rights movement sound to the fishermen, gardeners, and maids of McIntosh County.

Three

The Education of Thurnell Alston

1

The voice of civil rights sounded first within the mind of Thurnell Alston, years before he received it in the form of news reports from the outside world. He was born in McIntosh County in May 1937, the fourteenth child in a family of six sisters and thirteen brothers. His mother prepared shrimp at a canning factory, earning a few cents a day: "My mother used to walk from here all the way down to Valona to head shrimps," said Thurnell. "Some of the time she has walked as far from here to Darien. My mother tell me a lot of time they had to hide in the woods, young girls, because white guys be coming along, know they be coming along that time of the morning, nothing but womens. They had to hide in the woods, walking to work." His father was a pulpwooder and a turpentiner, a gruff and bristling man: "He had a lot of friends, but he was very stubborn and very mean. And over the years he walked around and always carries a gun—on account of snakes or different things out in the woods or even back home. And everybody knew it. I mean, truthful, a lot of people didn't want to surprise him or nothing like that. And then he had eight older boys you know. And that's a big thing when you come with all these boys. And we never went out with big fear of any kind. I mean from *nobody*."

An unusually wet year created a disaster in the pulpwooding business in 1952 when Thurnell was fifteen; hundreds of black workers, including Thurnell's father, were laid off without pay. The owners were bankrupt, the workers penniless. "We had a very rough year the rainy season of 1952–53," said Thurnell. "Can't get the truck in the woods; can't get the wood out. The owners of the pulpwood wanted some kind of compensation; nobody was making any money. They didn't give us no welfare or food stamps—it didn't exist."

A group of black men, including Willie and Thurnell Alston, called on the sheriff to ask for help, for food, or for the extension of credit from local stores. But Poppell sent the blacks away, saying he would look into it, and when they showed up again, protesting that their children were hungry, the sheriff leaned back and stated expansively there simply wasn't a thing in the world he could do for them.

On top of this lie, the sheriff later was heard to remark: "Only way you can control the Negroes is to keep them hungry." Thurnell was staggered: "I know he said that, and he never denied it. I know he was just talking, but we *were* hungry. We were *hungry*."

Still just a boy, Thurnell could not respond; it was simply a blow he absorbed. But he was intelligent and watchful, and he began then to keep track of the attacks on his dignity—and on the dignity of his community—against the time that he would be capable of action. The education of Thurnell Alston consisted of a series of rude awakenings, until the day he had heard and seen enough and could not, in good conscience, remain passive any longer.

The family survived that winter, but Thurnell forever after felt aggrieved. It was his first lesson in the extent of the sheriff's power and cynicism, and of the black people's naive dependency. Despite favors he received from the sheriff over the years, Thurnell never forgot his first harsh glimpse of the man, and he held himself slightly aloof from the only white man in the county who made a show of caring about the McIntosh County blacks.

2

Shivering in the dark, the teenaged Thurnell Alston rode in the bed of an old pickup truck in January 1955 beside his father and a dozen other McIntosh black men. This was to be his first real experience of work. It also was his first perception of himself as a colored laborer.

They were driven by a white employee of the logging company out of the coastal forest, across the inland farmland to the logging forests of Brantley County. The men slumped silently against the sides of the pickup; they lit cigarettes when it stopped for gas. The boy held his hands under his armpits and shoved his feet into a pile of burlap on the truck bed. His stomach shrank around the black coffee he'd had for breakfast, which had scalded his tongue. His father had downed his cup of coffee while looking out the door of their cabin, as Thurnell dressed in front of the wood stove. "Let's get going now," his father had said as if angry with him. It was to be the boy's first turpentining trip. His mother had hugged him and kissed him on the neck. Having no gloves, he had refused to take her small ones. And now, in the back of the truck, his father wasn't looking at him.

At sunrise the fields were silver with frost. The boy's friend slid close to him, and they sat with their knees pulled up, huddled forward against the cold, and admired the beautiful cars on the road. His friend whistled and pointed: "They talking about hard times? A white boy just drove by in my *dream*." Thurnell looked at the warm flushed faces in the cars behind the truck: businessmen with fur collars on their car coats, country lawyers wearing bow ties. He could guess what they thought as they cast half an eye across the men in the truck: niggers. He huffed down into his jacket, leaned against the ribbed metal, and watched the light sky blur past.

Outside of Waynesville, one of the black men knocked on the window of the cab and pointed to the side of the road. After another mile the old truck slowed down, the white driver rolled down his window and stuck his arm out to wave cars past, then drove onto the shoulder. Two of the black men stood and hopped over the side of the truck, then a third and a fourth, while the driver lit a cigarette and looked across the road the other way. The men walked toward a stand of pine trees midway across the field. Thurnell looked to his father—he wouldn't have minded going to relieve himself, because the rest rooms at the gas stations in the little towns were for white people. He raised his eyebrows slightly to ask, but his father gave a slight shake of the head, an almost imperceptible scowl, before staring ahead again. It meant, to the boy, Go if you have to, but it's undignified. Thurnell took a deep breath, sat up straighter, and waited until they got to the logging camp.

In Nahunta they rattled to a stop. The driver went into a diner and leaned across the counter, joking with the waitress. He ordered from a menu and sat on a stool. The black men watched him through the window. Thurnell's father climbed out of the truck and went down an alley to the kitchen door of the restaurant. He brought the boy a cup of hot coffee, sweetened with cane, and a slice of pie. Thurnell gave half to his friend. Inside the restaurant the driver made a call to the crew boss; the men felt him watching them through the window. He counted them with his eyes while he talked.

In the pine woods beside Hoboken, Thurnell and the men dismounted into the still air. The fir trees were blue and frosty, the forest cavernous. Two white men came out of a cabin, laughing, and one called affably, "Hey, boys!" Thurnell had begun to shiver again—the cold and the hunger and the caffeine. From the cabin chimney rose smoke smelling like hickory. The white men wore padded, zippered jackets and rubber boots. "Build a fire, boss?" asked one of the McIntosh men, grinning with cold.

"Come on now, y'all," said the affable one. "You boys get started; you can build you a fire this evening." He gestured to a rack of axes, picks, and pails.

Thurnell's job was to clear a path for the men like his father who wound deep into the woods, farther than you could see or call to. They left, tramping together, shouldering axes, and swinging buckets. Sometimes they sang, rumbling bass voices over the snapping pine needles. He seemed to hear them long after they disappeared, until he realized that the notes in his mind were the low tones of the forest itself. He also gathered pails of resin and emptied them into larger buckets, then carried or dragged the sloshing buckets back into camp. His hands were freezing all the time. He used them stiffly, like wooden spoons. His father helped him wrap burlap around them, but he still had to beat them against his sides: a flapping dummy. The men came back one by one, or two by two, puffing under the weight of buckets balanced on poles. Their pant legs dripped with swamp mud, and the brown needles tufted their hair, beards, and sweaters.

"You doing all right, boy?" they asked, glowing with work.

"Yes sir," he said, but when he straightened to stretch his back, the tall whispering trees tilted between him and the men again and he was alone. Bears lived in these woods, and coachwhip snakes they said could eat a man. From the matted floor of the forest, the sky looked torn by the great steeples of pine. Singing, the men hiked toward the green center of the forest, but he stood on the outskirts, flapping. "It was very hard work, turpentining," he said. "You cut the tree with slashes, tack a tin up there in a V shape for turpentine to stream down. My father was cutting the notches. If you're turpentining, you're bending and chipping notches from one tree to another, have to leave three in the morning to be there by daylight."

After the first week his friend was carried to another camp. Thurnell saw him once, from a distance, obscured by the pine trees: his friend stood alone in the back of a truck, gripping the sides bare-handed and falling when it lurched onto the gravel drive.

They didn't quit work till nightfall and then had to root around for kindling so they could heat Campbell's beans in a can. They all slept in a pair of windowless shanties, on the floor on filthy straw and blankets. Strangers kicked him in their sleep and cursed with whiskey breath.

At the end of a month his father gave him five dollars. In Atkinson, on the ride home, he bought a pair of shoes for two dollars for his younger brother. They paid eighty cents each for a bus ride to Brunswick. They paid his father's uncle two dollars each to drive them in his new green Chevrolet home to McIntosh. That left him twenty cents. And he'd never been warm. And he'd always been hungry. And he'd left school for that.

3

Thurnell worked for his father for six years, then ran from turpentining. He walked sixty miles along the highway from Baxley to Brunswick, hid in the home of an older sister, crouched in a closet when his furious father came looking for him, then went out and found better-paying work: pulpwooding. He felled pines, gums, and oaks; dragged them to a warehouse; and cut them up. Within a few weeks he was sharing money with his parents and encouraging his father to retire. He would support them, he offered, but his father declined, walking down the road alone now to catch the truck to the inland forests.

Thurnell pulpwooded for several years until he found a modern job as a machinist with Babcock & Wilcox in Brunswick, a coastal city of seventeen thousand. He was trained in his mid-twenties as a boilermaker and earned more money than he'd thought possible. In the black hamlets of McIntosh, he was becoming a wealthy man. When he visited McIntosh, he let word of his success precede him.

Segregation existed at Babcock & Wilcox, though, and it ruined his feeling of achievement. "We had white water fountains and black water fountains, white bathrooms and black bathrooms, white cafeteria and black cafeteria," said Thurnell. "I mean they shows you that right after they hire you and you take a physical and they give you a tour of the plant. I was shocked because that was a person that, you know, carries you every places in the plant and shows you what you going to be part of, everything you going to be working on there, and what they have to offer; and they shows you that."

Here was a modern, efficient, successful American factory that included—matter-of-factly, as just part of the layout—a colored this and a colored that, a colored entrance, a colored time clock, and a colored toilet. It was all presented to him matter-of-factly, too, as if it existed for the convenience of the black work force rather than in concession to the bigotry of the white. It did not surprise Alston, but it grieved him. He figured he had been hired as just one more nigger, an extra nigger, one more for the line. Maybe there was a shortage of niggers the day he walked in wearing a suit, completing the application, looking like a trained ape; so they took him.

What sickened him most at Babcock & Wilcox were the segregated water fountains. He worked long hours in furnace heat, not shying from the arduous exertion of the work, but his thirst was not equivalent to the thirst of the white workers, for it was not to be quenched like theirs. The *white* water fountain was refrigerated, electric, the water pure and cold. The *black* water fountain beside it offered tap water simply piped in from outside. It was as if the blacks were horses, to be watered from a bucket. As it had been, according to legend, for Helen Keller at her famous pump, so it was for Thurnell Alston, the beginning of a word forming inside, the stammer of an idea. *Wa. Water.*

Work was hard. He was a man. He needed cold water.

"To me it was just . . . I seen restaurants, you know, where eating areas for black and white; Archie Davis and all them had black and white: black goes in the kitchen and eat, white goes in the restaurant, and even in a restaurant, I don't know. It was just something . . . the water you could get out of the black water fountain wasn't even cold. You know, it was just water. But the white water fountain, it came out of a machine, a cooler, that's cold water. And everybody that work there that wanted cold water had to drink hot water out of the black fountain. As big a company as Babcock-Wilcox—they had about eight or nine plants. And this was in 1963.

"And if you have a problem with a white person there, even if you won the argument, then you have to give him the satisfaction of, 'Hey, okay, now I get to go drink some hot water.' "

Thurnell would not drink the water. He found he would not force himself to bend and slurp it, the warm reddish water, piped in straight out of the ground.

As a boy in McIntosh, he had overheard Sheriff Poppell making wisecracks about letting the black people starve, and he had listened and was hungry, and the hunger had placed him outside the joke, left him at odds with it; he was like the only man in a movie theater who misses the punchline and finds himself surrounded by laughing faces that suddenly appear to him fleshy and distorted in the flickering light. As a teenager on the back of a pickup truck, he had seen himself counted like a head of cattle by a white foreman talking on the telephone; and being a boy, he had watched and absorbed it. But he was a man now. He began his own private, instinctive boycott, one that began in his spine: he wouldn't bend to sip the allotted black man's water.

In the mid-1970s, black people would begin to say of Thurnell Alston, "The man will stand up. The man stands up." At that time, they would mean, of course, that he would stand up for what he believed, stand up to the whites. But the words described Thurnell simply standing up, which was funny because it was the way things began for him: standing up, thoughtfully, at the head of the line at the hot, rusty black water fountain at Babcock & Wilcox, with thirsty others waiting their turn, unwilling to stoop and bend and push his lips forward to take the warm water offered him and his race.

"I was starting to notice all the discrimination at home, too," he said. "I really felt that you can't straighten out nothing nowhere else if you can't do it on the job with the people you work with. And I'm talking *after* integration. My Lord, something have to be done to get rid of all that junk."

He went thirstily and angrily on his lunch break one day with a handful of other black men to demand audience with the plant supervisor. They interrupted the man at his desk, in quiet enjoyment of his own lunch, but he received them civilly, without exaggerated surprise or feigned interest. Thurnell began to talk: "Look here," he said, "we feel we have discrepancies in the black and white situation here," and the supervisor stopped him and held up his hand, then spoke into the intercom to summon a union representative to join them.

In the sudden coolness of the glassed-in office, Alston faced the unruffled gaze of the white man who politely had brushed off his lips and laid aside his sandwich and now looked at Thurnell without curiosity but without dismay. Alston had come straight off the line, unwashed, streaked with sweat, hair mashed down and dusty from his helmet, speaking in a fast and high-pitched voice, bursting in and beginning without preface: "We're going to request a federal investigation, and we've talked to some people about coming down to look into things here." He had the feeling that he was doing nothing more than towering, disheveled, over the poor man and shouting, Yes, I'm a Negro! We are all Negroes!

The white man, however, behaved with civility rather than

superiority, and did not draw attention, through any movement of the eyes or nostrils, to Thurnell's uncouth appearance, to the dark stains of sweat and oil on his blue jumpsuit, his wild eyes, his matted hair, or his stutter. Of course, the man worked in a factory and could not, in fairness, expect men to appear before him neatly groomed; but all the black men in the small group had ample experience of white men distancing themselves from the distasteful physical presentation of Negro workers, when the Negroes were involved in the very work assigned by the whites.

The supervisor, in fact, seemed to stand aside from the racial caste system for a moment and look at things as a factory problem, as if workers had come to complain about a glitch in the machinery. The union rep took a chair and made notes on the meeting and promised to get back to him; the supervisor stood, thanked him, and reached across the desk to shake his hand; and the committee of black men crowded around Thurnell in excited discussion after they exited. He felt himself a man among men—a novel sensation to him, given his race, his poverty, and his youth. Shortly after the meeting, the company asked him to be a union steward, and he became Babcock & Wilcox's first black union steward. He was twenty-six years old and suddenly was looked on as an intelligent and purposeful man, a source of strength and leadership.

4

In the same years, Thurnell met and married Rebecca Pinkney. He was twenty-six when they met, a full-grown and serious man who had been earning his own living for nine years already. She was a schoolgirl, ten years younger, still full of daydreams and playfulness, waiting to fall in love for the first and greatest time.

Thurnell, employed as a boilermaker in Brunswick, was distracted by her. He appraised her, manfully, from a somber distance.

"I think, let's see, Rebecca was about sixteen when we met. Fast little girl. I mean I was glad, I was a young man anyway," said Thurnell Alston.

"I was painting her mother's house, not for the money, just to help some of the older people in my spare time. She had a big house; she had a lot of kids. Her mother was kind of jealous [protective] of Rebecca. Every now and then Rebecca would run through and say something and keep running, to keep her mother from saying anything. You know how little girls is, they're nothing serious, just talk.

"She'd be coming down the road, coming down 17 when I finish, and sometimes her mother say to her, 'You here? No you're not.' And I keep right on painting. When I get through with something, we sit on the porch and we talk. So basically her mother got to the point where she had faith in me, so we used to sit on the porch a lot of time to talk until I finished painting the house. And you know she fast. Fast, fast, fast.

"When she was about three or four months pregnant, we got married. And from then on that was about it. That was Thurn. And we didn't have no problems. She made a good wife. And I thought I was a good husband. We made little arguments, but I have never strike her and she have never strike me and we love each other twenty-five years. I'm quite sure everybody have arguments, but that's all we ever have. We maintain to have that much respect for one another."

In the era of the shoe truck, Rebecca Alston, whom everyone but Thurnell called Becca—he, rather sternly, stuck to Rebecca—lived the life of a mother duck surrounded by ducklings. Her life filled up with children: four sons were born to her and Thurnell: Thurn, Anthony, LeVan, and Keith; and four foster children were taken in by them. Chickens in the backyard, dogs all around, mother-in-law and sisters-in-law and brothers and aunts in cabins and trailers in the pine woods about the house—Becca, a twin, and one of fourteen children, was related to most of those in the black community to whom Thurnell was not related.

She stood frying catfish in an iron skillet on a hot summer morning, while little boys lay outside the kitchen door, tummy-down in the dirt, driving small metal cars and making accelerating and crashing noises with their lips, and older boys tinkered with old bicycles. A slew of half-related boys frequented the house. They were brothers, cousins, and second cousins. By ten in the morning, the fine dirt in the yard was warm to the touch. The bushes buzzed with cicadas, and the cars going up and down Highway 17 looked brassy in the sunlight. Friends and relatives honked their car horns when they passed the Alstons, and that frequent beep-beep was the friendly background music of their lives.

Becca had a round, pumpkin-colored face, light brown eyes, and freckles. (There had been a white great-grandmother, it seemed, and Thurnell occasionally blamed this or that unfortunate trait in Rebecca's personality on her mixed blood.) She had a gold front tooth with a star in it, like an extra flash of humor when she laughed. She left the golden catfish dripping into paper towels on the counter and came outside into what felt, briefly, like cooler air, to sit on a kitchen chair in the yard and fan herself.

"My mother was a strict sister, child!" said Becca."She raised fourteen of us. She got three sets of twins. My twin is the worst one in the family, the worst one! That boy? Whoo, Jesus! I say Mama must have leave him up there a little too long.

"My daddy got killed when I was eleven, and Mama raised all of us. Thurnell didn't live too far from us. I knew who he was, but he didn't know me. He found out though. I guess he figured in his mind, 'Say, this is a *fast* little girl.' But he wound right up with this fast little girl. I'm right here, sure is.

"He used to paint. When he was painting the inside of our house for Mama, I'd be the last one to bed, just being fast. (I tell you I don't want to raise no girls. I know just how they'd be: *fast.* Have a girl take after me?—I swear Thurnell would *hurt* the child. I rather be safe and have boys.) I was a young chicken, and Thurnell was a full-grown man. And Mama would say, 'Girl? get your old fast ass up there to bed!'

"But I always said I wanted a man at least five or ten years older than me. I don't want no young giddy-go because I know what'll happen to me and that giddy-go. Me and him will get married, and I bet you we won't be married for two weeks. I used to run around with a lot of giddy-gos, I had my little boyfriends, but Thurnell the only one I deeply down been caring for.

"Thurnell was a loose man then—oh, Thurnell had his womens. But he been as serious as that right there ever since I been knowing him. In '63 he got my company. He come round here to Mama and ask for my company. I said to myself, 'Yeah, this the guy. Look at all them free womens out there—he didn't have to wait for me.' But ain't but one love. That's how it be with me and Thurnell. Ain't nobody gonna turn my mind from him, not nobody.

"We were together about five years before we got married. When we got married, nobody knowed it. I was sitting around my house just like this: I had my old skirt, my hair plait-up, my bobby sockses and my tennises. He was working with P.J. that morning and he show up here with cement all over him and said, 'Let's go for a ride.' And we drove to the courthouse.

"When we got back home I went on into the house and started taking my clothes out of the closet. Said, 'Thurnell! Come on in here and help me tote it out!'

"Mama was there. She say, 'And just where are you carrying your fast ass?'

"I got my pocketbook and pulled out that little slip of blue paper they give you. And Thurnell say, 'Miss Retha, we married!'

"'Lord!' she say, 'Well, well, well, Lord! Why y'all ain't tell me?'

"'Mama,' I say, 'I ain't know myself.'

"Anyhow, we come on down here, and I went to get my clothes out of the car. His mama came running out, say, 'What y'all done did?'

"Thurnell say, 'Me and Rebecca just got married.'

"She jump up. 'Whooo Jesus! You coulda telled me! I could been done straighten up everything and had dinner cooked!'

"Thurnell took my clothes and stuck them in his room and went straight on back to work. I sat down and talk to his mother, then got in the kitchen and started cooking. I been here ever since. It just seem like it meant to be."

Thurnell and Rebecca Alston lived in a cinder-block house facing U.S. 17 across a front yard of pine trees, dirt, weeds, broken lawn furniture, chickens, and pieces of plastic toys. The house was long and narrow like a trailer. The light bulbs in the overhead sockets (there were virtually no lamps) were yellow porch bulbs or green party bulbs. The small rooms were dark and leering and smelled of smoke and grease. Eight children—four of their own, and the four foster children—moved about the crippled furniture and slanting rooms, pulling clothes from heaps on the floor, tying their shoes on outside.

Thurnell woke up early and wandered around the dark, stuffy house in an undershirt and dungarees, smoking a cigarette and drinking a can of Coca-Cola, his long, thick hair mashed against his head on the side he slept on. The house was heated by an old wood-burning stove; on cold winter mornings the rooms smelled of stale smoke, the windowpanes were ashy, and the eyes burned. Children emerged from the two back bedrooms, leaving damp, tangled knots of bedclothes behind them, their hair, like their father's, oddly piled up on one side from sleep.

Thurnell removed a pair of pants and a long-sleeve shirt from hangers he'd placed them on the night before, hangers that hooked over the top of the door to his bedroom. He ironed the clothes in the dining room, where short, thick brown drapes shut out the light. He stood before the chipped, rusted mirror in the bathroom, under a flickering bulb, meticulously shaping and evening out his long gray-blue hair before leaving the house.

In summertime the heat inside the cramped house was an ancient heat, the heat of the Amazon. Becca Alston sat on a kitchen chair in a sleeveless cotton nightgown, pulled a foster girl to her, and began hacking with a brush and comb, separating stalks of hair, then weaving tiny coarse braids secured with colored rubber bands, while the foster girl cried, "Ow! Ow!" and her sister yelled, "Do me, Becca! Do me!" When Becca cooked, the loud sizzle of frying sounded like rain in the streets. She banged the utensils sleepily, like a Rasta man on tin drums. The kitchen floor was made of buckling dark-brown linoleum; insects swarmed across the counters; the color television ran fourteen hours a day, even when nobody was home. Larger-than-life white boys and girls, with straight teeth and hair like gold satin, wearing stiff, new, bright clothing, skipped across the screen; kitchen floors sparkled like blue sheets of ice; and larger-than-life bathrooms held porcelain fixtures glowing like the full moon and stars. Meanwhile, teenage boys lined up at the ironing board in the hot, dingy brown dining room and pressed new blue jeans and shirts for school.

At home after the children left for school, Becca, in cotton shift and rubber thongs, desultorily straightened a bit, then fried something to have ready for dinner—a chicken from the yard, which she throttled herself; a fish from the river, which she cleaned; a side of beef from the freezer; or a handful of okra coated with eggs and flour. Then she sat in the sweltering, dusty shade of the carport in a metal glider with no cushions, visiting with a neighbor who had drifted over. As the dazzle of noon approached, they swayed back and forth, drank cans of Coke, cooled their bare feet in the fine sand of the driveway, and loudly agreed about things.

Thurnell Alston was a thoughtful man and an angry man, and it was probably these unreconciled halves of his character that gave him a nervousness, a fitfulness, a haste, an unexpected roughness; an occasional high hysterical pitch to his voice when he felt outraged or was engaged in some tomfoolery; a hand in and out of a coat pocket, a glass of Scotch held between long, trembling fingers, an inability to stay seated or to stay in the house for long. He stammered when he spoke. He was impatient and jittery, although he had a knack for slowing down, shutting up and listening for a moment when his neighbors spoke of their hardships in life: nodding his head rapidly—"I hear you man, I hear you man"—focusing with bloodshot eyes, drawing on the trembling cigarette, and letting the news penetrate. It was a natural social grace—one of the few he inherited—and people felt close to him as a result of it. He was like a skittish horse, eager to be off, who nevertheless would accept a sugar cube, quickly, taking in the giver with long rueful eyes.

Thurnell Alston's high, jittery voice had the scratchiness of smoke in it, and his speeches were strewn with anxious little smoker's coughs. He began a story, had misgivings, gave a little cough, started in a new direction, and coughed again. His narrative style, overall, was like parallel parking on a busy street: he proceeded in fits and starts, backed up, edged forward, backed up, while other ideas zoomed past close at hand.

His speech was a mixture of educated usage and backwoods conjugation, and this half-and-half combined within a single sentence. Past tense and present tense sat side by side—"He walked around and always carries a gun." The clumsy grammar didn't serve him well. Clearly, the King's English as a complicated and subtle tool had not been well placed at the disposal of the bright and curious black boy, one of a horde of children to emerge from a sharecropper cabin ruled by a tough man named Willie. Yet some sort of rote, schoolroom grammar *was* hammered into him (by poor black teachers from families like his own, graduated from struggling black colleges, who taught a textbook English they themselves spoke stiffly and self-consciously). This stiff, self-conscious, carefully conjugated English was hammered into him; and at the same time the rich local talk—the humorous, knowing, metaphorical, riddle-filled, and present-tense Gullah talk—was hammered out. His glorious rags, so to speak, were removed, and he was handed, instead, a U.S.-issue factory-made suit several sizes too small.

Thus, he had misgivings in midsentence, despite the hurried cadence of his talk, and shifted back and forth between an early native tongue and the white grammar of his schooling. The result of being between one and the other, given the ambitious and subtle mind of the watchful boy, and man, was that he rarely matched words to thought very happily. In fact, in an inverse relationship, the more he desired to express something of deep importance to himself, the more tongue-tied he became, the more frequent the fits and starts, the worse the stammering, until—judging the parking space too small—he abandoned the attempt. It was the very incoherence that signified largesse of thought.

Still, locally, he was acknowledged as an eloquent man, in part, because he *had* half-mastered white grammar; but in part also because he battled courageously to bring thought into words, to sketch out inexpressible modern ideas without excessive reliance on biblical parables. Thus, when he expressed the notion that all men were brothers, the people knew he did not mean "brethren" and he was not talking about Jerusalem or Heaven. He was becoming a sort of secular preacher. He was a Christian like the rest of them, as well as a churchgoer and a choir singer, but when he spoke to crowds, it was his stammering call for American justice that stirred them up; and when he addressed white officials, the black people knew that Thurnell was not stammering in fear.

"There's a lot of people have been intimidated in McIntosh, but there was no fear of things for me," he said. "I would tell it the way I see it. Regardless of who they are, I mean they could kill me for it because I'm going to say it anyway. And I got that from my father. Because he was very outspoken whenever he spoke. And it was very seldom, if he's in a crowd, you never know he's there; but whenever he say something, I mean they listen. And I get that from my father because he never was scared of anything, never really was scared of anything."

Four

"Howdy Folks, This Your Lucky Day"

1

When the black people from the quiet and unworldly hamlets began to complain and confront the sheriff, they faced a man flanked by henchmen and coconspirators, as well as deputies; a man rich in both civic law enforcement abilities and felonious talents. For 50 years before the construction of Interstate 95 on the East Coast, northerners on vacation cruised down old Highway 17 through McIntosh County toward Miami. They were the county's greatest source of wealth. The dynasty of Sheriff Tom Poppell grew and thrived out of proportion with almost everything else in Georgia because of this moveable feast of Yankees on wheels.

The Yankees soared across the Georgia line by the thousands, in high spirits. The children opened new boxes of crayons and worked in new coloring books; their legs looked skinny and white sticking out of shorts in November. The families sang songs and counted state tags, and the kids and fought over who got the window.

In moments of repose, the curious children laid aside their comics and dolls and car bingo games and stared out the backseat windows. In the wooded northern half of McIntosh County, black families were seated on kitchen chairs in dirt yards, shelling peas or drinking beer. In a clearing, baseball players without uniforms or caps zigzagged after a ball. In the side yard of a cabin, an old woman bent to a spigot and filled a bucket, and barefoot toddlers chased chickens under a rickety porch, and men poked with sticks at a smoking cookpit in the middle of a vacant lot. Sometimes the northern children had a game of waving at strangers: the black strangers standing under the pine trees waved back, while their dogs or kids raced the cars; the white children kneeled backward in their seats to watch until the wood-and-dirt settlements were concealed by forest as the cars zoomed south into Darien.

In Darien, the New York–to–Miami traffic was relentless. The traffic was a metallic river, flashing back reflected sunlight, churning and lurching and giving off fumes. Half a dozen locals were killed every year on their way across the street to the drugstore or the post office because some damn fool from New Jersey forgot to read the signs that he was entering a town. "HIGHWAY CARNAGE CONTINUES" was a frequent headline in the *Darien News*. But Darien harnessed the traffic and grew, lengthwise on either side of the highway, precisely the way a town grows on two banks of a river. The bumper-to-bumper traffic turned the waterwheel of commerce.

The heyday of Darien and of U.S. 17 lasted from the 1930s through the mid-1970s, an era during which a multitude—a plague—of locally owned two-bit tourist businesses thrived along the route. About two-thirds of them were legal, too.

There were souvenirs in profusion. Gift shops displayed alligator wallets, little bags of local cotton, seashell wind chimes, Log Cabin syrup in tins shaped like log cabins, and beaded Indian belts. Some aisles held pirate ships made out of shells, miniature picnic tables made to hold jars of condiments, shot glasses on wooden stands labelled "Attitude Adjuster," and cigarettes in glass tubes labeled, "Break in case of emergency." Tiny china French poodles were connected to one another by diminutive gold leashes. Local kitchens had prepared paper sacks of fresh fried pork rinds, mason jars of barbecue sauce, or Vidalia sweet onion relish. Coca-Cola serving trays, billed caps with Mr. Peanut on the front,

Confederate flags, and bumper stickers with slogans like "American by birth, Southern by the grace of God" were widely available. Local ladies' club cookbooks included recipes for "Ritz Cracker slaw," "Sweet pickled okra," "Congealed Coca-Cola Cranberry Salad," and other recipes that began, "Crush one bag of Oreo cookies." Countertops displayed pickaninny rag dolls and salt and pepper shakers in the form of Negro laundresses.

The northern white families made pit stops in Darien and let their children out to run in the sand parking lots of neighborhood fish houses. Inside, the grownups tucked red-check cloth napkins into their collars and ordered fried shrimp and devilled crabs (both from local waters), coleslaw, hush puppies, and sweetened ice tea. Often the families spent the night in the Old South Manor, or Plantation Estates—one-story motels sticking back into the pine woods. They toured Darien's four blocks briefly on foot the next morning, pointing at the Spanish moss, the river harbor and shrimp boats, the seagulls, the sheriff's office. They ate lunch at Archie's—fried chicken, country-fried steak, fried okra, and pecan pie—before heading out (with unbuckled belts, the car groaning) over the Darien bridge south toward Florida.

Archie's Restaurant opened in 1938; Archie Davis, the son of the founder, inherited the restaurant and rebuilt it in red brick. Handsome in a slack, indifferent way, with upswept black hair so straight and fine the track marks of a comb were visible in it, he has the careless suntan and outdoors build of a sportsman. His voice and movements are desultory; he wears loafers and a comfortable madras shirt and loose, soft khaki pants with change jingling in the pockets. He is the sort of man toothpicks were invented for. He spent his life servicing the tourist traffic.

"As boys, we'd sit along the curb and count tags. 'You take Connecticut. I'll take Massachusetts,' he said in a lackadaisical south Georgia tone of voice, uninflected, calm, and slow, the way northerners talk just before dropping off to sleep. "We had a major New York–Miami highway right here [pronounced "rot here"], right through town ["rot thoo town"]. You had your rich Yankees going south in the fall of the year and going north in the spring. Then you had your paid drivers going through when the old folks took a train or a plane. That turned into your man and lady tourist toodling down the coast. Then you got your man and wife who worked at the Ford plant going on a little vacation to Florida.

"We've had people stopping with us for forty years," said Davis, a man somehow able to recline comfortably in a straight-back metal-legged kitchen chair. "I knew them. I loved them. They paid our bills. They helped to raise me. We had four people in here the other day from Philadelphia; the man said he used to eat with us during the war, never went through without stopping."

The long northern cars drooped with wealth as they roared into the South, riding low over huffing tires, or so it seemed to the locals watching for them. In the northern half of McIntosh County—fifteen miles north of Darien—a wide selection of roadside entertainments and refreshments awaited the tourists and retirees the moment they sailed over the county line. PEACHES! PECANS! VIDALIA ONIONS! FRESH SEAFOOD! Great hand-lettered, stilted signs encouraged travelers to stop, and produce was displayed on wooden carts under striped awnings or in whitewashed shacks. There were signs promising "KOSHER SANDWICHES!" or "KOSHER HAM!" because there was no one in the county who knew that *kosher* meant, among other things, no pork. *Kosher* was simply a word that, when added to a sign, mysteriously caused lots of Yankees to pull over. Some of the signs were misspelled: Fresh Oystsers! said one, and Shimps! another, so that when the Yankees slowed down and looked, they were often chuckling.

The drivers parked and got out in good humor, in the mood for a bit of local color, a chat with a local type. The taste of a Georgia peach was the very taste of vacation, and the corrugated skyline of southern pines relaxed the eyes. Perhaps the driver amiably called out, "How you?" in a mock southern accent to a skinny, cigarette-smoking proprietor in undershirt and overalls. Ambling over to the carts to see what a quarter would buy, while his wife sought out the restroom, he asked, "How far to Jacksonville?" and the local man sprang to life, happy to converse in drawling twang.

The signs had been misspelled on purpose.

In McIntosh County the pecans, the peaches, the peanuts, the onions, and the seafood offered from roadside stands tended to be shoddy merchandise, not fresh, some of it not even local. The real business of the roadside stands was gambling, and the gambling was rigged. These businesses were the most prosperous in the county.

The northern end of McIntosh County was the Kingdom of the Clip Joint, and the only way the Yankees could be sure of traversing it safely was to roll up their windows, lock their doors, stare straight ahead, not stop for strangers or gas, and keep on driving till they arrived in Darien. But many stopped, bought a little something, played a little game. To this day, no one knows how many thousands—how many tens of thousands—of cash Yankee dollars of vacation money and retirement money were lost on that mile-and-a-half stretch of fruit stands under the pine trees, because gambling was a felony in Georgia, the victims were warned not to report it lest they themselves wind up in jail, and those who overcame their fear and *did* report it made their report to Sheriff Tom Poppell. "We had damn fools," sighed Doug Moss, "who called the sheriff *from* the clip joint."

Doug Moss is a bearded, beer-bellied, motorcycle-riding man with a short, brown ponytail secured with a rubber band; a private investigator employed by Atlanta law firms; a Vietnam vet, from army reconnaissance; and a former police detective in Brunswick, the next city south of Darien on the Georgia coast. "The rule of thumb for catching tourists," said Moss, "was: 'You don't outsmart a Yankee. You outdumb him.' Some of them were pretty decent little restaurants out front. A family comes in and sits down, Mom and Dad and the kids: 'Where y'all from? How's the food? We got a little game over here if y'all'd like to play . . .' Whatever game you were playing, you would win—until you were playing for big money."

The fruit carts and pecan stands offered poker, slot machines, dice, shell games, and "razzle dazzle," a game of chance that has been described by carnival experts as the most vicious game ever seen on a carnival midway. The white men who ran the clip joints, like their merchandise, were not all local either. Many were carny operators who had traveled the back roads of America for years, working Las Vegas, Atlantic City, and Phenix City, Alabama. They migrated into McIntosh County, where, as in the other national centers for gambling and prostitution, they had the law on their side. Their talents included offering three throws for a dollar at a pyramid of bottles they knew how to arrange in such a way that when *they* threw the ball in a demonstration, the bottles leapt into the air like young porpoises, but when a *customer* had a turn, the bottles would not topple if a nuclear warship were aimed in their direction.

Of the main operator of the gambling operations, a local man, it would later be said: "His ma died, his pa died, his grandma died, and his dog died the same year Sheriff Tom died, and the only one he grieved for was the sheriff."

"Howdy y'all. Going to Florida? Purchase of five dollars or more give you a free throw of the dice."

"You from New York? This your lucky day! You the tenth customer this morning—give you a free chance to win this bucket of silver dollars."

"Kids want to see a card trick?"

"Yes ma'am, the whole United States just about knew about Long County and McIntosh County, Georgia," said former governor Lester Maddox, who took office in 1967. "I'd been getting a lot of complaints from people in New York and different parts of the country. It had been going on for years." Lester Maddox is an aggressively affable, bald, red-faced man with twinkly old-fashioned steel-rim eyeglasses. This once venomous and outspoken racist surprised everyone in the late sixties by serving as a decent and honest governor: he appointed more blacks to public office than had any predecessor; was committed to education, prison reform, and integrating the county courthouses; and waged war on the corruption on the coast.

"People would buy a five-pound bag of pecans," he said, "and maybe half of them was fresh and the rest of them junk. They'd have their cars drained out of oil or their tires punctured while setting at the pecan stand and here, fifty feet down the road, sits a gas station that'll sell you tires or rebuild your engine.

"I didn't want a police state in McIntosh County," said the former governor recently. "The first time I went down there I warned them people I'd rather put Sheriff Poppell in jail than you business people, but something's going to have to give. You're hurting the young people in this county, the good people, and the state. That quieted it down for quite a while, then it came back. I couldn't get it cleaned up."

"While passing through your state Monday, Route 17 I believe, my wife and I decided we would like some pecan candy," began a letter dated March 12, 1971, addressed to the Honorable Governor of the State of Georgia, one of thousands received over a period of twenty years.

> We stopped at a small shop. . . . I found the door locked but right away it was opened by a man. I went in and picked up the candy which was 3 bars for a dollar.
>
> As I started to pay, the man, approximately 45 years old with a bandaged right ear, asked me if I would like to roll the dice.

TRADE BANK 10 POINTS OR MORE WINS					26 BONUS	TRADE BANK 10 POINTS OR MORE WINS					
10 POINTS OR MORE WINS	40 1 POINT	19 2 FOR 1	38 3 FOR 1	36 2 FOR 1	20 2 FOR 1	18 3 FOR 1	37 2 FOR 1	16 1 POINT	26 OR 30 NEVER WINS	POINTS NOT TRANSFERABLE	5 MINUTE DELAY ENDS GAME
	15 1½ POINTS	41 1½ POINTS	13 4 POINTS	48 10 POINTS	8 10 POINTS	43 4 POINTS	14 3 POINTS	42 2 POINTS			
	22	12 5 POINTS	35	45 5 POINTS	11 5 POINTS	21	44 5 POINTS	34			
	33	47 8 POINTS	24	10 5 POINTS	46 6 POINTS	32	9 7 POINTS	23			
	27	17 ½ POINT	31	25	30 RAISE	28	39 ½ POINT	29			

Gambling game board, a form of "razzle dazzle," confiscated by the GBI from McIntosh County in 1973. Reprinted by permission from Chief Bill Kicklighter.

I did, and rolled so that I was $4 ahead. He said I was lucky and if I wanted to bid the money up and accumulate 10 points, I could win up to $1,600. In the meantime I had made 9½ points. With ½ point to go to win, I very foolishly kept on playing. In the meantime my wife had come in and although she is very averse to gambling, with only half a point to go she said to go once more to see if I could recoup my losses. Needless to say, I lost out and that was that. My money was gone and I went out of the store really mentally sick. I realized I was very foolish and had no one to blame but myself. I feel if I can save someone else from being ripped off as I was I would feel this letter was worthwhile. I lost $260 which I could ill afford since it was my vacation money, and being a retired federal employee since 1959, it did not come easy.

By the way, the money he kept piling on the counter did not look real. It was lighter in color.

The man who unveiled the inner workings of the pecan stands of McIntosh was GBI Special Agent Bill Kicklighter. He is today Chief of Police of Doughterty County, in Albany, Georgia. He is handsome in a clean-living, blue-eyed, Marine Corps sort of way; he looks like Frank Sinatra, like a fit, trim, crewcut, and sportsmanlike Sinatra. He has a southern drawl which consists of one part southern white, one part Ludowici, Georgia (his hometown), and one part just plain Kicklighter. He says "thoo" for "through" as in "Let me get thoo with this phone call," and "ever time" for "every time," and "I have to wrestle with this thang," for "I'll have to think it over" and "he liked to got killed" for "he might have been injured."

"Most of this stuff," he said, "I know of first hand.

"During the early sixties I was on the Memphis, Tennessee, police force," he began. "It was a very professional force, good equipment, good people. I'd come home in the summer and at Christmas time. My grandparents had built a house in McIntosh County near the coast and that's where the family would gather. Gambling was real bad, and the pecan stands and clip joints in McIntosh County cheating the tourists. It used to frustrate me no end, me being a police officer visiting my home state. They'd have trooper cars stationed in front of these clip joints. If a carload of tourists pulled in—and it was obvious: station wagon, out-of-state plates, bag of oranges tied up on top—this trooper would get out of his car, go up and warn them that this place was a gambling joint. The trooper would explain that gambling was a felony in Georgia and try to talk them out of going in there. I thought that was a totally ridiculous way of handling this thang: 'Why the heck don't you arrest those people and get them out of the county?' I couldn't stand the idea of the troopers tied up all day on Highway 17. It looked to me like something funny was going on. Of course I lived in Tennessee then and I wa'n't familiar with the political situation in Georgia, but I thought, 'That's not the way we'd a-handled it in Memphis and I can't believe they'd handle it anyplace that way.'"

Kicklighter moved home to Georgia and joined the GBI in

Hinesville. "The Governor's office had files on that area going back twenty years," he said. "The main kingpins were Colonel Ralph Dawson in Long County and Sheriff Tom Poppell in McIntosh. Nothing moved that they didn't approve it. The two of them literally ran the area.

"Now the way these places worked was you go in there, you buy a bag of pecans, and the fellow tells you any purchase of a dollar or more entitles you to one free roll of the dice. They had a little basket of silver dollars, two to three hundred of silver dollars, turned by a little motor, and they'd tell the people, 'One roll of the dice and you have a chance to win these silver dollars." Everybody later told me, 'It was running me crazy hearing those silver dollars clanging and clanging against each other.'"

In 1973, Kicklighter oversaw raids on the clip joints. The confiscated game boards showed that the most popular game on the coast was one called razzle dazzle.

According to Matthew Gryczan, the author of *Carnival Secrets* (1988), razzle dazzle first appeared in the United States in the early 1940s. "Like the devil, razzle dazzle appears in various forms and under many names," he writes. "Police files are loaded with reports of gullible people from all walks of life having been cheated out of thousands of dollars each, playing razzle."

The key to razzle dazzle is a conversion chart, which assigns points to each throw of eight dice. The odds against winning are astronomical.

To play, you throw 8 dice, add them together, and check the chart for what their sum is worth. If they add up to 48, for example, they are worth 10 points and you are an instant winner! Much ado is made over this possibility.

"Here's the whole thing," said Kicklighter. "There's only two points on that whole board that's going to win. With eight dice you got to roll eight ones or eight sixes. Some of the FBI agents and I were sitting around one day, figured the chance of winning was something like one in a million." In fact, the likelihood of rolling eight ones or eight sixes is one in 1,672,000 rolls.

And what will you earn for the totals you are *most* likely to roll with eight dice, such as 26 or 30, which occur once in 13 rolls? The conversion charts in McIntosh County carried a few fine-print warnings and rules along the right-hand margin, including "26 or 30 never wins."

Matthew Gryczan, in *Carnival Secrets,* gives countless tips on how to win carnival games. His tip on razzle dazzle: "Never play this game. Advise others not to play."

The most insidious aspect of the game was that the operator cheated in the player's *favor* as the game began, so the player racked up points right away: Before his wife had time to wonder why he was taking so long to use the toilet and buy a jar of honey, the lucky vacationer had shelled out sixty-three dollars already, had won eight points, and was ready for his seventh—and possibly winning—throw. He only needed two points to win the game and thousands of dollars.

How *had* he achieved so much so quickly against impossible odds? The operator had swept up the eight dice, adding aloud—*incorrectly*—faster than the player could follow and helping the player to triumph in his good luck: "Six, 12, 17, 23, 29, 35, 41, 47! Forty-seven is worth, let's see . . . eight points!" But *had* the player actually tossed seven 6s and one 5? Perhaps—but 209,952 to one says he didn't. And the distance he still had to traverse from eight points to ten points and victory was the distance from here to eternity.

A player paid a dollar for his first roll, two dollars for his second roll, four dollars for his third, eight dollars for his fourth, and so on. As he began to lose, he stayed the operator's sweeping hand and totaled the dice aloud *himself.* The operator most generously allowed the player to do this. At $64 a roll, adding aloud, the player announced his total of *twenty-eight* (once in twelve

Game of Chance with Eight Dice

Number Rolled	*Expected Frequency*	*Payoff*
8	once in 1.7 million rolls	10 points, INSTANT WINNER!
9	once in 209,952 rolls	7 points
10	once in 46,656 rolls	6 points
11	once in 13,997 rolls	5 points
12	once in 5,090 rolls	5 points
13	once in 2,121 rolls	0 points
14	once in 983 rolls	3 points
15	once in 499 rolls	1½ points
16	once in 273 rolls	1 point
17	once in 160 rolls	½ point
18	once in 100 rolls	0 points, extra rolls
19	once in 66 rolls	0 points, extra rolls
20	once in 46 rolls	0 points, extra rolls
21	once in 33 rolls	0 points
22	once in 25 rolls	0 points
23	once in 20 rolls	0 points
24	once in 17 rolls	0 points
25	once in 15 rolls	0 points
26	once in 13 rolls	26 Never Wins
27	once in 13 rolls	0 points
28	once in 12 rolls	0 points
29	once in 13 rolls	not on board
30	once in 13 rolls	30 Never Wins
31	once in 15 rolls	0 points
32	once in 17 rolls	0 points
33	once in 20 rolls	0 points
34	once in 25 rolls	0 points
35	once in 33 rolls	0 points
36	once in 46 rolls	0 points, extra rolls
37	once in 66 rolls	0 points, extra rolls
38	once in 100 rolls	0 points, extra rolls
39	once in 160 rolls	½ point
40	once in 273 rolls	1 point
41	once in 499 rolls	1½ points
42	once in 983 rolls	0 points
43	once in 2,121 rolls	4 points
44	once in 5,090 rolls	5 points
45	once in 13,997 rolls	5 points
46	once in 46,656 rolls	6 points
47	once in 209,952 rolls	8 points
48	once in 1.7 million rolls	10 points, INSTANT WINNER!

rolls)—according to the conversion chart, that was worth . . . nothing. The next roll would cost him $128. But he had only two points to go.

"I had $5,000 in my pocket I had drawn out of the bank when we left Long Island yesterday evening," a man reported to the GBI in 1968. "We were going in the car, I had my family. We were going to Florida on vacation. We had spent less than $8 getting from Long Island to McIntosh County.

"When I went in there I figured I could buy the whole damn building for less than the $5,000 I had with me. It was a little old shack with nothing in there, and to tell you the truth, I got the feeling we weren't really gambling, we were playing for fun. The dang fool could count three times faster than I could.

"I had laid down $4,300 in less than twenty minutes when I realized, 'Hey, I'm never going to win.'"

The occasional editorial or sermon blasted the illicit businesses at the fringes of the county, but after a few days the grumbling always abated. Meanwhile, Sheriff Poppell's crooks and fugitives—some of them local, some of them from out of state—approached white Darien with clean-shaved, hats-in-hands, soft-spoken attitudes: "These operators moved in and became pseudo-locals," remembers a Darien lawyer. "By some elements they were looked upon as scum, but by other elements they were looked upon as, 'Well, you've got your local barber, your local grocer, your local slot-machine operator.'"

"My father had a general store in Eulonia, way out in the county," said another Darien man. "The clip-joint and truck-stop people were always good neighbors, absolutely the best. People have a hard time understanding that, but they were always friendly and courteous, never rude or pushy. Keep in mind we were way out in the county and they were just a phone call away, always happy to help."

"Yes the crooks were friendly, nice people," said Charles Williamson at the *Darien News*. "They integrated into the community. They would come into town and subscribe to the newspaper and go to the grocery store. One of them had a son who's a lawyer. I had one to come to me, said, 'Listen, I haven't made a contribution to the Lions Club. Could I give you fifty dollars for the Lions Club?'

"And I said, 'Here's your receipt for donating fifty dollars to the Lions Club.' "

Some of the shaken victims, relieved of all their money, made their way into Darien and stopped at the *Darien News* office. There they encountered the only man in town not only aware of but willing and able to do something about the clip joints: Charles M. Williamson, the newspaper's publisher. Kind and tremulous, he is a lean, tall, skinny white man with a small, round pea of a head and the kind of face that may be described as "wreathed in smiles," concentric circles spreading outward toward his boyish stuck-out ears, the rings of laugh lines radiating kindliness. He is the kind of man who probes gently, "Are you a Christian?" and switched into Bible talk—"thy" and "thou" and "the King of Glory!"—with absolutely no change in his thin, humble, beseeching posture or in the tone of his soft and earnest voice.

Williamson and his wife, Maude, published the county's weekly newspaper, the *Darien News*, for thirty-five years. The paper is the sort of small-town weekly with headlines like "RIDGE RE-ZONING SITUATION HEARD BY COMMISSIONERS" or "INDUSTRIAL AUTHORITY NAMES NEW DIRECTOR." A column entitled "The Question Box" appears in each issue and entertains questions from readers like, "If there is a heaven, how come the astronauts have never seen it?" During the school year, a weekly list of the school lunches makes the op-ed page, and Christian inspirational verses are scattered throughout.

"Most folks around here call the paper the 'Darien Mullet-Wrapper,' " said Vic Waters, a local musician. "But I have always called it *The McIntosh County World Astonisher*!"

Yet, during the heyday of the clip joints, Charles Williamson and the *Darien News*—at great risk—took on the corruption. "After Phenix City, Alabama, was closed up, there were people who came here," said Williamson in his quiet, hesitant, well-meaning way. "They came here and they began to operate what we call clip joints. U.S. 17 was a main artery of traffic to Miami. The people from the North would come sliding through here and many of them would stop. And it was a confidence game, a con game. They would serve them up bacon and eggs or a ham sandwich and say, 'You are so very fortunate, sir. You are our ninth customer today and that entitles you to a free lunch.'

"'Oh really?'

"It was a confidence game and the people were really taken. Among them were people like a retired detective from Long Island, New York. When people realized what had happened, they'd stop off at the sheriff's department. They'd say, 'Listen, this place up there is run by crooks! They beat me out of my money!'

"'*Really*?' the deputies would say. 'Do you mean you're admitting that you were *gambling* there? There is no gambling in the state of Georgia. It is illegal to gamble in the state of Georgia. Now, if you're telling us you were gambling, we can lock you up right now. Otherwise, you can get the hell out of here.'

"A lot of the people came to see me. There was one straight deputy at the sheriff's department who referred the people to the newspaper office." [Confronted with this bit of information about one honest deputy, both Doug Moss and Bill Kicklighter had the identical reaction of looking startled, thinking a moment, grunting, then offering, "I sure as hell don't know who *that* would have been."]

"The honest deputy," said Charles Williamson, "would take them outside and tell these people, 'Why don't you go see Mr. Williamson at the paper? Maybe he can help you.' So they would come and see me, and I would get out a pencil and a piece of paper, and I would ask, 'Who are you? Where did you come from? Where did you stop? How much money did you lose? How did they get your money out of your pocket?' Now this was twenty-five, thirty, thirty-five years ago. And many of them lost $1,200, $1,400 when they pulled over to get a sandwich. Retirees lost their savings.

"I just started documenting it. And I'd get a witness and I'd collect them. Nobody was going to do anything about it. At some points I would get so exasperated, really . . ." And here the pink-faced man with the boyishly stuck-out ears tried to get a Christian grip on his un-Christian emotions. The battle raged momentarily as a kind of facial tic, then the gentle man emerged and renewed the story with a softer, slower voice:

"One of the first ones that happened, I said, 'Now, you just wait right here.' And I went up to the jail and spoke to the sheriff and I said, 'Listen, there is a man down there that has been fleeced out of his money and I want him to get his money back.'

"'Oh, I'll come.'

"So within a very few minutes the guy that ran the clip joint came, and the sheriff was there, and the sheriff said to the guy that had been clipped: 'Is this the man that you are accusing of clipping you out of the money?'

"'Yes sir,' says the man. 'He's the one. He clipped me out of $1,200.'

"And the guy that ran the clip joint says, 'No sir, I don't believe that you lost but $900. Would you care to step outside and talk to me a minute?'

"And the guy looks at me and at the sheriff and asks, 'Is it all right if I talk with him privately?'

"'Hell yes,' says the sheriff, 'Go ahead on and talk to him.'

"And he comes back in and says, 'Well, he gave me back $900 of my money and I'm glad to get it, so I'm going on down the road.'

"Well, after that I never bothered the sheriff anymore.

"But I continued to collect their statements," said Charles Williamson, "and I contacted friends of mine at the *Atlanta Journal* and let them know what was happening. They drove down from Atlanta in a car with a New York tag on it and stopped at six of these places that were running wide open, and went back to Atlanta and had a double-decker headline on the front page of the *Atlanta Journal*: "THOUSANDS OF TOURISTS FLEECED ON U.S. 17 IN MCINTOSH COUNTY."

"So the McIntosh County grand jury came into session, and the judge charged the jury, said, 'You subpoena the editor of the *Darien News* and make him answer for the allegations that he is making in his paper because it is reflecting poorly upon the county.'

"I presented all the statements I'd collected, or as many as the grand jury wanted to hear. And the foreman of the grand jury said, 'Well, we weren't aware of all this, but it's taken about three hours. It ought to be about time for your lunch by now.' He told that to me! You know what the grand jury report was? 'We recommend that all parties in McIntosh County work for the good of McIntosh County.' "

On November 18, 1971, the offices of the *Darien News* caught fire in the early hours of the morning and burned to the ground. Investigation confirmed that it was arson; no arrests were ever made, but the newspaper staff never doubted that Sheriff Tom Poppell was behind it.

"You know," said Williamson in his smiling, humble, heartfelt way, "sometimes fights come and find you out and all you can do is stand and face them. I was still young enough when it all happened that I thought—and this was a mistake that I made—I thought, 'Well gosh, once I expose these people for the lechers that they are, they'll take up their tents and be gone forever.' But that isn't what real corruption is like, and that isn't what they'll do. They fight back and they have the money to do it. I didn't have any big business, but I wound up losing all I had. Kathleen and Charlie were little, and I was brought to the place where, 'Lord, I can't protect them and I have no law here that is going to protect me.'

"All the difficulty we've ever had with the newspaper has been with the news. We've never had any difficulty out of the expression of our opinions in editorials; trouble has always come out of printing just the facts. The *facts*."

2

McIntosh County's most famous roadside attraction was the S&S Truck Stop: a humble, slipshod, unpainted, trashy-looking little place sitting on a quarter acre of sandy land under a few pine trees facing Highway 17. Red, rounded, old-fashioned gas pumps sat out front, dry as a pair of sinks in a hardware store. A green-and-white striped aluminum awning shaded the doorway, under a fat hand-painted sign reading S-S Truck STOP. Inside was a room with a lunch counter, a few tables and chairs, and a window fan. It looked as if you might sit down and have a tuna sandwich and a cup of coffee while waiting for your car to be serviced. But you sure couldn't.

From Jacksonville, Florida, to Dallas, Texas, what truckers had to say about the S&S Truck Stop in McIntosh County was: They don't sell diesel and they won't fix your tire and you can't get yourself a cheeseburger and it's the busiest truck stop in the state.

"Truck drivers would go out of their way for the S&S," said Doug Moss, the private investigator and former police detective. "Trucks on the Miami-to-Houston route have managed to stop by. Hell, trucks going from Detroit to New York probably have managed to stop by.

"I stopped there once or twice in my lifetime," said Moss. "I was driving back from Savannah with a guy and said, 'Why don't we stop to eat at the S&S and check this place out? See what these people look like.' And they didn't have any food. I don't know if it was the day, or the particular time of day, or if they had a kitchen and it was closed. Some cute, scantily clad ladies sat with us, wearing, I guess, short-shorts and tank tops. They started chatting with us and asked us what we wanted. We said we wanted some cheeseburgers, french fries, and a Coke, but they didn't budge. Then one of them started rubbing my friend on the neck. We left shortly after that."

"They had gas pumps out in front of the place; no gas sold there in years, if ever," said Bill Kicklighter. "I sent a man in there. He went to the bar and sat down and ordered a beer. Person in charge said, 'What'll you have?' He asked for a hamburger. She said, 'Honey, the only thing you gon' get here costs thirty-five dollars, and you get it in the back room. You're going to have to go on down the road if you want a hamburger.' "

In years to come, coastal law enforcement agents would focus on the S&S Truck Stop as the hub of Sheriff Poppell's illicit businesses, specifically: prostitution, narcotics, gambling (including the running of a lottery in the black community), counterfeiting, racketeering, murder, the fencing of stolen property, the sheltering of criminal fugitives, and white slavery, or the employment of prostitutes against their will. "This list," the special agent in charge of the investigation noted helpfully, "is not intended to be all-inclusive."

What could have been left out, jaywalking? The Special Agent might as well have quoted T. S. Eliot and said, "McCavity, McCavity, there's no one like McCavity. / He's broken every human law. He breaks the law of gravity."

A successful, affluent, high-profile Savannah attorney remembers the S&S fondly: "The S&S? *Oh,* yeah. The year I was president of the Civitan Club in Savannah, we drove down the coast to the S&S for a club outing, kind of a field trip. Naked girls in harem costumes met us at the door. There was blackjack, dice, slot machines, screw movies, the works; and trailers out in the back for those adventurous enough. We had a hell of a good time, we came on back, some damn fool told his wife, and that was the *last* trip the Civitans ever took."

3

Sheriff Thomas Poppell flourished in a system of favoritism, nepotism, and paternalism known as "the courthouse gang" or the "good old boy" system. Georgia was infamous for much of this century for its highly evolved system of influential courthouse gangs. "Four or five counties down there along the coast practically controlled much of what went on in Georgia," said Lester Maddox. "Those who ran the county courthouses had their own empires in a lot of places."

Georgia has more counties than any other state in the union except Texas—159 little counties with names like Jeff Davis and Lee, Bacon and Coffee, Seminole and Cherokee, Lumpkin and Bleckly, tacked to the map by sparse little county seats like Vidalia, Jesup, Blachshear, Swainsboro, Folkston, Ludowici, and Darien. The little towns have wide, empty main streets—so wide and so empty that the downtowns allow parking perpendicular to the curb. And there are rusty awnings over vacant storefronts and—a block from downtown—dirt streets, porch swings, vegetable gardens, and half-asleep dogs in the middle of the road with their tongues dangling. Folks know one another in those towns and counties. They give directions to outsiders trying to find them like, "You come on down, you come on down, stop at the Piggly-Wiggly, get out and ask somebody."

It was not hard for born politicians to rise to power in a Georgia county courthouse. For one thing, not many folks were interested in the courthouse anyway. But having risen to power within the courthouse—whether or not anybody else coveted it—the local good old boys found that they had gained more than local authority: they had acquired statewide importance and influence. This was due to the remarkable institution of the county unit system.

When radical Reconstruction was dismantled over a hundred years ago, Georgia electoral law was rewritten in a populist spirit, making of all the tiny rural counties a powerful voting bloc. The Neill Primary Act of 1876 established the county unit system, a sort of electoral college for the state's primary elections (the only elections that mattered in Georgia). The county unit system resembled, in fact, the conversion chart in Razzle Dazzle. The conversion went like this: the 8 most populous counties in Georgia got six votes each to cast for a primary candidate for state or national office; the next 30 most populous counties got four votes each; and the remaining 121 little counties got two votes apiece. As a mechanism for fair distribution of voting strength, it was a disaster, since three tiny rural counties could nullify the vote of a major urban county; but the county unit system was not intended to apportion voting strength equitably: it was designed to place the balance of power in the rural countryside, in towns like Ludowici and Darien.

The historian William Anderson wrote the following in *The Wild Man from Sugar Creek* (1975), his fine biography of Governor

Eugene Talmadge, the ultimate manipulator of the peculiarities and downhome tastes of Georgia politics: "Georgia had uniquely thwarted the rush of history in 1876 by creating an addition to her primary electoral system which guaranteed rural domination of state politics. The popular vote was, in effect, disfranchised. Also voided was the vote of minority groups who had fled to the cities. As Georgia entered the twentieth century, the County Unit System became the cornerstone of her politics. While her economy began to slowly industrialize and her people to urbanize, the power in the State would remain steadfastly stagnant in the staunchly conservative multitude of counties.

"Management of the system fell into the hands of the county politicians, each of whom demanded homage and promises at election time. They held their sway over local voters through numbered ballots, the secret ballot not being a state law."

In addition to gaining statewide and national electoral influence, the courthouse gangs, once installed, tended to deviate from the obvious purposes of running their counties into the hidden purposes of earning more money than the everyday business of the counties permitted. The courthouse gangs tended not only to monopolize the local sources of wealth but to locate, exploit, and ultimately control the illegal sources of wealth as well. Nowhere was this accomplished with more flair, daring, and finesse than in McIntosh County. Sheriff Poppell earned a pleasant income for enforcing the law in McIntosh County, and he did a good job ("You didn't have to lock your doors," people said), but he earned a *magnificent* income for *flouting* the law in the county. Because he did the first capably, the law-abiding citizens, safe in their beds, didn't trouble themselves much about the second.

The courthouse gangs ran the counties smoothly for years, enforcing race, class, and gender distinctions, while eschewing modern industrial development with its threat of civil equality, higher wages, and the migration of outsiders into their counties. A handful of white men controlled each county, succeeded themselves at every election for decades, packed other electoral and appointed posts from among their family and friends, and filled up their own pockets with fortunes. They were, in a sense, middlemen, guaranteeing their county's votes to state and national politicians, in exchange for favors they were then able to pass along to the constituents.

A rather elegant example of this middleman setup was Ralph Dawson and the turkeys: The State Board of Education sent turkeys to Long County, next door to McIntosh, each year—enough turkeys to feed all the schoolchildren a fancy holiday cafeteria lunch before Thanksgiving vacation. At Thanksgiving, according to sworn affidavits collected by the GBI, retired city solicitor and local strongman Ralph Dawson would send over to the high school and the elementary school. "He'd say 'Go over there and get those turkeys,' " said a former GBI agent. "His men would go over to the schools and load up police cars with turkeys. The kids'd eat dried beans or whatever was left and go home with no Thanksgiving meal. Ralph would have his people carry the turkeys around to the needy families in the county and give them out. He'd have the turkeys delivered in police cars, so people would know Ralph sent them. He hadn't done a thing in the world for those turkeys. They weren't his in the first place. But people'll tell you: 'He gave me a turkey every year. The colonel looks after po' folks. That's why I love him.' "

Tom Poppell also generously dispensed goods belonging to other people. "Local people who leased equipment from other counties knew that once they crossed the Darien bridge, they were home free," said a white Darien businesswoman. "When the payments stopped coming, the owners of the equipment came across the river looking for their property. They'd run smack into the sheriff sitting in front of his jail enjoying the sunshine. He always knew they were coming. 'Boys,' he'd say, 'the way I read it is, possession is nine-tenths of the law.' "

"Everybody in McIntosh liked Tom. That was one of the

things about him," said Doug Moss. "I had a close relationship with McIntosh County in the 1970s when I was with the Brunswick police force. The McIntosh County Sheriff's Department was always ready to cooperate with us on investigations, as long as it didn't involve one of their locals. If we brought in a home boy, Tom would say to him, 'Son, why don't you go to Alabama and cool off for a while?'

"We had many a chase up [U.S.] 17 out of Brunswick," said Moss, "trying to catch crooks before they got to Darien. When they reached the McIntosh County line, we'd turn around and go home. We always said, 'That's it. They made it. If we want that guy, we're going to have to extradite him.'

"State troopers would pull over drunks and bring them into the Darien City Jail. They'd be writing the tickets out front in the office while Sheriff Poppell was letting them out the back door.

"And there were a lot of wild hogs in McIntosh County at that time," said Moss. "Tom thought all those wild hogs were his. He was all the time arresting out-of-state hunters that touched one of his hogs. I was told, 'You get in more trouble shooting one of these wild hogs than shooting one of the Negroes in McIntosh County.' And I don't use exactly the language they told me that in either."

"He had complete power," said Charles Williamson, the publisher of the *Darien News*. "And his father, the sheriff before him, old Ad Poppell, was just a nice old man who walked around town with a pair of gloves, spitting tobacco. He never hurt anybody. He had no corruption within him. He just got elected and he always said, 'I got enough kinfolks and damn fools around here to elect me so I guess I'll have to go into politics.' But his son came along and was apparently enlightened as to how he could make a lot of money without a lot of effort."

Five

Deacon Curry, Deacon Thorpe, and the Little Deputies

1

The secret life of the black people of McIntosh County unfolded inside closed cabins; and within the humble little Holiness churches, where perspiring worshipers in radiant clothing jumped and chanted in unison; and inside the weedy roadside juke joints, where moonshine and marijuana changed pockets by the light of neon beer signs; and at the icy metal tables of shrimp-processing plants, where old women in galoshes walked in place to get warm; and along the dirt roads that snaked through the twinkling pine woods and burst out under the vast white sky at the shoreline of the marsh; and at night on the ocean, where black captains tied their shrimp boats together, and drank whiskey and played cards in the hold, by the light of swinging kerosene lanterns, while the summer constellations slowly wheeled overhead.

It was a world practically impenetrable to white people, with a harsh, quick, humorous language nearly indecipherable to them. The white people, needless to say, weren't interested anyway. But there was one white man who *was* interested in the hidden life of black folk, and he employed spies eager to flap their tongues and tell their wild tales in exchange for his very special kind of patronage. He was, in his way, a genius, a quick study, this white man Tom Poppell, so that a small bit of information went a long way with him. After a minute or two of listening to some well-meaning, breathless old Negro standing in his yard after dark, he was able to thank the man and return to supper, his napkin still tucked into his belt where he'd left it when he'd excused himself; and he was able to go to bed later that night, and every night, fully abreast of the news, fully informed. And the old black man, replacing his cap and hurrying off, could fairly well count on a fresh turkey come Christmas, or a quart of something at election time, or a phone call direct from the sheriff's office the next time a truck wrecked, or instant and official forgiveness if his son or grandson got into some kind of trouble.

The High Sheriff was Darien's point man, the role model for racial decorum in the county. He employed blacks, he was friendly to blacks, he shared the bounty of wrecked or sabotaged trucks with blacks, and he gave rise to the living legend of McIntosh County as a place without race problems.

The black people, on whom little was lost (there were geniuses and quick studies among them also) knew quite well there were spies in their midst. The spies were known (unbeknownst to the spies) as "Tom's little deputies." In fact, it was one of the few things that escaped the sheriff's understanding: that the black community knew precisely who the spies were and yet did not ostracize or excommunicate them.

It was a poor, oppressed Christian community, the black village within McIntosh, exhorted by its own impoverished preachers to love and not to hate, to forgive and not to begrudge. Thus, the people tolerated the "little deputies," allowed them their pennyworth of pride, their molecule of power, allowed them even their vain belief that they were performing important undercover work. That the work happened to be the intentional betrayal of the black community was generally understood, but the cruel facts of poverty and joblessness surpassed it in importance. These were the people who mopped the floors, handled the garbage, killed and plucked and debeaked the chickens, and slaughtered and disemboweled the hogs. They could not afford to turn down work. Spying for Mr. Tom was, in its way, very dirty work, but the work was steady. And there came with it perhaps a hundredth of a percent of the sheriff's power, which, in an outcast community, was desirable to some.

"Now the sheriff's father, Sheriff Ad Poppell, he pretty much stayed in Darien," said Thurnell Alston. "McIntosh was about 70 percent black during that time, and most of them lived outside Darien. The whites in Darien were pretty much surrounded by blacks. Sheriff Ad Poppell, if he got a warrant for you, he send word by somebody, somebody riding horseback, and tell you to come in. He didn't go round and get you. Regardless of what you done, even if you killed somebody, he wouldn't come out and get you because Ad, he wasn't out there to get killed. But when he got you in jail, then he can control you. But as long as you don't go to jail, you don't have any problem with him.

"But Sheriff Tom, now, developed a kind of control right in the black areas. He had people in the area, he had people in every place of the county and every place of the region who are his robots. They do what he say do. And if they don't do what he want done, then hey, take them out, give them a good beating. They take care of the vote selling for him, too.

"Every now and then he'd bring one of these guys a little badge. The sheriff give them a *badge*. 'You a deputy. You my *special* deputy.' They really didn't have no more authority than a piece of paper, but the sheriff give them some little jobs: 'You see cows, hogs on the road, you run them off.' It was just the privilege, psychologically. In every community he had a little badge. And those guys were ashamed of it, to show the badge, but within themselves they were proud of it.

"You could always pinpoint these people. I didn't like, you know, seeing people being used against their own people. That's all it did consist of, is being used against your own people. He had a lot of them scattered out there."

Only Sheriff Poppell felt at home in every cul-de-sac and cove in the county, at both the north and south end.

He glided along the leafy sand streets in Darien in his Buick and turned north onto U.S. 17, bumping onto the rocky dirt dead ends in the pine woods, the Negro areas, with his car windows rolled down and his elbow stuck out, waving affably to one and all. He knew all the grown-ups by name, black and white, and knew to whom the children belonged; and in times of sickness, trouble, and death, he was the first one tapping at the screen door, hat in hand, voice lowered.

In times of nuisance, misdemeanor, or disturbance, he was also the first one there, never needing to show his gun or raise his voice. "Let's you and me go have a talk," he said to the drunk or thief or juvenile delinquent; and there was, truly, no menace implied as the sheriff opened the back door of a waiting patrol car. Even blacks could quiet down and climb in without fear, for Poppell was as open to bribery from them as he was from whites.

The black people didn't have money, but they had land, hundreds of acres of prime Confederate land waved into their family lines by General Sherman. An understanding existed between the modern sheriff of McIntosh County and the black people descended from the freedmen: an arrest warrant or an indictment might be mislaid permanently, or even formally dropped, in exchange for their land. The black people felt some confidence in knowing that a deal of some kind would be struck with the sheriff, who was becoming an extremely wealthy man. Titles would change hands in return for clemency and freedom, more valuable to the blacks than the richest land. Thus, the sheriff gained the loyalty—and the property—of the black families whose sins he forgave, whose debts to outsiders he severed, and whose crimes he forgot.

"The sheriff did so much for the colored. That's why I like him," said Deacon Danny Thorpe. "Get in trouble, lot of times he go in there and help them out. You know there's a little slickness goes on in everything. I don't care what you doing, there going to be somebody around to find fault, but he was a friend to us. There wouldn't be a world if there wasn't *some* sharpness going on, that's right."

"He has done some things for me," Thurnell Alston admitted. "I was about to lose a trailer, nothing anyone could do, went to talk with the sheriff: I've still got the trailer. People respected him for that. And *he* never forgot the things he did for you either."

"People respected him in a way that was hard to surpass," said Sammie Pinkney. "And he took care of his people. And then, it didn't matter what part of the state you were in. If you ran into a problem, all you say is, 'You call Mr. Tom.' And that was it. A lot of folks who needed welfare and couldn't get it, could go to the sheriff and he'd say it's okay. His sister ran the welfare department. Of course if he *didn't* want you to get welfare, you wouldn't get it. But he did a lot of favors for folks, particularly black folk. He'd loan you money. He never hardly carried a gun, never carried a gun. Just the way he approached folk, would go to them and talk to them in such a way there were no arguments."

A half-toothless, black-wigged, shy, heavyset, middle-aged black woman named Mary Harmon, now squeezed into a cotton shift with straining zipper, once was a mischievously pretty and shapely lady who worked in moonshine. "Be in the 'shine house," she said, lisping, her false teeth loose in her mouth. "He come in there and I say, 'Sheriff, I buy you a little drink!' I give him a pint or a half-pint. Ain't nothing to that. 'Shine houses be all over the county, and he'd be right there; he wanted to tend to his business. He was a good man. He was all right."

Mary Harmon lived in one of the rotten, gray Negro shacks in Darien, across a dirt side street from the jail. The holes in the side of her house were patched with cardboard, aluminum foil, and string, and it looked as if one good kick would topple it. It looked like a vacant-lot fort constructed by neighborhood children, but it was her house.

"He certainly got me out of trouble," she said with effort, the teeth clicking, as uncomfortable to her as too-tight pumps, so that one almost wondered whether they were borrowed dentures. "I was in Palmetto, Florida, one time, picking oranges. This particular night, me and my boyfriend Joey, we went up the street. I didn't want to follow Joe down to the diner—there's a place you can sit out there and drink your beer to the diner—and I didn't want to go down there that night. I wanted to stay at this country restaurant. So this guy was up there messing with me, and I didn't want to be bothered with him. He said if I didn't do what he said do, he was going to tell Joe that I was running around on him and cause him to be fierce.

"I said, 'Don't you do that.' He run up into me. And I said, 'If you going to do that, you wait until I come back.'

"And then honey, I got a knife about that long. I come back, I say, 'You still going to tell that lie on me?'

"He say, 'Yeah, I'm going to do it.'

"He push me and I done like this with him and cut his arm, cut his arm like that. He called the law.

"Hurry on home and got in bed. I never been in trouble. I went on home and get in my bed. Police come there, got me out the bed, took me down where the blood on the ground at Palmetto, went in the station, sat down there, started to cry. The judge sit down. 'Now you being a parent, you going to need some time.' I had my little boy with me, which is grown now. They done put me out in the county, at the jail house, but they give you time to call.

"I said, 'I ain't got nobody *to* call.' I said, 'I tell you what you do. You call Darien, Georgia, and call for the sheriff there, Tom Poppell. He'll tell you I never been in no trouble but just for drinking or clowning. And he will tell you to let me go.'

"And they did that, and I hear him when he come on the line, Mr. Poppell. He say, 'What Mary Jane doing down there?'

"They say, 'She in trouble for cutting a man.'

"He say, 'That man had to did something 'cause she ain't never been in trouble down here except for drinking. Turn her loose.'

"And the man—he's not a man would help you out—probation judge or something, he said, 'You got a pretty good recommendation down there. Your sheriff must be tough.'

"I say, 'Yeah, he rule us.'

"And he said, 'Well you out now. You just have to wait two days and then you clear.'

"That's right, that's why I love him.

"When I come back to Darien I went to the jail house, went into the office, and asked for Mr. Tom Poppell. Man say, 'What you want?' I say, 'I like to speak to him.'

"And he come out the back room and say, 'Well hello, Mary! Damn it all, what the hell you doing in jail down there?' That the way he put it.

"I say, 'I thank you.' And he shake my hand.

"He say, 'Don't go off and get drunk now.' That exactly what he told me. He really did. That ain't no lie. That why I love him."

Sheriff Poppell had the black community of McIntosh in his pocket. He seemed to be their great friend, and in a great many instances, he was. Yet the racial status quo was maintained, and he stayed in office.

He was a *personal* friend to black people, helping many out of difficult scrapes; but for the community as a whole, for progress, for justice, he did less than nothing. The precise machinery with which the southern caste system was being maintained was therefore harder for the black people of McIntosh County to pinpoint: there was no snarling hatred, no overt abuse, certainly no police brutality as in so many other southern communities. It was all done with a concerned kindliness and affability. Sheriff Poppell was their friend.

"The sheriff was a political power because he always manipulated and controlled the black district, the Crescent district," said Charles Williamson, the *Darien News* publisher. "And in so doing, he perpetuated himself in office. That's just smart politicking. I'm not being critical of it; I'm just telling you the facts. He was popular in other places, but he was *powerful* in Crescent. Black votes could be more easily influenced—I won't use the word *coerced,* I don't think there was any great coercion—but votes could be controlled back there.

"To this day, a person wants the black vote, well, he goes to the black churches. And the leaders of the black churches, the black leaders, come together and say, 'This is the person who will benefit us the most. He is my friend and he'll be our friend and therefore we will support him.' Whether he's black or white makes no difference. Poppell was a white man, but the black people voted to support him because he sold himself to the black people. He had the wherewithal to acquire their friendship. Whatever it took, he had it.

"Black people have controlled the politics in McIntosh County for all of my life," said Williamson. "There's never been a time that the black people didn't control the elections. We are practically fifty/fifty. Voting as a bloc is what makes it powerful."

"Yeah, yeah, I've heard that all my life. Yes, okay, they're the swing vote," said a voting rights lawyer in Atlanta, David Walbert, who would, in time, forever change the electoral system in McIntosh. "And tell me the good of a swing vote if your choice is between two arch-segregationists."

But Kathleen Russell, a *Darien News* editor, said: "We've always called them the sleeping giant."

"He ran McIntosh County with an iron fist," said Doug Moss. "He was a benevolent dictator, but he was a racist. He had black police officers, probably some of the first in the state, but I believe he had them in order to control the people. McIntosh County under his tutelage was a very depressed area. I think he felt if the county got in too much money, too much industry, too many outsiders, they'd lose control. And he kept his eye on the black community. If a black person got out of control in McIntosh County, he simply disappeared. We used to say they took a swim across the river wearing too much chain."

"There lots of people disappear that people don't know about," said Thurnell Alston. "A friend of mine was out in the country digging, and they dig up human bones—none of them even deteriorating, the head and all of them not even decayed. I think everybody in the county knew the sheriff had people killed. He was too powerful to do it himself. He always have somebody to have it done. He know about it. He know whatsoever went on. He *knew* that it was done or he *ordered* it done, one out of the two.

"These people haven't been nowhere else. The sheriff just really had them hoodwinked. They're just ignorant to what's going on. The sheriff was running this county just like an old plantation. When Tom said dance, you dance. When Tom said die, you die."

2

In one extraordinary instance in the mid-1960s, Sheriff Poppell did not have the patience to wait for the black people to come up with something and for the little deputies to knock at his screen door to report it. *He* read the newspapers; he knew there were changes afoot in America; he knew it would profit McIntosh to be able to point to its own racial progress. So he settled on a black political strategy himself and then informed the black community of it.

The first official black community organization in McIntosh County was conceived, founded, and named by Sheriff Tom Poppell.

He named it the McIntosh County Civic League and chose its members. He chaired its first meeting and named its primary goal: to place a black man on the McIntosh County Commission. He chose the candidate himself and enlisted the nominee's agreement. He then created an opening on the county commission. He did all this not whimsically, but in order to comply with federal guidelines governing federal revenue-sharing monies for which McIntosh wanted to apply. Applicants for federal funding in 1966 were required to show evidence of minority participation in the preparation of the grant request and evidence of minority representation on the recipient governing body. McIntosh County, needless to say, had neither. Not to worry, said the sheriff.

Overnight he created the McIntosh County Civic League; within one week the civic league had nominated a black man for public office; within two weeks the black man was seated on the county commission; within three weeks the completed grant request was mailed to Washington; and within six months McIntosh County had its federal money and frail, sweet Deacon Henry Curry, seventy-eight years of age, sat politely and inquisitively on the McIntosh County Commission, hands in his lap, blinking his large round eyes, the first black official in McIntosh County in the twentieth century.

"The people joined the organization; they didn't even have the slightest idea what was really going on. I joined it myself," said Thurnell Alston. "I was a member and I thought it was something good because they let us meet at school and that was very unusual, that they let us meet at school to organize, let us use the school to have our meetings. Then I started thinking, started realizing that what we had there was just another of Tom Poppell's symbols.

"He was pulling all the shots. He attended the meetings. The individuals did the things themselves, but he teaching them to do it, or suggesting things for the organization that need to be addressed. And he got his black for his federal funding.

"Of course, we felt good about Deacon Curry. We hadn't had a black there for I don't know how many years—not in my lifetime we never had a black. But I mean no telling what all they did with that federal money when they received it. The black community never saw any of it. Deacon Curry was *there* and wasn't any more the wiser of what was really going on. During that time they didn't have no really strict guidelines on the money. You just got it, you know. If they want to, they could bank it personally.

"It had to be very hard for Deacon Curry," said Thurnell. "That was before integration. But the sheriff had done it in such a way that nobody could point a finger at him and say, hey, that is the black that the sheriff selected for the board of commissioners. What he did, he came up with an organization and then this organization backed Deacon Curry. And that was the last act that this organization did was to back Deacon Curry. Then they start deteriorating.

"I'm telling you," said Alston, "that's about the greatest lying that I have ever known in my lifetime."

Henry Curry was, to his own mind, a simple and uneducated man, a son of slaves. Gay Jacobs called him a Ph.D. of the ocean; his church congregation made him their deacon; and his adopted sons and younger men in the county came unannounced to sit by his chair and listen to his thoughts, which he shared, while his old fingers tirelessly knit the fishing nets. But to his own mind he was a simple, not a clever, man. He was a fisherman; he dressed cleanly but poorly; he lived neatly but in poverty, while rejoicing in all he had been given. His calm spirit seemed composed of the same vast, simple, unending, glowing elements of sky and sand and salt and ocean among which he'd spent his whole life. He was a kind and ethical man, unworried about the unfair distribution of riches, looking instead to heaven.

And this was the man plucked out of his armchair by Sheriff Poppell and seated on the McIntosh County Commission, so that the sheriff and the county could say to the federal government, yessir, we've got a black, sure do—look here.

Startled by the sudden attention from white Darien, believing himself sorely unqualified, Curry exposed his lack of education to Poppell: "I didn't want to do it," he said. "I told them I didn't have the education, but they insist. They didn't have any colored on the commission board. They persuade me to be a commissioner so as to open the door." With reluctance and some anxiety, he went, and the young and middle-aged white commissioners greeted him in a friendly fashion—they knew he was a fine old fisherman and had hauled in plenty of shrimp in his day—and they tossed him a friendly goodbye when the meeting was over. They thought they did him a great favor, bestowed on him untold honor, and Curry thought so, too.

For two years Henry Curry faithfully attended the commission meetings and sat, and the quick, half-shifty business swirled around him like muddied water hiding dangerous rocks beneath the surface. In two years they never clearly explained a thing to him, nor deferred to his outlook. He understood early on that his color was adequate, was all that they needed from him. He'd been tapped for this post not for his wisdom, experience, or even age, but for the black-skinned grizzle-haired fact that his parents had been slaves and his great-grandparents, Africans. This, too, he might have accepted, seen as just, except that they would not let him speak—or did not listen, really, when he did speak—so that he seemed to himself not a representative of his people but an adornment for the commission table, sheer ornamentation like an artificial plant or a centerpiece. And this was beneath his dignity.

"Gentlemen," he said at his last meeting, at the end of two years, speaking deeply and slow, although the others already were scraping together their notepads and pens and heading for the door. "This will be my last appearance amongst you . . ." He told Sheriff Poppell he would not accept another term of office, and he troubled to explain why: "The human family has five senses, every one of them important, but which one you have the most confidence in? Seeing. The actions. Actions speak louder than words. You can't hear actions. But you see them. You can look at people and tell exactly how they feel toward you." But Poppell, bored, had turned back to his idling car in Curry's yard.

"Amongst those commissioners there shouldn't be no secret," said Curry. "Whatsoever one know in there, the others ought to know. I see several times that two or three or four of them would get up and go in there alone. Now I couldn't know what they were saying in there, they could have been setting a trap for me, as far as that goes. If they had any problems, they ought to bring them before the board and we all discuss them. I was on there for two years. I didn't want to run again because I saw they were only in favor of certain people."

So it was that the patriarch, the pearl, of the black community sat in governance at a table in the county courthouse, the first black man since Reconstruction to hold authority, and yet none of his gifts flowed into the life of the county. And when he departed, the whites took about two seconds to replace him, thinking it was so easily done.

3

When Henry Curry—in hurt and aggravation—resigned his position and went home to his wife and his fishing nets, Sheriff Poppell already had his eye on Curry's replacement: another black deacon and retired fisherman, another frail, sweet, elderly gentleman. But this one—unlike Curry—was eaten up with humility, stoop-shouldered with the desire not to offend. The sheriff drove onto the front yard of the most distressed and unhappy Deacon Danny Thorpe, where he bid Curry get out of the back seat and go knock on the door.

"My uncle, Henry Curry, was the first black commissioner, and Mr. Tom Poppell and him came up on me and wanted me," said Thorpe, in his placating voice, in his tiny gray house on a mud yard lined with flowers. "How come my uncle didn't last but two years on the board was he move from out of the district, move to a different house, so he couldn't run no more for that district.

"I didn't hardly want to do it, though. I didn't think I *could* do it," he explained. The old man retreated backwards through his small rooms crammed with furniture, his hands held in front of him to ward off Curry's request. Sheriff Poppell suddenly filled the doorway and ducked under the door frame into the still, hot, brownish room. Then Thorpe bumped backwards into a dining room chair and sat down in it, Curry pulled up a chair and sat down at the head of the table, and Poppell stood above them. "They asked me not to say no," said Thorpe, "and I didn't say no, and I tried it, and I liked it all right."

Thus began the sorriest chapter in the good deacon's life, as he left the dark cocoon of his home and church and went down U.S. 17 into Darien, all the while looking to Sheriff Poppell for guidance. He was like a newly landed immigrant and Poppell his smiling guide and translator: all the signposts and warnings the poor immigrant had followed in his homeland were missing or garbled, so he leaned ever harder and closer on the arm of the guide, who kindly led him down, down, down into a moral underground from which he would never completely escape. He served from 1968 until 1976. The memories he retained—quite unlike those of sharp-eyed Henry Curry—were of powerful white men having been "nice" to him.

"I got along pretty good," said the old man, while his lipsticked, bewigged, sweet-smelling elderly wife purred with pride in the chair beside him. "The chairman was a good white gentleman, and he was real friendly with me. And things I didn't understand, he helped me out with."

"I didn't know at first, you know, how he would make out," said Belle Thorpe, beside whom Danny Thorpe appeared positively boyish and full of potential, "but after he got into this job I felt pretty good because he was recognized. We have lots of nice plaques. And he did a good job; seemed like everybody liked him."

"Sheriff Poppell the old man, Ad Poppell, was a good sheriff," said Deacon Thorpe. "And that's why it was kind of easy to work with him and his son when they have those elections. Tom Poppell and I vote many people in for him. Wasn't exactly right, but yet and still I did it, and he like me for helping him out. That's why he did so much for me."

A typical form of corruption on the McIntosh County Commission was a commissioner's approving the use of county equipment and labor to further the projects of private landowners: private roads paved, land cleared, septic tanks installed, fill dirt removed, or supplied, at county expense for friends of the commissioners. White Darien quickly learned that Deacon Thorpe did the sheriff's bidding in these matters.

"A lot of time they worked me pretty well," he remembered. "So much calling. You see, they call in to ask you, and you have to write it down or you wouldn't remember all of them. So-and-so wants so many load of dirt, so-and-so want me to dig. That's the way they did it, so, see, that's why a lot of people didn't want me to come down or quit with it, because white and colored told me that I did more for the county than any county commissioner they had. And they all before was white."

He gave earnest, sincere service; he did his best; he did as he was told; he followed the rules as they were explained to him. Unfortunately, the unwritten rules of operation of the McIntosh County Commission under Sheriff Poppell (who, though not a commissioner, participated in the meetings as if he were the immediate past chairman, yawning and departing when he got bored), the operating rules of the commission were at about a ninety-degree angle from the rules in the law books. The presence of Deacon Thorpe on the commission allowed the white commissioners to slow their own transgressions down a bit and coast along legally for a time, cheerfully referring their friends and constituents to the Honorable Commissioner Thorpe. "He'll help you out," they said. All operations ran smoothly, and everyone—other than Danny Thorpe, hoping to please—understood completely what he was doing there.

Charles Williamson, the *Darien News* publisher, recalled a historic moment that placed Thorpe and him at the center of a controversy. Williamson was a soft-spoken, trembly, religious man, a kind of photographic negative of Deacon Thorpe; the two of them would have made a fine pair of opposing bishops on a chess board. In another life, in another world, they would have made an elegant duo of old professors, making a slow circumference of their shady campus arm in arm, deep in discussion of some arcane matter, encircled by pipe smoke. As it was, they became, very briefly, allies against corruption, although Thorpe wouldn't remember it the way Williamson would. It came to mean—and to cost—a great deal more to Williamson, whereas to Thorpe it was part of a bewildering array of events occurring virtually in a foreign language.

The incident concerned a nightclub in Crescent called the Moonlight Cove, which stayed open on Sundays, illegally offering liquor, gambling, and prostitutes. "The state patrol was regularly arresting sailors from the naval air station in Glynn County who had visited the place on Sundays," said Williamson. "They were intoxicated and they'd say, 'Well, see here, I've been out to the Moonlight Cove, and that place is owned by the sheriff and it's all right for me to go there and drink and nothing is supposed to happen to me.' " It was clear the place needed to have its license revoked. A local probate judge contacted the chairman of the county commission, and a special commission meeting was called.

Williamson said: "The commissioners all said, 'Well, that's Danny Thorpe's precinct.' He was the only black county commissioner. But there again he was named by and approved by the powers that be. He always voted however the powers wished him to. So they said, 'Danny Thorpe. It's his precinct.'

"The other two commissioners said, 'Yes, that's Commissioner Thorpe's precinct, and we want him to second it because that's not our precinct.' And Mr. Thorpe sat there very quietly.

"Now this was a white establishment, and after much waiting for Mr. Thorpe to second the motion, Mr. Thorpe says, 'Well, I couldn't second the motion because that's a white place, and I've never been into it and I don't know anything about it.'

"The chairman of the board said, 'Mr. Thorpe, you don't

have to go there. There's the documentation and the evidence that they are violating the law, and it's your precinct and we want you to revoke the license and second the motion.' (It didn't make good sense that it was his precinct anyway; they didn't have to go by precinct, as they quite well knew.)

"And Mr. Thorpe said, 'Well, I couldn't do that. I've never been there.'

"So you know somebody has really got their finger on him. The other two whites said, [drawling] 'Well, if Mr. Thorpe the black man would second the motion, we would certainly vote with him. We could do it unanimous.'

"Chairman said, 'I have to have a second to the motion. We cannot vote on it until I have a second to the motion.'

"Nobody would say anything. The room was packed. I was there as a reporter," Williamson said. "You know how reporters are. I said, 'Mr. Chairman, could I have a word?'

"He said, 'Well certainly, go and have a word, because I'm going to have to bring an end to this meeting. I can't get a second to the motion.'

"I said, 'Well, I'd like to speak with Mr. Thorpe.' I said, 'Mr. Thorpe, you've heard what's happening here. They are going to put all of the blame on you if this license isn't revoked.' I said, 'You need to make that second to the motion because you certainly have got good reason to, and it would be a terrible thing to allow this place to continue in operation when it is in your power to stop it. These other county commissioners—one has made the motion and the other two say they will vote with you if you second it, but the truth of it is, none of us are ever going to know whether they would vote that way if you don't second the motion. I urge you. Please.' People in attendance applauded when I sat down."

Then Mr. Chester Devillers rose. Devillers was the high school principal, a square-jawed, graying man. He was extremely serious and vastly competent. It was a rare man or woman in town who did not somehow feel—when conversing with Principal

Devillers—like a schoolchild called on the carpet for a reproach and perhaps, if they were unlucky, a detention. Williamson said: "Mr. Devillers said, 'Mr. Chairman, as principal of a school that has white and black children in it, I want to say we don't need that kind of a place operating in the district. Mr. Thorpe, you need to do your duty.'"

Danny Thorpe twisted his mouth this way and that, twisted his lean bony body this way and that like a long, friendly grasshopper that has been caught and pinned to a piece of cardboard. There was no escape, only misery, while at home far away his dear wife tunelessly hummed as she straightened up the cramped house, preparing things nicely for his return home from his day as an important official.

"Before Mr. Devillers had finished speaking," said Williamson, "Mr. Thorpe said, 'I second the motion.' And they did vote unanimously to revoke the license. Of course, the place closed for about a week maybe, then opened for business again. But all I can tell you is a short time after that the *Darien News* burned down at 3:45 on a Sunday morning November the 14th, 1971. We lost everything we had. They rang my phone in the middle of the night to tell me the place was on fire."

And what remained with Deacon Thorpe of that episode when he fell back on his old instincts for once and behaved honorably? "No, I didn't do it, I didn't do nothing with that," he said. "No, I don't remember that event because I didn't have nothing to do with it. I know it did happen, but I don't know if I was even on the board at that time. It's *been* a good long time . . ."

Deacon Thorpe stepped down from the county commission in 1978. "I resign because I see there certain things in county commissioner. You can't do everything you *big* enough to do because it against the law. So I was kind of helping out a good white friend of mine, and I done a little too much for him and they were going, you know, to put me in court for doing that. There so much you can do and so much you can't do. I give him a little too much dirt or something like that, that's all.

"The other commissioners didn't do as much as I did because I had a good backer at that time with Tom Poppell. He let me do a whole lot I wasn't supposed to do. So, however, I feel if I stay any longer now there I have to be prosecuted. So I decided I better come down."

Meanwhile, there are still a few tributes, even today, to the work of the well-meaning and misguided old gentleman. "Last April, I was the marshal—one of the colored marshal—at a parade in town," said Deacon Thorpe recently, perking up. "It was two marshals, one white and one colored, and we rode in the limousine they had in the parade." And Belle, beside him, nodded and exhaled, "Ummmm hmmmmm!" in smiling pleasure at the remembrance of seeing him there.

Six

Praying for Sheetrock

Off the road and far from money, the old people of McIntosh County quietly have sat, moving their lips and remembering their lives for hundreds, maybe thousands, of years. The ocean makes a person contemplative; it is brassy and rank and young, whereas human beings slow down and age beside it. It would be easier to grow old, you feel, if the rest of the world did not outlast you so ostentatiously, every spring gaudier than the one before.

Before the whites came, before the blacks, the Indian elderly must have sat, relishing in memory their fine moments, inwardly reveling, just as today, on high, small concrete balconies overlooking the Florida beach, American elderly people sit on foldout aluminum chairs and lock to the horizon from their high perches, while the ocean wind ruffles their hair.

There is thus the history of the place that can be written factually and straightforwardly, full of regiments and musketry and battle charges, dates and locations, explorers and beachheads and native warriors. Deeper than that is the history of the place that is known locally and not often told, except among insiders; these stories are referred to in a close-mouthed, roundabout way, such as the tales of U.S. 17 and the High Sheriff. Deeper still are the numberless secret and eccentric tales—unwritten and untold (unless one pries and sits and waits, and comes back another day to sit and wait again for a candle to be carried into a pitch-black, long-sealed-up room of the soul)—that also are part of the county's history. These are the private chronicles that people relate to themselves, the most secret plots and narratives. They will dissolve with the people's deaths if they are not shared, like glorious cave paintings never discovered by spelunkers, gently erased by rising water and mud.

For some, like Henry Curry, the inner paintings told the story of gaining and living in freedom; and for other, humbler ones, the paintings told the story of seeking food and warmth.

A short, dry-throated, cackling old woman, Frances Palmer, of undetermined age, the daughter and granddaughter of slaves, was born near the start of the century. In her old age she swathed herself in layers of long johns, pullover shirts, sweaters, cotton hosiery, and skirts, with a flowered house dress on top of it all. Her gray hair a thin, moist mat under a greasy kerchief, she scooted close to the blue jets of her gas heater even when hot autumn wind set the golden woods chiming around her house. She hunched forward in her chair to see her TV. When she laughed—a screeching *eee-eee-eee!*—her face blinked shut: the soft, lumpish forehead and chin closed in upon the nose, and the yellow eyes glistened.

She spent most of her days in her chair by the heater, rising occasionally to stomp in her son's boots to the kitchen for juice. She walked as if clubfooted, having stood for decades ankle-deep in ice, peeling skins off shrimp for a few cents a hundred. While Curry steered, competent and free on the open sea, shaking loose the clinging, crawling shrimp from his nets onto ice in the hold, Palmer curved her back and froze, standing in ice in a gusty warehouse; she barely survived on the wages and grew crippled from the work. So she hobbled like a Chinese noblewoman with bound feet. Her hands were clenched so tightly they were like stumps, from the thirty years of work on the frozen shrimp delicacies. It took two fists to raise a paper cup of juice to her lips.

In her old age Miss Fanny was content, especially when sitting in the upholstered rocker by the heater—an upholstered old woman with her substrata of clothing, plus shawls and blankets. She nestled in, sighed, and squinted at the TV. Sometimes a silly thing happened on TV—a cartoon cat chased a dog, or Lucy got closed up in a foldup bed. Sometimes a chattering bluejay alighted at Fanny's living room windowsill; or a spray of dry leaves and dust spun down the hallway from the open door; or a great-grandchild darted in to sit, gazing at her pocketbook until Fanny dug for a quarter, then smeared her old cheek with his dark lips and fled. At these moments the old woman's hoarse screeching laughter filled the little house.

On other days, though, she woke up sick and dragged soddenly from the bedclothes, a sour, nauseous taste in her mouth. She got dressed stiffly, crookedly, and ate some poor excuse for breakfast like a single hot dog with a slice of white bread. Because she was old and toothless and she scuttled around in her son's worn-out boots, there were days when no one called on her, even though she could hear car doors slamming in the distance. Then she sat gruffly before the television in her nightgown and left the windows shut as the afternoon slanted past.

On her weary days, when she sat hunched up and sickly, Fanny Palmer thought back to her grandmother, who had been a slave.

African slaves had been in the Atlantic colonies since 1619. By the mid-eighteenth-century, slave ships in the harbor of Charles Town were off-loading hundreds of slaves monthly. But the London Trustees who bankrolled the founding of the Colony of Georgia were reluctant to introduce slaves there. While most of the Georgia colonists clamored for slaves against the decision of the Trustees, the Scottish settlers of Darien penned the earliest antislavery petition in North America, *The New Inverness Petition of 1739,* which read, in part: "It is shocking to human nature that any Race of mankind, and their posterity, should be sentenced to perpetual Slavery."

Nevertheless, in 1749, London approved the importation of slaves to Georgia. And in 1755 the first slave ships arrived from Jamaica, Gambia, Senegal, and the Ivory Coast. By 1790, 70 percent of the population of the Georgia coast were slaves. And within months of the arrival of the first shiploads, the Darien Scots—signers of the heroic *New Inverness Petition*—purchased slaves and pushed them to the fields.

Miss Fanny was soft-gummed, bleary-eyed, and spirited, and her voice was full of metal and gravel—scraping, raucous:

"She had a little black hat and her hair just as *white,* white as snow, just as white as snow. And she been in slavery when it first start, when it *first* start. My grandma been a hundred and fifteen when she die. She say she had a *time* in slavery. She say, Whooo, she had some white peoples then! When the boss man call her in the morning, she say she shuffle her feet. God knows she didn't feel like going, she shuffle her feet. Say the boss man call her two times and say, 'If you ain't up, I'm coming back there and you better get up!' Say she got up. Oh Lord, she got up.

"My grandma used to go with her dress tied up round her waist and a big foot tub on her head, going down the road. And the boss man behind her with a strap. In the bucket they had guano to throw on the fields. And that boss man follow behind. Plat! Got to work or he beat the devil out of them. That in slavery time. Yeah, they got to work. And she had her little chile tied 'round her back. That were my mother, hugging her tight 'round the neck, a string around her little legs, a band around her waist—she tied to my grandmother's waist. And the poor little child—that my mama—cries, but that's all right, you better not stop. And all day long four or five white mens walking up and down the fields with whips that plait up [braided with leather straps]. When they cut you, the blood come. You can hear 'em: 'Oh Cap, oh Cap, I'm working.' And you better not stop. You better not stop, cause if you stop, they'll kill you. They kill some of them, my grandma say, they lynch them and they hang them out on trees; it were a shame to see. Sometimes they would try to run away, then they had dogs to catch them. She say they have a hard time in slavery time.

"You know you can't tie no child to your back, and hoe and pick, is it? My grandma say they work her till the tears fall from her eyes. Some had beds to sleep in and some on the floor. They get plenty of moss. You get your little child and y'all lay down on that moss. And when that big old clock strike, everybody rise, everybody rise. And that boss man, that white man, come there with that whip and get them up off that bed.

"Grandma say that field be full of good people, and plenty of people working and singing. They sing they little songs. Ain't know nothing about no church. When the thunder roll, boss man say, 'That God driving across the big bridge.' And the lightning: 'That be God striking his cigarette.' My grandma say she couldn't go to church in slavery, but she say, 'Let me be *turn* church [born again]!' I mean she *really* be turn church. When she die, she hold on and she say, 'Come on death!'

"My grandma say the Yankees! the Yankees the ones that make 'em free them. You ever see a Yankee? My grandma say the *Yankees* the ones that free them. She say she was a glad soul then. She say, 'Children, all we that been in slavery got something to tell God when we go home. Get the Negro up before God, every tongue going to tell the story, every tongue going to confess.

"'You got to tell God all your troubles about this world below,' she say. 'I got a lot to tell him and plenty more.'

"She say that be a time."

A work bell clanked in her memory. "Clanka-a-clang! Dinga-dinga-ding," she sang, telling it. Now her eyes glazed over and wept and all her limbs fainted with weariness even when she just shuffled down the hall to the bathroom or tried to reach the phone before it stopped ringing. Alone in the house for hours or days, sucking apple juice out of the Dixie cup she crushed between her two paws, she had ample time to relive her childhood; she recalled being a bare-legged young thing waist deep in the cotton field, threatened with a switch waved by a fierce, hooting grandmother who raised children to work, just like she herself had been raised: Bed. Field. Table. Field. Church.

Fanny had a laboring childhood in a world that consisted of her cot, the field, the kitchen, and the church. She lived within a circle of stout, husky-voiced women like her mother and grandmother, sun-blackened women who handled ploughs (usually without mules to pull them; they pulled them for one another) cooked vats of field peas with a twist of fatback and sang like wailing angels in church every weekday night and twice on Sundays. Beyond the circle of the tall women who surrounded Fanny, the twin enemies of sin and starvation advanced—just over her elders' shoulders, judging by the way they warned and threatened.

Women just like her mother and grandmother rode by Fanny's cabin when evening came, in wagons pulled by mules on the way home from distant fields. They shaded their eyes, jiggled half to sleep, woke and smiled, and hollered when they saw her: "Hey, little Miss Fanny!" She was a frightened scarecrow child who dug in the front yard and secretly hoarded the smoothest stones, lining them up and calling them babies; who wept and pleaded with the last and biggest sweet potato to please come out and kindly get into her basket before her grandmother got home.

Night, dawn, noon, dusk, night. Bed, field, table, field, church. Sleep, pick, eat, pick, pray.

Hair like black straw, parched skin and eyes, eyelashes brown with dirt, Fanny owned one dress (owned by ten before her), which she dredged through suds every night after church, dozing off on her feet, then threw over the line in the yard when prodded, and dragged from the line every morning in the dark. Her feet hardened like leather shoes, and she watched every dawn from her knees in the cotton rows.

Bed, field, table, field, church. Bed. Field. Table: a hollow gallop of wooden bowls on a wooden table. Field. Church: a chase through dark woods and clinging vines, barefoot behind her grandmother, who carried a pair of church shoes for the girl in one hand. Bed. Field. Table. Field. Church: dry, upright, mumbling heat. She slumped against her sisters and snored. Bed. Field: endless. Table. Field: dirt filled her fingernails, eyes, ears, nose, hair. Church. Bed. Field: she weeded, hoed, and picked until the sky and air whirled brown and thistly around her, and her small fingers moved, delicately plucking so as not to get pricked, even in her sleep. Bed.

The hoarse, straining voice continued:

"My mother had about nine girls and six boys. I was the youngest one. My mother was a preacher and a midwife, and she was traveling on, so me and two sisters lived with Grandma. Grandma tried to bring us up like she come up. She raise us up to go in the field. She give us so much and so much to work before breakfast. She ring the bell and we all get up—Dinga-dinga-dinga. We wouldn't do nothing but drink a cup of coffee and go into the field. That four o'clock in the morning. We go into the field and we mind the bird, call the lark off the corn. And it be cold. She would tie the moss from off the tree on our foot for shoes. It were *cold.* When the moss give out, she get a wide piece of pine bark and put that on my foot. We had to tie our little dress up around our waists, and I mean we had to work something else! We had to mind them boys. Next after that we had to mind the rabbits—oh Jesus, the rabbits eat the potatoes. And we stay there till sundown.

"At sundown we wash up good and go to church. We wouldn't ate no supper. Can't cook then, got to go to church. Now we come back from church, tired out sometimes I would fall down on the ground behind Grandma, and she be going, and I wake up and catch myself sleeping, I jump up and I run. Oh, I'd run through the woods, oh Jesus. I say, 'Do Jesus help me, help me get grown!'

"After that, four o'clock that bell ring, we in the field while the moon is shining. Working and hoeing by the moonshine. That's the truth. And singing. 'Save My Soul from A-Burning in Hell!' Oh we used to sing them songs; it make the work fast. 'I Want to Go to Heaven When I Die!' We singing. And we work. Grandma would give us a tas' [half acre] of ground to hoe. We work that before breakfast. We have a yellow cowbell—dingaling-aling-aling, dinga-dinga-dinga. We must eat. Time we done eat, we go back to the field. Then we knock off about two o'clock in the evening, and we go in another field to look out for the crow. On the corn, those crows be sitting on the corn. And we sit there till sundown. Then we go to the house.'

"I be so tired sometime don't know what to do. You get to bed and dangalang-dangalang, get up. Ain't had no kind of fun growing up; ain't had time to have any. But I had a good mother and a good grandma. We go in the woods with tin buckets and we fill them with huckleberries. We make plenty pies out of them and berry dumplings. You get your flour, and put you some flavor, and the butter, and they be fine.

"Yeah, I come up tough. I carry my little Sunday shoes, and I clean my shoes. Ain't get but one pair of shoes out of two years. I had a nice grandmother. Everything she teach me, I'm living by that. She would pat me in the night, me and my sisters, and she would tell us how to go through the world. She say, 'After a while Lord going to bring things a little better for us. After a while you going to see plenty of cars and airplanes and God going to give us all of them to use in the nice big world. But after that, don't forsake Him.'

"The lady that stay next door to my grandmother say, 'You trying to bring the children like your mama bring you in slavery times. That moss ain't doing those childrens' foot no good, it cold.' Mama say, 'No, I ain't bringing them like that. But I ain't got, and I am learning them to work for they living. When I'm dead and gone, I won't worry about them cause they can work for their living.' So she tie the moss. One time I get new shoes, and I don't put those shoes on my foot—I leave the moss on my foot; I want the shoes to go to church. Mama say, 'You going to know how to fight for yourself and how to fend.' "

The nights in her cabin with her own bare-legged children ("eleven head of children") sleeping willy-nilly on blankets on the floor, the oldest boy hauling in more wood for the fire, and her own sweet husband asleep in his chair while she sewed nearby seemed all there was to know of wealth, of happiness. She'd given them corn bread and flour-thickened stew for dinner; then children of all sizes roamed around the room for a while, undressing slowly in their fatigue, shoving each other, laughing, draping their wrung-out socks and underthings over chair backs, then rolling into sleep. She smiled past her sleeping husband at the oldest boy dragging in more logs. But the quiet hour was dearly bought: by 4:00 A.M. her husband would have been an hour in the forest, swearing and swinging and toppling the giant longleaf pines; she and all the oldest would be standing in the ice before hoses and knives at the metal tables of a Darien fish factory; while the youngest ones spent their days at her sister's, even the babies toddling into the fields to scare the crows with switches.

The scratchy voice, rasping and full of effort:

"My children would plow up all this field and sharecrop in the morning. I got all my big children catching the bus that go to the factory, shucking oysters. You go to work from three in the morning till five in the evening. My biggest girl been ten years old when she go to the factory; my next girl been eight. I raise all my children up just like that, from the factory.

"We work from dark till five in the evening, come on back, some cook supper, some go to the washhouse, some of us washing on the washboards, some of us down on the floor scrubbing. When we done our wash, I get my songbook and my children, and we walk two miles to church. Come back, get a little nap, cook breakfast, go to the factory again. Times was tight, there wasn't no money, and eleven head of children is something to feed.

"I'm going to that factory rain or shine, rain or shine or lightning. I had two little children, and I carry one and put him in a little box. I do every one of my children just like that, in a box. I'd stand up in that factory with ice piled up on my leg. I was working in the shrimp and standing in ice—standing in ice from three o'clock in the morning till five in the evening. I ain't had no good shoes on my foot, had them little slippers. When I get off, I don't seem to have a foot on my body. And every doctor I go to he say, Is it time for the change of life? Do I have hot flashes? I tell him I don't know nothing about no hot flash. My blood wasn't nothing but water. I couldn't eat; I had a straw through a bottle, and I sucked that straw for a year. July when it be hot I have to have a blanket over me; the cold was done gone through me. Anyhow, God helped me, because I should have been dead. Many young women come along like me be dead and gone, and I right here."

Her voice grated, like a stereo needle scraped back and forth across a record, a protesting, static-filled noise. There was no single, clear tone to her voice, but half a dozen simultaneous rough-timbered, minor-key pitches, all rumbling together to make a single guttural word. "You cut off the tail and peel him," she croaked, "peel the shrimp and put him in the can, a quart can. You get one can, you get twenty cents. It would take about a hour to make a can. Two of us have to work that can to get a can. That ten cents a can. Fifteen cent for a full quart of oyster. It take most all day to get a dollar.

"Ain't had no kind of heater. A government man come one day, say, 'If you don't get some kind of fire or something for these people, we'll have to close you down.' I declare, because plenty of them half-died, plenty *is* half-died, plenty of them gone. Well now, I say, the Lord hold me here for something! After the government man tell them, they get a heater. They stick the heater up in the corner. But there be so much of peoples that one-half couldn't get to the fire. And that half be trembling. The head man come in, say, 'All right, don't stand front of that heater too long!'

"My husband and I got married Easter morning, six o'clock in the morning, and we be together fifty years. He never did slap me, never beat me, ain't never left me, and I never seen him mad. Hoover times, times be so tight, and they would give us the naked flour—no meat, no lard. He tried to get just what he can, and he didn't keep nothing from me. He tried to work 'round the white people. Some of the people in Darien ask me now about my husband. He used to cut ties [planks] out of pine trees, but he didn't get no money. He cut a hundred ties, and that ain't but a hundred dollars. You cut down the tree and you bust it up and you got two ties out of a tree. That two dollars.

"I had two big tins and one would be full of corn bread and one would be full of biscuits. A stove of potatoes, a pot of fresh okra, and a pot of peas—I mean, I used to *feed* them. A young man said, 'I know your children ain't starving and you doing the best you can. Well, I'm going to marry that girl there.' That was

Annie Mae. I say, 'Oh no, no, let my daughter go.' That was a sweet child. I say, 'Time too tight and I ain't got the money to fix my daughter to marry.' He come back the next evening, say, 'I been working, and next Sunday I'm going to marry her.' I say, 'I ain't got the money.' He say, 'I'll buy the dress and the shoes.' He bought the dress, he bought the white shoes, and he bought the veil. A cousin come and make the pretty arch. Her and him come and stand in the door just like that. The preacher married them. Then she married and gone; I didn't have no more trouble with her.

"I been to a woman's house, she fixing to go to church, she say to her daughter, 'No, don't put that dress on'; the girl say, 'No, I don't want that!' She fling the dress in her mama face; she go get the other dress and throw it on the ground. I glad I ain't had no children like that, 'cause just what I put on my children they wear. Ain't none been in jail. Ain't none of them thief. They all trying to fight for they little self, they all got they little home.

"I had one stubborn one though. The others be in the field; I come to the house to carry some water to them in the field, and she be in the room putting on some clothes. I say, 'What you putting on them clothes for? Take them things off!' and she pulled them off and she beat me to the field. They all say, 'We got a tough mama, *tough* mama. But every one of them get a husband, and ain't none of them had a baby on them. Ain't none of them been in jail, and every one of them is church workers. I thank God for that. I raise a good family. And of that eleven head of children, my husband ain't get one of them but his.

"Sometime my children come to me, you can hear the band playing, they say, 'We going on the picnic.' I say, 'What picnic?' I say, 'I'll picnic you. If y'all don't get you back in the fields, I'll picnic you.' "

When Fanny Palmer had been in her new little wooden house a year, she still could detect the odors of lumber, paint, and varnish from the days of its construction. She sniffed for them. One closet still had curlicues of sawdust on the floor. She would never sweep them up. They were precious to her, like traces of talcum powder on the floor of an old nursery when all the babies have grown and gone.

Men came from all over the county and nailed the box of her house together while she and her youngest son—a retarded man of thirty-five—stood by. Her old house, a sharecropper's shack, stood tilted in the backyard of the new house. She had raised her family in it, but it was falling to pieces, sinking into the ancient, overgrown tobacco field, the rows of which once had come right up to her door. The cabin had been like a black patch on a green striped sheet, but the black people who had lived in the shack knew—as the white owners of shack and field knew—that without the patch, there would be no stripes; without the sharecroppers, there would be no crop.

The cabin had become like part of the woods itself. The sunlight lay in pale yellow lines on the wood floor, as it would on the floor of the forest, because it came through the gaps between the planks in the roof. The inside walls of the house were one side of ancient, crusty two-by-fours, and the exterior walls were the other side of the same planks. The windows were open squares covered with wax paper. On winter nights, Fanny and her son put on sweaters, coats, hats, gloves, and shoes before getting into bed. Her husband, the night he died, said to her: 'Get you a house, for you and the boy.' But there appeared to be no way she could get a house, though she and her son were freezing to death. Every winter in Georgia, old people in these shacks freeze to death. Fanny put on a whole closet full of clothes and lay down shivering. But then God made a miracle.

"I been getting ninety dollars Social Security, that all I been getting. I put down forty dollars to the hundred. I get a hundred, I put 'em down; get a hundred, put 'em down. Sometime I didn't get nothing to eat, but the other house been old. Sometime I would need a shoe; sometime my boy would need a shoe. I wouldn't get me no shoe. I would get my boy a shoe. Then I see a young fellow that used to stay over there. I say, 'Could you build my house for me?' That my grandson. He say, 'Grandma, you can't build no house 'cause you ain't getting nothing much and we ain't able to give you.'

"I say, well, I'm going down to God and ask God to help me. He say if you come to Him in earnest, He going to help you. You make one step, He going to make two. I say, 'All right God, I'm going to make the step; you know I need the house, my house falling down.'

"All right, the next year they raise my check to $125, so I start a man on the house. He do a little bit at a time. He come at eight o'clock and be gone at nine, and I don't see him before the next day. That just the way he be doing. It be getting cold. I ask him one day, 'When you think you'll let me get in the house?' He say, 'Well, next year, in January.' I say, 'Well, praise God, there ain't no place for us to sleep.' I lay down and ask the Lord, say, 'Lord, I ain't got no husband, ain't got no mama, got nothing to help me, and I done make the first step. So are you going to make the two?' I *ask* the Lord.

"All right, next a young girl come here one day, a white girl. She say, 'Miss Palmer?'

"I say, 'Unh hunh?'

"She say, 'When you gon' get this house done, Miss Palmer?'

"I say, 'God knows.'

"She say, 'Miss Palmer?'

"I say, 'Unh hunh?'

"She say, 'God sure is good to you, because I want you to sign a blank for me and tell us what you has got and all your business.' I signed the thing and she gone. It been a month before I hear from why I sign.

"One day a man come by here from Savannah—he be going down that road there. He say, 'I'm looking for a lady call Miss Palmer.' My boy say, 'That my mother, she here.'

"He say, 'Miss Palmer?'

"I say, 'Unh hunh?'

"He say, 'We got information about a little house that ain't got nobody to build it. The government want us to help you finish it.'

"I say, 'Thank you God!'

"So the next week he send some boys and they make these rooms and put in a toilet. Now ain't that been God? That was the Lord. You got to love everybody. I love the white just as good as I love some of my own color. Now that's a white fellow what come to me.

"But then we got to struggle. Ain't had no Sheetrock, and no more money, and the house can't be built. And that man say, 'You won't find a woman, white or colored, that could build a house like that with no money.' I ask them to take the tin off the old house, but it wouldn't go 'round a house this big. So they put a little tar on it for me.

"I lay down and I cried, say, 'Lord, they can't finish my house; we ain't got no Sheetrock; please help me, Lord!' The night me and my boy come in this house, that night I took sick. I been so sick till I didn't know. I just been taking cold going from the house. Ain't had no Sheetrock. I say, 'Well Lord, don't know how we're going to get the Sheetrock. Praise God, I done take the first step; I *need* you to take the two.'

"So a young girl come here from the state road, say, 'Miss Palmer?'

"I say, 'Hmmmm?'

"She say, 'Where your son?'

"Say, 'He gone.'

"She say, 'Lord! If your son been here, there two trucks wreck on the state road with Sheetrock, and the people carrying it and they charging them nothing. I mean that *good* Sheetrock—they be going up north with it.'

"So I phoned a house up the road, and one of my grandboys been home. So he took his truck and he gone, and he bring a load and pile it up in there. I say, 'You think you can get any more?' He say, 'Yeah!' So he gone and he bring another load. So now when the man come to put it up, he say, 'How you get this Sheetrock, Fanny?'

"I say, 'Ain't God is a good God?' I say, 'That truck wreck!'

"He say, 'This Sheetrock will cover all the house. This Sheetrock would have cost a thousand dollars.'

"It cover all the house and left two sheets, and my granddaughter gather the two sheets. Ain't that been a good God? *Ain't* that been a good God!"

Part Two

Mayor Sumner said to me, 'Sammie, I been knowing you all your life.'

I said, 'Yeah, I been knowing you too, but I'm not the same Sammie you used to know. I'm a different person now; my thoughts are different. I was a young boy at that time. I'm a man now.'

And Sheriff Poppell said, 'I never had any trouble out of your daddy.'

I said, 'Well, you won't have any out of me if you leave me alone, but I'm not my daddy.'

He said, 'You were a cop up in New York.'

And I said, 'Yeah. But I'm home now.'

—Sammie Pinkney

Seven

Shoot a Man in Broad Daylight?

1

The season of great change began with a shooting on March 22, 1972.

Mary Harmon (rescued from a Florida jail by a phone call to Sheriff Poppell) stood flirting with an old friend outside her shack in Darien. Patched with cardboard and aluminum foil, the house sat across the street from the rear entrance of the white brick city jail. Mary was thirty-eight. She had a few yellow teeth and a few silver ones interspersed, like a keyboard; a head of black hair; and a body that still resembled—in heavier outline—the abundant and smooth contours of her younger womanhood, the slopes and hills and resting-places that men longed to follow and lose themselves among. It was a queen-size bed of a body and required about the same quantity of stretched flowered cotton fabric to cover it. "She was a *good*-looking woman," said Sammie Pinkney. "Men *stay* behind Mary."

It was spring. The bare hickory trees had become curly-tops overnight, as if they'd stepped into beauty parlors the evening before with their empty branches and emerged suddenly bushy-headed, with tightly curled, shellacked-looking permanents. They appeared slightly ridiculous for a few days, as if fluffily overdressed for the get-together. Then within a few days the dogwoods and pear trees shyly emerged, all beribboned, braided, and perfumed; and tulips stood up in the yards in colors so bright they seemed almost musical. Yellow forsythia bushes shot up here and there in yards like fireworks. And there was the democracy of the azaleas: the cheapest tin trailer with its pounded dirt yard could present the year's best, startling the eye with bushes of flaming magnificence, so that the trailer settlement, the chained dogs, the used tires, and the bare-legged children all took on a brief reflected beauty, a Caribbean exaltation of life in the middle of poverty.

On that hot spring Friday afternoon, Mary Harmon planted her buxom, loud-mouthed, cocky self, barefoot, in her own dusty yard and refused to go indoors. She was sleepy and tipsy and was taking more pleasure in saucily arguing with the would-be beau, Ed Finch, who had just arrived, than she was likely to experience indoors with him, wrestling and resisting on the slovenly sheets of the daybed. So she stayed outdoors in the sugary air and put her hands on her hips and answered him impertinently when he begged her, in low tones, "Come on, let's go inside the house." Such impudence had been hers for a long time, since she was a teenager in smeared vivid lipstick and too-small pumps and a too-tight skirt; since she was a pigtailed child brazenly refusing to perform some chore and laughing with her little pearls of teeth.

"Mary was a nice-looking woman," said Thurnell Alston, "I mean, in her day. But she start drinking and all that junk. She just a little tramp. She was that type of person that anybody—you know—it didn't make no difference. Ed Finch worked for the city on the garbage detail. He was about 6′1″ or 6′2″, must have weighed 230 pounds—fairly large, very muscular, big-boned, wide mouth, round face, hair cut short. He didn't carry too much weight in town, wasn't real popular. His brother was a crook."

"Ed was a little taller than I was," Mary said later. "Color a little lighter, gray hair. He was neat and clean. Couldn't see out of one eye. He was a friend of mine, a nice friend of mine. I would say he wasn't a *special* boyfriend of mine, but he was a nice guy to me."

So Ed pleaded and Mary refused. And he begged louder and she refused louder, laughing, kneading the dirt with her bare feet wide apart and swaying the great hips, the massive rear; and there was pleasure in it, it was flirtatious. "Get away from around me!" she snapped, and he said, in low notes, "Come on Mary, let's go inside." Two doors down, other friends stood in their dirt yard, and they also were drinking and bickering on this colorful spring afternoon.

"Starting off like this, what the problem was," said Mary, "on this particular day I wasn't going with anybody, and he come by to see me. When he'd get his paycheck, he'd come by and bring me a bottle, you know. But we still wasn't *too* close, but we was still friends. Understand?

"All right, on this particular day, I have two friends across on the other side of the raggedy house, and I stay on this side. And my daughter was home. And I come home. So Johnny and Mary—that's another Mary—over on that side raising a lot of cain—they been drinking. So I come on home. That time Ed Finch come around me, and then he wanted me to go in the house. I said, 'I'm not going in the house, Ed,' and he got this look on him. He real jealous of me. He just wanted to go in the house, and I wasn't ready to go in the house. You know what I mean?"

Fussing and drinking and shouting and scolding, the voices rose; and across the street Darien's chief of police had stepped outside the rear door of the jail for a coffee break in the dull day.

"So this *po*-lice named Mr. Guy Hutchinson come out of the jail," said Mary. "Guy was a big old kind of person. He real big. He didn't take no for the answer. He have a nickname, Hard Rock."

"He was kind of short and stubby," remembered Pinkney (from the perspective of six foot two). "Let me see who he favor: he was sort of like Archie Bunker on TV, but not that white of skin. He was kind of reddish. They call him Hard Rock, and he was mean."

Hutchinson was irritated by the lazy, drunken clanging of the voices of barefoot people on a workday afternoon. He yelled at the black people in their own yards to shut up, and when they acted as if they hadn't heard him, he crossed the street to tell them again. "He was over there standing by his police car," said Mary. "After all this John and Mary hollering over there, here come me and Ed Finch kind of loud. Telling like it is, but I wasn't mad. And so this Hutchinson came in the yard, and me and Ed still there. He got on Ed. He tell Ed to hush, and Ed ain't going to hush. But Hutchinson didn't have no business—we hadn't called him. We didn't send for him. The police don't have no business coming to the house to bother me."

"I just told you to hush," said Hutchinson.

"I ain't ask you to tell me what to do," said Ed Finch.

"I am warning you that you are disturbing the peace," said Hutchinson, and Finch replied, "Yeah, well you can go to hell."

Finch then walked off toward the side of the house, cursing to himself, and Chief Hutchinson followed and grabbed him by the arm. When Finch whirled around, the chief raised a can of Mace and sprayed it at him, and one-eyed Finch dropped to his knees.

"My daughter Lillian was sitting over there, and she say, 'Mama, come on,'" said Mary, who had observed the action to this point. She grabbed me and carried me in the house. She done stashed me in the house because she scared. And she know the balance of what happened."

When Lillian went back outside, Ed Finch was crouched at the faucet trying to wash his face. Hutchinson approached him from behind, they wrestled briefly—Finch reached for a hoe lying in the yard, then Hutchinson stuck his .38-caliber revolver into Finch's mouth and fired. He then dragged Finch, bleeding, across the street to the jail. Finch was locked in a cell and left alone.

Having been shot point-blank in the face, jailed, and denied medical attention, Ed Finch was charged with aggravated assault—a felony—and drunk and disorderly conduct—a misdemeanor. He was also charged with having obstructed a law enforcement officer in the lawful discharge of his duties.

"I had my hoe because I had my yard clean and it was full of leaves 'side the house," said Mary. "I can see the hoe now. It wasn't no wooden hoe. It was an iron hoe all the way around. I do know that Ed had that hoe. I see Ed pick up the hoe, hit at Hutchinson. Then Lillian carry me inside and I hear the pistol. Then they carry him to jail, and nobody go down to see him, even me. I didn't go because I been scared, because I didn't want mixed up with nothing.

"They wouldn't let me get up," she said. "Made me stay inside because I was kind of half- . . . had a little drink, you know, and Lillian didn't want no trouble out there. But I wasn't doing nothing wrong, not a thing wrong. I just be drinking, and they come bother me because the man tell me to get in the house.

"All I know I stayed in the house. I do remember this much: when I *did* come out the house, a lady come on the porch as far as I remember. I didn't see Ed out there. Ed wasn't there. That's right. Ed Finch was not there. A lady named Lankford come to the house and ask me, say she heard that Ed got shot. 'Well,' I said, 'I didn't see it, but I know he got shot; but I didn't see it.'

"I don't know how word spread so fast. Weren't nobody there but me—I was there, with Mr. Ed and Hutchinson and the landlady. And how do you explain word spread so fast? I really don't know.'"

Perhaps it was because the story was so simply told—a dozen words could tell it—or, if the time were short, four words: "They done shot Finch."

Ed Finch spent Friday night in jail with a fresh bullet in his jaw, choking on blood in his throat, blood drenching his clothes, and spitting fragments of teeth. In the neighborhood outside, as a pink dusk full of flowers and birds drifted through the streets, the news penetrated every house. "You hear police shot Ed Finch?" "Don't believe they called the doctor." "Do the reverend know?"

After suppertime, the black people of Darien came back outside and stood unhappily around in the streets, under a sky striped turquoise and black, looking toward the jail where Finch lay dead as far as anyone knew. Illumined from beneath by yellow streetlights, the dogwood trees seemed made of paper, each white or pink petal cut with child's scissors, softly rattling like paper when the wind blew. The black people stood and spoke in quiet voices under the dogwood trees.

They lived lives of civilized repression, separated from white Darien in dignified and orderly fashion according to state and municipal laws and the prevailing social codes. But clearly an attack such as Hutchinson's upon Finch was not allowed: the blacks were not, after all, to be slaughtered like hogs; the fiction was to be maintained of two separate societies living rather gingerly side-by-side, each with its own hub of social and business life. Such a vicious and unprovoked attack by the chief of police against a citizen was a violation of the unspoken social contract that allowed the whites and the outcast blacks to live in peace.

Of course, sudden messy violence was not unheard of in McIntosh County: black men had been shot point-blank, hanged, and even—during slave times—burnt to death. The sheriff was known to ride untouched on a sea of violence that rose and fell at his beckoning; but those murders—of transients, of underworld people, of gambling and robbery victims, of prostitutes, of drug dealers—were committed far from the residential areas. Bodies had been found in the pine woods, as had new ownerless cars; bodies had surfaced in the marshes. But those crimes followed a pattern of angry justice all their own. The sheriff had the propriety, the good manners, to keep such acts far from the flowery streets of Darien.

But shoot a man in broad daylight? across from the jail, with patrolmen lounging around if reinforcements were required? Shoot a man for fussing with his girlfriend? and even *she* said they were just funning? Then lock him up without letting a doctor look at him? No matter which way the bystanders handled and turned the story, no matter how they dissected and considered it, they could not contain a rising sense of outrage and abuse. The crowds in the street grew, and grew louder, as more neighbors came forward with their bits and pieces of information: "I saw Ed and Mary in the yard." "I heard the shot." "There's blood over there in the street." And where was Hutchinson now? Where was the mayor? Why hadn't anyone called the doctor? And was Finch still alive?

Long after dark, after the last stripes of turquoise had been inked out of the sky and the last wild-eyed, whooping children had been culled from the yards and streets and sent to their baths and their beds, the mothers reemerged wearily. They scuffed in slippers down their two steps—the screen doors slapping behind—and into the streets to rejoin the circles of people still outdoors, still exclaiming. With darkness, the sand streets glowed with the whiteness of streets in northern cities after a snowfall. Fenced-in dogs barked at the strange unrest, and loose dogs in the road ran ecstatic, snorting rings around each other. The voice of one person or another grew loud for a moment, drowning out the rest, then the low drum of voices proceeded. These moments of shouting louder and gaining attention with an original—or even not-so-original—loud staccato declaration—"She say she didn't *call* no police"—were the briefest possible instances of leadership and of courage: Yes it's me and I'm hollering, the voices seemed to say, aimed at the dark and serene, deaf, dumb, and blind white neighborhoods just beyond the backyard fences, where the neat, nicely painted wooden houses seemed to snooze with their curtains down like closed eyelids. But no one could command the crowd's attention for more than an angry phrase or two—"Say she *invited* Ed Finch *into* her yard"—before the crowd's attention shifted; each briefly heroic voice returned to the low, drumming chorus as a new voice yelled out above the rest.

Beneath the hurt and anger—the mothers in their damp dresses, with their rough hands, could hear it—was a sort of splendid excitement as well. It was that uncommon case, that rare thrill of justified fury. Men could raise their voices and yowl under the stars and the telephone wires, men who usually stood silently absorbing, and no one could say their sorrow ought to be reined in. This night of shared pain and confusion leaped up like a bonfire, everyone hurrying to join it. Yet there was something beneath the grief—the mothers could feel it—of arousal and excitement.

The night was not unlike a night of tremendous snowfall in the Midwest, when schoolchildren and their parents stay up to watch the eleven o'clock news to learn whether schools and city offices will be closed the next morning. If there is going to be snow, many secretly feel, then let there be plenty of snow, let there be weighty snow, let there be so much snow it buries the city, and people must light fires and wear pajamas and drink hot chocolate and share food with neighbors they never otherwise talk to and dig themselves out slowly, over several days. Just so, many people in Darien secretly felt, if there was going to be a disaster here, then let it be a true disaster; let us rise to our greatest manhood and womanhood; let leaders emerge among us; let us pit ourselves against Them with a heartbreaking cry for justice that even the deafest of the whites cannot help but hear. Without a great disaster—what if we learn Ed Finch pulled a gun? what if he shot first? what if the story of the shooting is untrue, arising from Mary's drunk imagination?—then we must return to our jobs or to our joblessness with swallowed outcries, separately.

"Do Reverend Grovner know?" "Do Louise know?" "Miss Carter say she *saw* the shooting." "Call your daddy and tell him." Overhead a million stars were scattered now, like sand flung onto blacktop. The people poured out their bitterness, dropped their differences. Men with jobs and manicured lawns stood beside men without shoes. Old ladies shoved up their front windows, stuck out their small heads wrapped in hairnets and called to the people in the streets: "Do Reverend Grovner know?" "Do Thurnell know?"

"Someone go and call Thurnell."

The minority blacks in the town of Darien instinctively looked to their stronghold, the black county. They agreed to drive out of town into the unwary outskirts and meet at the Alstons': it was centrally located, a common stopping place; everyone knew the Alstons, and a good percentage of the people were related to them; and Thurnell, in his midthirties, was a churchgoing family man, a skilled boilermaker and a union man. His opinion on the matter was worth having. And his phone was out.

The angry hubbub and bitter muttering built as people with cars drove in the dark through Darien out into the sleeping county. They pounded on the door. "Thurnell! Thurnell! Get up!"

Sleepy little Alston boys had been herded off to bed many hours earlier. They had kissed Daddy goodnight with their toothpaste mouths, and Mama had picked up their milk glasses and cookie plates from in front of the TV and turned off the lamps behind them as she gently shooed them down the hall to their room. She and Thurnell had followed them to bed not long after, and now she, Rebecca, twenty-three years old, was the first to awake to the sound of cars crackling onto the gravel driveway. "Thurnell, get up!" she hissed in fear and edged down the hall to protect the children, fearing the voices to be those of white men. Then she heard his name called supplicatingly, "Thurnell! Thurnell!" so she hurried back up the hall to her bedroom to get a robe, put a brush to her hair, and give her sleeping husband a shove before unlocking the door. There stood a crowd of friends and cousins and acquaintances from Darien, red-lipped in the dark, tearful and furious. Thurnell came out of his bedroom in a T-shirt and gray sweatpants and thongs, his hair bunched to one side like a beret. "What it is, brother?" he said.

"They done shot Finch."

"Say *what?*"

Perhaps the crowd had reached a threshold number at that point, ready to act, and their cars had pointed them to the Alstons' so that it felt as if this were the house they'd been trying to reach all evening. Perhaps it was because here, deep in the county with only black homes around them, they were freer to raise their voices and protest without excessive fear that the cause might be mistaken, might not be worth the pandemonium. Or perhaps it was because Thurnell Alston did not think first of relaying the message onward, did *not* say, "Do Reverend Grovner know?" but instead received the message himself, accepted the story from them, and sat down at his kitchen table to study the situation. The closest men took chairs nearby, watching him. All in all, the angry black Darien citizens—having waked up half the black county, and seating themselves, now, at Alston's table—suddenly felt that the message had been delivered.

"Okay then, okay then, okay, okay," Thurnell said. Awake now, he was agitated, stammering; his hair stood on end, and his hands shook as he lit a cigarette.

"Okay, okay then," he said. "We need to talk about what we

going to do. Somebody need to call the jail, find out if Ed is alive. Merritt, go ask 'round back can you use her phone." Rebecca made instant coffee and opened bags of chips. Little boys appeared shyly at the kitchen doorway in their pajamas, rubbing their eyes and smiling because they knew no one could fault them for coming to inquire. Men lifted them, and Becca absently handed each of them a slice of bread. They grinned at each other across the men's backs, at the late hour. Merritt returned and reported that Finch was alive but that was all he knew.

"Okay then, okay, okay," Thurnell was saying as everyone watched him. The commotion in the room dropped off to nothing save for heavy breathing. The little boys twisted around in the arms of their big friends to see what everyone was looking at. Everyone was looking at their father.

Black McIntosh County gathered around Thurnell Alston's kitchen table the night Ed Finch was shot. In many ways it would be seventeen years before they left again.

2

"Okay then," Thurnell was saying, seated in a kitchen chair, rubbing his hand over his hair as the standing crowd circling his kitchen table gazed down on him, and his own boys slowed their munching on cookies and turned in the arms of the men who held them, to look. "We know Finch is alive. We don't know how bad he's hurt. What we're going to tell people is to meet at City Hall at nine in the morning. We're going to find out if the man have received medical treatment, and we're going to get to the bottom of the story."

"We sat down and we talked about it," said Alston. "We made some phone calls; I called my brothers; we called some people from all over the county and explained the situation and told them we were meeting in Darien. Some guys wanted to find out would we be violent. So we told them this was nothing about being violent. We hope there wasn't going to be any violence, but just bring some stuff to really be prepared to protect themselves if something comes up."

In the small hours of the morning, after the last newborn had been fed and diapered and put back to bed for the last time till dawn, phones rang and lights went on in the cabins and house trailers deep in the pine woods where the black people lived.

"Why did they come to me?" said Thurnell. "I don't know. Every time I went to church, I was telling people about some of the things we should do. So I guess they were just thinking maybe I would be the one could start some kind of reaction."

Toward daybreak throughout the county, with voices and lamps low, men oiled their guns and women looked to their food supplies and counted their kitchen money as if preparing for a long siege. This had felt like a long time coming. In the morning the city people walked over to City Hall, and the county people drove down Highway 17 into Darien, grim faces behind the windshields of old Chevys and battered trucks, a slow cortege that lengthened at every dirt road as more cars and trucks pulled out and headed slowly south.

More than 200 black men and women circled City Hall, parked, and waited for the mayor, James W. Caldwell. A larger number of newer cars and trucks circled theirs, in which white men sat wearing sunglasses, holding loaded shotguns. In this, as in all matters, Sheriff Poppell had been well advised beforehand. This was not his fight, being officially a city problem, but the prospect of hundreds of armed Negroes in the center of Darien was disquieting to any thinking man, so he had alerted his people.

"We had two hundred or three hundred people, blacks, show up at City Hall Saturday morning," said Alston. "It was amazing to see that many people, just somebody call, telephone call. People come from twenty miles away. Everybody was just that hot about it. Not only men; we had a lot of women there also. That really shocked me because once a woman get something to start going with, it's hard to break her. And they look just as nice that day as you want to see."

Thurnell's carload got out to stretch their legs and wait for the mayor to arrive. A white man strolled over to Thurnell and advised, "I hope y'all ain't going to start no stuff, because the sheriff done authorized the stores not to sell ammunition to no blacks." He nodded at the men standing at either side of Thurnell, turned, and walked back to the watching whites. Then there was sarcastic laughter among the blacks as the story was handed down the line: "They think we come all the way *here,* from all over the county, *carrying* guns and ain't got no ammunition?" cried Thurnell. He and the others scoffed at the image of black men politely lining up at the white stores, by the hundreds, to purchase cartridges: "Shall I wrap it, or would you like to load your gun here?" The white men must think them children, or fools.

"Mayor Caldwell was working at the Ford place," said Alston. "We got to town and he wouldn't even come to the office, so we had to go over there to the job and get him. He unlocked the door for us. We could only get seventy-five or eighty people in the building, and you couldn't walk back out the door there was so many people and so many cars parked there in front. And everybody came prepared, if you know what I mean. But the mayor disappeared. He unlocked the door and he was still in the building, but we couldn't find him. We had to send a group to round him up and bring him back, and then we had a meeting and I was the spokesman for that.

"Rebecca wasn't with me that day because the children were small. Merritt picked me up that morning. I didn't know I was going to be spokesman; I had just gotten ready to do whatever. But when I got there, Merritt and the rest of the group said they wanted me to be the spokesman. So I went in and took a minute to find out more detail about what happened, what went down, what didn't happen, what was the explanation for why they didn't send him to the hospital. I said there was no need me going in there, didn't know nothing about what happened. I mean I wasn't *there,* and knowing only what they told me. So they filled me in and it wasn't no problem then."

"We want an investigation done into this thing," the young Thurnell Alston said. The mayor and the handful of unarmed city councilmen and clerks looked miserably out over a packed room of angry black people in a realization of their collective worst nightmare. The black community of McIntosh County had long been obliquely described, by whites speaking among themselves, as 'the sleeping giant.' On this day, for the first time in a hundred years, the sleeping giant had been prodded awake. It was now blinking its dark eyes to focus on the line of skinny white men in khaki slacks and golf shirts in the front of the room.

City Hall consisted of a long, poorly lit, cheaply paneled room about the size of an Elks' or a Veterans' Hall in a small town; it had the rundown, dingy feel of a poolroom. And it was hot in City Hall that morning, a typical spring day on the coast, the azalea bushes smelling like simmering pots of jam. The radiant clouds lay flat against the pale sky like towels spread on a hot beach; up and down Highway 17, normal Saturday morning activities of garage sales and car washing began.

Inside City Hall row upon row of black men faced front. These broad-shouldered, muscular men—men shaped by the labor of felling trees, hauling nets, and pouring tar—stood crammed together facing the skimpy row of uncomfortable whites, and in that confrontation there was felt to be power within the black camp. The sheer numbers spoke of power, and the blacks were at ease among themselves, close together. This chafing of forearm against forearm occurred in their churches; in the dark juke joints; in the work of pulpwooding, shrimping, and turpentining; and at the backyard barbecues. These were people who had been rubbing up against each other all their lives. The subtropical climate and the hot shacks in which they lived forced them—from earliest childhood—outdoors, to a community of the streets and dirt yards, and then manual labor placed them shoulder to shoulder. They stood calmly now, unaffected by the crowding; and had there been cause for agitation, they could have reacted simultaneously.

And the white public officials knew the black people were armed, knew that each sweet-voiced black man pleasantly raking and hoeing a field or garden had within reach, in a bedroom bureau or in the glove compartment of a truck, coolly nestled behind rags and maps and matchbooks, a loaded revolver. The surrounded-minority mentality of all the white officials added to their sense of being under siege. The black crowd inside City Hall seemed to flow seamlessly out the doors and into the county, with every upturned black face for fifty miles—every soul looking up from plow, saw, or stove—adding to the length and breadth and depth of it.

The mayor and councilmen would have preferred to be anywhere in the world but in that room on that particular morning at that moment in history. It was not out of fear so much as out of physical discomfort, claustrophobia, and a feeling of tedium, a feeling of being sat down and lectured to, a sheepish feeling of being held captive in one's own chambers by one's temporarily hysterical inferiors. Their immediate task was to placate the mob and to ride out the fury without irrationally provoking anybody with a gun.

The white officials were physically intimidated rather easily. The white men—unlike the black—took no comfort in their own proximity to one another. They had sharp elbows and gooseflesh and did not brush together accidentally without leaping apart apologetically. In their airy, high-ceilinged churches they sat with half a foot of polished wood pew between them; at their dinner parties they reclined in comfortable chairs; and as for the leisure hours of summer evenings, they spent them indoors in air-conditioning with their wives, quietly reading or watching television. There was no life of the street for McIntosh County whites above the age of about twenty or twenty-two. The shooting of Ed Finch was, in fact, a kind of assault upon this outdoor life, this public mating ritual, by a man who didn't get it, who didn't *want* it exposed to him. Now, facing the fabled sleeping giant aroused, breathing through wide nostrils and heavily armed, the white men each felt alone, bony, pale, and vulnerable—and so they were.

Thurnell Alston wore his dress clothes: his white satin suit with velvet trim, a white ruffled shirt with cufflinks, and pointed white shoes with gold buckles. He looked like a bridegroom or like one of the Temptations. "We want Ed Finch taken out of the jail to the hospital," he said, with surprising composure, with his iron-black face and black bush of hair. "We want the chief of police removed from office pending an investigation." The black crowd murmured "That's right," after each declaration, like amens in church, and even the white men nodded acquiescently and the clerk took notes. But the black people were not looking at the whites particularly: transformed by the moment, they were speaking directly to God. "And we want an *end* to these abuses by the police force!" cried Thurnell in increasing volume and the crowd breathed, "That's right."

"They told me they wanted me up front," said Alston, "because they really felt I was outspoken. I wasn't bashful. So what I really wanted to get out was just the main issues of what happened. Everybody trying to figure out as big as Finch is, and Hutchinson have a gun with him, why Finch would have grabbed that shovel. And why do you bring a gun into a person's front yard? And why the man had come into a domestic argument where both parties were cordial. And why they didn't get him medical care. We wanted an investigation of the incident and wanted the chief of police removed. These were some of the issues we were pushing.

"We had just a few little councilmen there. The assistant

chief of police trying to explain that tear gas or Mace or whatever the chief had sprayed Finch with doesn't work on everybody.

"And we said, 'You're telling us this about a man with one eye?!'

"Then they trying to talk about the 'old bullet' thing. See, it was a old bullet. If it was a brand new bullet it would have killed him. This bullet was old and green, and they trying to say the impact is not as great, that it didn't do no damage. He was still spitting up blood. It was coming out of his mouth right along. I don't really know what they had in mind for him."

Outside more people were arriving every few minutes, trampling the small square of lawn and modest rectangle of bedding plants surrounding the flagpole. A victory was reported to the crowds outside by the people sweating it out on the inside: Finch was, at that moment, being taken out of jail and driven to the hospital in Brunswick. The throngs cheered and shook hands and relaxed into a carnival-like springtime gathering, a canvas of black heads and red knotted kerchiefs, white T-shirts and blue overalls, silver earrings and gold teeth, red toenail polish and pink bubble gum. Teenage boys turned up the volume on their radios and sat on the car hoods, and the young ladies plucked daffodils from the courthouse square next door and poked them laughingly into their hair. And the white men got out of their trucks, stretched and squinted up at the hot sky, stood and chewed gum, and observed the scene wordlessly.

Inside, Alston was acting like a prosecutor. "We found out the chief of police was lying," he said. "Hutchinson showed up finally and I got him crossed up on a lot of his tales that he told. Because when I stopped asking a question, I would jot down what answer he gave me, then ask him a question on something else, then come back around a little while later and ask a question similar to the first and get a different answer. Everybody started seeing it that way, and everybody found out he was lying.

"The crowd was very quiet. And Chief Hutchinson acted

scared of me. As a matter of fact, we took his gun away when he got to the door. We got him suspended from his duties. And we got the city to agree to pay Ed's hospital bill."

And then Sheriff Poppell sent reinforcements in the person of his chief deputy, who entered by the rear door and moved to the front: uniformed, freshly shaved, unflappable, and armed. He preempted both Alston and the mayor and spoke to the packed room in a different voice—a calm, reasonable voice; he spoke in a powerful voice, the voice of a man relaying the wishes of the High Sheriff. He thanked the crowd for their concern and told them that they could leave now: Finch was being attended to and the problem was over. "We are going to get to the bottom of this thing, and you can go home now," he said. But the people refused to budge: it was not a county matter; it was a city matter. The chief deputy's lone gun lay impotently along his hip while the silver noses of fifty others pointed at the floor of the room, and there were hundreds more outside. The people were not going to disperse until Thurnell Alston gave the word to do so. It would not have been easy to exit, at any rate, because the crowd so far exceeded the building's capacity; so they stood quietly, acting as if slightly deaf, and for the first time ignored an order from Sheriff Poppell to go home.

"The sheriff sent his deputy, who said everybody's disrupting and violating the law," Alston remembered. "I told him I was from outside the city limits, so I'd let the village talk to him. I kept quiet then because I knew he was on good ground with me being on city property. But the village shut him up. I think everybody really rise to that day. Everybody know real well what was going on: that the sheriff send his knight in shining armor to send everybody home and that would be that. But it didn't work that day. People told him to tell Sheriff that *his* office was going to be next if anything happened. That we would be down *there.* That really surprised me, because the sheriff had the whole county sewed up all those many years. To hear that was really something to think about.

"Then I kept on throwing words back at him and he left, he backed out of there, and nobody ever came back down—no more Sheriff, no more chief deputy, nobody else came down there."

Could Poppell himself have dispersed them? Maybe. Probably. But he was too clever to show up and risk failure himself, so he sent his deputy. His refusal to appear in person seemed an admission that he had some doubts as to whether the numbers, firepower, and anger of the blacks would yield to his traditional authority, so he stayed away. And the crowds stayed put. It was, all in all, a situation to be savored.

"We got Finch out of jail that day," said Alston. "The county deputies came and took him to the hospital in Brunswick. But we all stayed right there in City Hall during that period of time; we sent somebody over behind the cops to the emergency room to find out how did it pan out, what was his condition after taking X rays. We found out it did break his jawbone and he couldn't eat anything. The bullet had knocked out teeth on one side and went and lodged on the other side, and they had to break open his jawbone to remove it."

So the city council acquiesced to all the black demands: Finch was seen by a doctor immediately and at the city's expense, Chief Hutchinson was removed from office pending an investigation, and the black crowd didn't disperse until Thurnell nodded to them to go. "I hated why we were there, but you know I really enjoyed that day," said Alston. "They told us all kind of tales and all different kind of things, but it was something that day. I really wish I'd had a tape or camera or something during that time, because I really enjoyed that. That was really one amazing morning, one amazing morning, that morning."

In the weeks and months following the events of that Saturday, the city and county quietly undid the work the black people had achieved: Chief Hutchinson was suspended from his position at the police department, as promised, but was quietly hired by Sheriff Poppell and assigned to late-night dispatch duties. And on April 18, less than a month after the shooting, the city council voted unanimously to restore Hutchinson to his former position as chief of police.

Ed Finch was released from the hospital, and the city assumed his medical bills, as promised; but immediately upon his release he was indicted by a grand jury consisting of twenty white men and one black man and was charged with aggravated assault, and obstructing an officer—a felony and a misdemeanor, respectively. The black churches raised money for lawyers' fees. Finch hired a flamboyant young black lawyer from Savannah, Bobby Hill, and on June 1, 1972, brought a civil suit against Hutchinson, Mayor Caldwell, and the city of Darien. "The Plaintiff was assaulted, shot, beaten, arrested and abused by Defendant Guy E. Hutchinson while on private property at the invitation of the owner of said property," contended the lawsuit. "Plaintiff was at the behest of Defendant Hutchinson subjected to great bodily harm and mental anguish and further left to die. . . . The conduct which caused the Plaintiff injuries was part of the pattern of conduct by members of the Police Department . . . [consisting] of a large number of individual acts of violence, intimidation, humiliation visited on Plaintiff and other citizens of the Black race by members of the Darien Police Department."

On December 11, 1972, Finch was convicted by an all-white jury on both counts of his criminal indictment and sentenced to twelve months on each count. His suit for damages against the police department and the city was dismissed following his conviction on the criminal charges. Finch served six months in jail before parole. He died in 1976. Hutchinson was shot to death in Texas.

The episode was a watershed, an awakening, for a number of people, including Thurnell Alston, whose natural leadership of the black community was, from that day on, a given. "I think that was about the first time that blacks ignored an order from the sheriff's department," he said. "I think a lot of people got enthused about that because we really start moving from there. You know how fellows will talk about some of their accomplishments, some of the things in their lives? Well, a lot of them remember some of the very bold things they say for the chief deputy to take back to the sheriff that day. I enjoyed that day. I think that has got to be one of my best days."

Hadn't offenses similar to the shooting of Ed Finch occurred in the past? Of course they had. The blacks bore lifetimes of insults quietly like ancient scars, most of them insults casually, rather than wilfully, inflicted, tossed at them by whites operating under the foolish assumptions of racism. Even to be talked to fondly, like a favorite hound, can leave a mark, and the black people bore up under this marking until they were psychologically a tattooed people.

Finch's shooting in 1972, however, was seen as exceptional, something not to be tolerated. The cynical misuse of power expressed by the shooting, the conviction of Finch, and the exoneration of Hutchinson exposed a rude and flippant freedom possessed by the whites that the blacks could only gape at. The whites then appeared utterly lawless to them, shamelessly flouting even the pretense of being law-abiding. The blacks had lived for a long time with that pretense. It was as if previously they had seen themselves and the whites as harnessed to the same millstone, as two races treading the same circle of days on opposite sides of the wheel; they believed that the whites had no more asked to be born to their particular status than the blacks had to theirs, that all fulfilled the roles God gave them. Suddenly, with Finch's shooting, it was as if the millstone were stopped and turned on end and the two races looked at each other over its pocked rim: What is going on over there? the black people had to ask.

"Finch never did end up joining our organization or doing nothing," said Thurnell Alston. "He was just a person that we saw some wrong had been done to him, and everybody in the county just jumped in and helped. That was a breaking point for me. I mean there is just no excuse for a white guy shooting a black guy in the mouth. If you're that close to me with a .38, hit me in the head with it for God's sake, you don't have to shoot me.

"I'll tell you what: I think that was the first time we really felt—in the Crescent district where I live—that we had more blacks than whites. The sheriff could do nothing with that district from that day until the day he died."

Eight

The Three Musketeers

Many years later, few whites even recalled Finch's name, and those who did remembered the episode as the tiniest blip on the long straight line of racial harmony reaching back across the century. But for the many blacks who remembered it, it was forever a historical event, a psychological event, a watershed year. What remained in their memories, undissolved, was the unheard-of scene, the unprecedented thing: that black people had poured into the streets and pushed angrily into City Hall, shouting demands, stating with their presence, with their bodies: This is enough. Beyond this you have gone too far.

And instead of shooting them or arresting them or turning hoses or dogs on them or heaven-knows-what, the white Darien citizens had assented, rather politely. The black people filling City Hall in the Finch protest had overwhelmed the whites. The outside world dropped away. Then the blacks filed out in orderly fashion and went home, taking up their traditional roles as they stepped into the sunlight. The moment faded and the fleetingly overturned caste system was righted.

A year after the shooting, Thurnell Alston, inspired by his role as spokesman in the Finch episode, ran against Deacon Danny Thorpe for his seat on the county commission. Voting was at-large and Alston lost. "Oh yeah, he fought me something fierce to get on that board," said Thorpe. "But I get the biggest crowd. That's how come I was winning. And then I had great help, though.

Tom Poppell really help me, because he'd go around and ask them white people to work and vote for me." Alston ran for Thorpe's seat again in 1975 and lost again.

But then another great offense occurred and in its wake another, and the black community—of a post-Finch mentality—rose promptly up to meet them, fearlessly overturning all the tables of previous racial understanding and coexistence.

The first disaster arose out of a mundane bit of county business, one of a series of items on a typed, carbon-sheeted agenda voted on by a local board. On May 26, 1975, the McIntosh County Grand Jury, under the leadership of a foreman named R. D. Gardner, appointed a new member to the McIntosh County Board of Education as part of its usual duties—namely, George Gardner, R.D.'s brother. And to create that opening, they displaced Chatham Jones, the only black member of the board of education. Thus, operating out of a system of patronage and nepotism, the all-white grand jury created in its own likeness the all-white school board to preside over the majority-black public schools.

Still, it was business as usual. That such a dry, yawn-provoking piece of county business should inspire such rebellion was a measure of how far the black community had come since the Finch shooting three years earlier: the startled white officials found they were dealing with a different entity now, a black population watchful, sensitive, and mistrustful. Hundreds of other votes, recorded in the minutes of numberless county meetings over the years, could have given rise to protest—votes of blatant favoritism and obvious discrimination—but they had passed unnoticed, unremarked upon, and were shelved away in file cabinets in the basement of the courthouse. The black community had not been ready to fight previously, but they were ready to fight *now*.

And there was more in the dismissal of Chatham Jones than

appeared at first. Jones was a soft-spoken man of Deacon Curry's generation. He had been a modest and inoffensive presence on the school board, but of late he had begun to leak information. He had voiced his suspicion that the public school budget was being shared with the all-white private school. Although this charge never became public and formal and never was proved or disproved, most blacks believed it. "The blacks at that time really felt that the board of education was funding the private school," said Thurnell Alston. "The Oglethorpe Academy was totally white; virtually every white child in the county went there except for some who couldn't afford it, and then there were civic clubs in town offering scholarships to it, too. Then our kids getting old books and the kids at the private school, brand new books. Things being sent from the state board, ending up at the private school. I mean they did it and they got by with it for years."

Alston rode this new wave of political unrest with his old friend and former schoolmate, Nathaniel Grovner, the minister of a local Holiness church and a schoolteacher. Grovner was a dark, skinny, college-educated man in a faded black suit and black tie, with small-lensed black eyeglasses that didn't sit quite straight, buck teeth, and a high-pitched squeak of a voice, a sort of southern, black Ichabod Crane.

"When the grand jury dismissed Chatham Jones, the black community took that as a shock and we retaliated," said Grovner. "It was racism, though that wasn't the reason given. I can't even remember the reason that they did give. We being in the majority in the school system and not having at least one black on the board, that really upset us."

Alston and Grovner revived the McIntosh branch of the NAACP with Grovner as president and Alston as vice-president. They also created the McIntosh County Civic Improvement Organization (MCCIO), with Alston as president and Grovner as vice-president. On behalf of these organizations they mailed official-looking letters of appeal and letters of protest to the grand jury. But the grand jury declined to alter its decision: Chatham Jones was out; George Gardner was in.

"Five years ago the jury then in session utilized the democratic process and appointed for the first time a Black member to the McIntosh County Board of Education," Alston and Grovner wrote to the *Darien News*. "The 1975 Grand Jury, all White with no Black representation, apparently elected to turn the clock of progress back (100) one hundred years by failing to reappoint the Black member."

"This Grand Jury has determined it can take no further action in regard to the selection," replied the grand jury. "At the time the Grand Jury made its selection, there was no conscious effort on the part of any member to discriminate against members of the Black community in McIntosh County."

Darien flattened in the white-hot summer heat, as if it were a stick of margarine left out on a warm counter. People said, 'It's so hot the mosquitoes are sticking together.' Coca-Cola water rose in uncollected glasses on restaurant tables. Government employees quietly shut their office doors and dozed, their belts loosened. Secretaries in the outer offices unhappily answered the rare phone call and tiptoed in their stocking feet along dim, warm linoleum hallways to the soda machine in the basement.

The locals who found a reason to drive somewhere drove slowly, their elbows stuck out their open windows, and the wind was like a rush of air from an oven. Clouds of gnats, suspended above the road, clung like hair nets to their arms as they passed.

Deep in the county, the dirt yards baked. Country people opened all their windows at night, hoping to attract a fresh, woodsy breeze, and they rose before dawn to slam the windows shut and close the drapes, trapping the cooler air inside. There was the distant sound of traffic on U.S. 17 and the intermittent spurt of a gasoline chain saw, but most of the fields were overgrown with weeds and the county was quiet. In the shrimp factories women stood knee-deep in ice and ripped at the pink shells. In the tall, narrow Victorian houses of the area called The Ridge, window air conditioners drowned out the calls of the marsh frogs and marsh birds across the road.

But the blazing summer nights of 1975, as darkness dropped, were full of spitfire and shouting, hand clapping and rage, as the black people—dressed to the nines—stormed into the black churches after work. Ministers thundered at them from above, choirs unleashed gorgeous, piercing songs, and the stamp of feet and shake of tambourines lasted late into the night. While white Darien slept and an occasional truck rattled down Highway 17, the black county was wide awake, its front doors open, windows up, lights on, cars coming and going, and little one-room, white-washed churches lit up and filled with hollering.

At the Shorters Chapel African Methodist Episcopal Church in Eulonia, Rev. W. M. Long and Brother Thurnell Alston presided. Every pew in the church was packed; well-dressed people lined the walls and crowded into the rear of the church; and a choir in royal-blue satin robes led the congregation in rich and heartfelt music. The choir held hymnals without looking into them and swayed heavily back and forth in unison, stamping once as they leaned left, stamping again as they leaned right, and the congregation in full voice joined in. And when Thurnell Alston, at the height of the meeting, went to the podium and faced the sweating crowd—sweating himself—and began to speak, stammeringly, high-voiced, and urgently, they received his words with hearts wide open.

The convocation resembled in nearly every particular a regular Tuesday or Thursday night prayer meeting, but it was, in fact, a political meeting of a new and hybrid kind invented by this antebellum African-American Christian community in isolation on the Georgia coast. Brother Thurnell Alston, rather than the preacher, gave the sermon, and ministers and choirs attended from churches scattered across the county, applauding one another's star sopranos. The collection went to the NAACP and the MCCIO rather than to the host church; and the "Remarks" portion of the service focused not so much on Holy Writ as on the political question, What is to be done?

These political prayer meetings went on night after night with larger and larger crowds, with rival choirs—green-robed, scarlet-robed, purple-robed—succeeding one another on the platform, the luxurious robes swirling and unfolding as the choir members climbed and descended. Beardless, soulful, round-eyed young men pried into heaven with falsetto voices until everyone in the packed house was near fainting with glory; and buxom, black-wigged, corsage-wearing ladies with lungs like the west wind (somebody's cook, somebody's maid—the white world never saw them like this) let loose and revived the people with cascades of shrieking melody until everyone was clapping, everyone was stamping, the church itself was vibrating and seemed about to ascend.

In the crowd and in the choir, a few individuals began to tremble and shake, crying "Thank you, Jesus!" as violent spasms shook their bodies. Some attempted to continue singing as the spasms violently wrenched them, as if someone offstage were jerking them by the arm, as if they were having an epileptic seizure. They gave themselves over to it and shook electrically. Nearby congregants spread out to give them room, reaching out with one hand to spot them like you would a gymnast; meanwhile, congregants at a greater distance fanned them with the cardboard fans. These fits were known as witnessing, and the people given to them—sometimes to the extent of slumping to their seat in a faint when the fit concluded—were the Holiness people.

Florine Pinkney, a relative of Sammie's who lived in a cinderblock house on a mud dead-end in the pine woods, was a member of the Voices of Deliverance Choir of the Junior Church of Christ Holiness Church. She remembered the political church services in the summer of 1975 fondly as "lively, lively, lively." She was subject to the epileptic-looking episodes, which bestow honor on the sufferer as a person worthy of receiving the Holy Spirit. "You just can't explain what it feel like, it just a joy in you," she said. "If you're having good church, you can't sit down. You got to get up. You can feel it, it just a spirit. It just a joy down in your soul. You feel that power. Some people sit down on it; but if you feel that joy, the Lord bring the joy out of you.

"You don't feel tired when it's over. It like something just take over you. You get hot. You never stay stop. The more you praise God, the more He bless you, the Lord bring you up higher. Holy Ghost gets in you, makes you want to shout. You put up your hand to praise the Lord, you feel Him in your hand, feel Him in your feet. It just a thing you can't control."

Night after night, with green summer darkness buzzing outside the open windows, with Thurnell Alston and Rev. Nathaniel Grovner on the pulpit, the people made a reckoning: In a county 50 percent black, there was no black mayor, city councilman, or county commissioner, nor any black sheriff, judge, or grand jury member—and never had been. Nor was there a single black store owner, clerk, salesperson, cashier, bookkeeper, bank teller, librarian, state park employee, firefighter, or mailman. In the poorest county in Georgia, there were no black employees at the welfare office or Social Security office, nor at the phone company, the power company, the courthouse, or the convenience store. They pounded the podium with their litany; they shouted at one another.

It was not all about Chatham Jones, as it had not been all about Ed Finch; rather, the long-endured, heavy baggage of second-class citizenship was being set down again, momentarily, giving the load bearers a chance to stand and stretch. Their neighbor's public misfortune created a breathing space, a bit of elbowroom in which to question the way things were being run. They met to discuss it, and the long-unspoken list of their private injuries pushed into their voices in the minor-key notes of outrage and urgency.

The hymns led by the choirs went into ten, eleven, twelve stanzas, with refrains, and the prayers offered by the ministers became lengthier and more ornate. As the hour grew late, the moon rose, and the marsh frogs beyond the sand parking lot began honking. Deeper in the county, in the pine woods all around, the old people standing on their front steps could sense it, as if a bonfire had been kindled deep in the forest.

2

Thurnell was thirty-eight years old that summer. He arrived home drenched and hoarse every night. With the brown gleam of bourbon-coated ice in the glass before him, he stood alone in the dark kitchen above a mottled clutter of soaking pots. Complaining, Becca would come in search of him, pulling her housecoat around her and softening her voice when she found him: "It's late, Thurnell, come on now." She jammed the Black Velvet back behind the glass punch bowl in the cabinet on her way out. And when he visited houses in the neighborhood to talk and then stayed late, refusing dinner, whole families stood in their front doorways, blocking the light, to see him to his car. He wasn't sure he had anything to offer besides his own restlessness and hostility, but it kindled theirs. And Rebecca's supper pots were warm on the stove and a place was neatly set for him when he roamed back home, feeling weightless, sleepless, mute. He put up the food.

Around him people labored, cooked, raised children, and cleaned house, all submerged in the slow, damp life of a coastal summer. But he and Grovner had gotten their heads above water far enough to look around and to see. Thurnell had been injured at his job at Babcock & Wilcox, had undergone several surgeries on his back, and had been retired as disabled and given a pension. Grovner, also in his midthirties, had his church, and he taught school in Glynn County. Thus, both of them relied on independent sources of income; neither of them had to fear economic coercion from the white community or from the sheriff. How this liberated the two of them, they were just beginning to tell. But what were they going to do about it?

Then, in the middle of that burning summer, another old friend, Sammie Pinkney, a former schoolmate of both of them, who had moved back to McIntosh County from New York City, cast his lot with theirs. Like Alston and Grovner, Pinkney had an independent source of income: he received disability benefits from the New York City Police Department, dating from the day he was shot on duty. His experience of the American West, of Europe, and of New York gave him the status almost of a prophet when he returned home to McIntosh.

"I was born here, bred here, graduated from high school here," said Sammie Pinkney, seated at his dining-room table. "I've been knowing Thurnell all my life. I left here to go into the military, was stationed in Georgia, Colorado, Germany. I went to New York, entered the police academy, graduated in the top 10 out of 380, then hit the streets undercover. I got hurt trying to prevent a robbery. A guy got between me and my partner, shot me and knocked me down a stairway; my partner shot and killed him. I've had seven surgeries on my back since then; they put me on pension and retired me. I came back to Georgia. I thought I might as well come home and relax and raise my family. But I found things to be so much under par. Good God, I knew things were going to be different from New York, but they were at least twenty-five or thirty years behind schedule. One black elected official at that time, and that was Deacon Thorpe."

He was a big man with a scarred face, a gold tooth, and a

voice with a deep, underground, rumbling timbre to it; but he was capable of swallowing up the hand of a child in his two gigantic mitts and speaking to her in the gentlest of tones. He liked to laugh and did laugh, lightly and pleasantly, but was ever on his guard, ever appraising, a man capable of absorbing vast abuse and capable, likewise, of paying it back. Pinkney was an intelligent man who in peacetime would cultivate peaceable arts—read, garden, cook, and raise children—but in wartime would not be found wanting.

"I remember as a kid I went to Darien," he said. "I was working for a white lady there. I was walking with her in town at midday. Some folks said: 'What do you think you're doing walking on this side of the street?!'

"The white lady said, 'Well he's with *me.*'

"'Oh! I'm sorry!'

"That's all there was to it, but I'll never forget it: '*He's* with *me.*' And that made it all right.

"As long as you stay in your area, or stay where you know you supposed to be, then that's the way, that's 'friends.' As long as you're doing the laundry every week or coming to cook dinner every day and go on back where you supposed to be, you could be 'friends.' But when it come to you sitting down at my table and having dinner, that's something different. And that's just the way it was. Whether you like it or not, that's the way it was. And any time you thought about you wanted to switch grounds, the grounds that have been established for you, then you have a problem. You have a problem."

When he returned to McIntosh the summer of 1974 and bought a brick ranch house in the lovely all-white area called The Ridge, he felt as if he—a wounded and decorated officer of the law—were likely to be stopped again on the sidewalk in Darien and questioned about his right to walk there, as had happened in slave times, when blacks needed permission slips from their owners to walk downtown.

"Little petty stuff that should have disappeared fifty years ago," he said, "hey, it's still buried inside everyone.

"I've been around the world one-and-a-half times. When I came home, I visited the school system, visited the businesses. There was maybe one black working at the bank; they were not working anywhere else. People were at one another's throats. Thurnell had run for office but couldn't get elected. Same people were still serving on the juries as had served years before. The Civic Improvement Organization was going on, NAACP was going on. They approached me, asked if I was a member. I said, 'Sure, I'm a member, but I'm going to join this chapter also.'

"About seven of us burned the midnight oil many nights: Louise Goodman, Thurnell, Teretha Skipper, Sadie Littles and her husband, Reverend Grovner, and me—that was the major folks. We gave it a lot of time and energy. Folks began calling me, Thurnell, and Reverend Grovner the Three Musketeers; some called us the Three Wise Men. We were in the process of becoming a major force in the political arena."

Sheriff Poppell was well aware of their meetings, his little deputies working overtime to report. After a private meeting in someone's home, the Three Musketeers and the others drove home slowly in the dark, along back roads, and found themselves tailed by police cars. The patrol cars followed closely behind, bumpety-bump, for many miles; then without warning, blue lights flashed, sirens wailed, and the black people were pulled over, there in the middle of gray fields, and ticketed for speeding, for weaving, for failure to yield, or for missing a taillight. The deputies leaned over and pointed flashlights at their faces. "Been to a meeting?" the deputies asked.

Sheriff Poppell seemed to know their strategies almost before final votes were taken. No matter whose cabin they met in or how deep in the woods, and no matter what the pretense—a potluck supper, calling on the sick, a poker game—the black people glimpsed, when they exited the cabin at some early hour of the morning, the taillights of a deputy's car that had just cruised slowly past and now went jolting down the rough path as if on regular rounds. That was the work of the little deputies.

"It wasn't possible to be secret from the sheriff," said Alston. "We had some of the people that were the sheriff's goons. Pretty soon the sheriff was getting more information than we had even talked about. We talked one night about running somebody for municipal court judge. The next morning, in Darien, the man we had talked about running against, the current judge, said a deputy had come to his door in the middle of the night and told him about it.

"We got to the point we started doing things regardless to what happens. If they want the stuff to carry back to the sheriff, we didn't care anymore. Before we get through the meeting, we always say, 'Okay, now you guys run and tell this. This is the high points of what we have discussed. We are planning on doing this and this and that. Run on back and tell the sheriff.'"

"I went back and forth to New York every other weekend," said Sammie Pinkney, "and I knew I was being watched: 'He must be doing something. He's got a new car, going back and forth to New York, not working.' Wherever I went, a cop car would be following me. They'd follow me from here to Savannah. They wouldn't stop me, but they'd follow me. Apparently, they felt I was involved in something. One day I just got tired of it. A deputy followed me right into my yard, got out and looked around my car. I asked him what he wanted; he wouldn't answer. I drove to Sheriff Poppell's office and asked him to call the deputy, but the deputy wouldn't answer his radio. Sheriff said he didn't know anything about it.

"I said, 'If you send him to me again, you're going to have to come get him.' That was the end of it.

"I picked up bits and pieces from the newspaper about Poppell's doings for a political science class I took at Brunswick College: someone in class taped it; Sheriff had a copy of it that afternoon. He asked me to come see him, said, 'Sammie, what is the goddam shit you saying about me at the college? Don't you know I can sue you?'

"I said, 'What are you talking about?'

"He said, 'I got the goddam tape of what you were talking about.'

"I said, 'You mean the presentation I made to my class about McIntosh County? It's all in the newspaper. Go ahead and sue me; I'll sue you and the county too.'

"He said, 'I never had any trouble out of your daddy.'

"I said, 'You won't have any out of me either if you leave me alone, but I'm not my daddy.'"

Sammie Pinkney enjoyed church as much as the next man, as he sat on a front pew and brought his hands together in song; but he was killing time, as far as he could tell, unless the Lord Himself, drawn by the magnificent, tearful hymns, was going to intervene personally in McIntosh County politics. Alston and Grovner reiterated the same half-dozen painful facts every time they stood up at the podium, then the congregation, in catharsis, swept the facts away with another mighty hymn. When the service was over, the people shook hands in the sand parking lot, bundled their sleeping children into their cars, and drove home, while Alston's powerful calls for justice flew up to God.

In August, an impatient Pinkney sat at his dining-room table one morning and made a few phone calls. He made long-distance phone calls. He hired a lawyer.

Nine

Circuit Riding into the Past

1

"At that point we were in a creaking old edifice right in the center of Brunswick," said Thomas Affleck, an attorney with Georgia's controversial legal aid network, the Georgia Legal Services Program (GLSP). "It was a typical legal aid kind of office with things like an elevator that would stop every time a fat person got onto it—you know, it would go up about three floors and just stop. Periodically throughout the day you'd hear the emergency bell ringing: there was always somebody too heavy for the elevator.

"When I first arrived, the managing attorney gave me the tour. It was, as I say, typical: my office had the institutional green walls with, you know, coffee splashes on them, and a bookcase that if you leaned too heavily against it, the whole thing would collapse. And I found this crumpled document down in the corner of the bookcase which turned out to be—when uncrumpled—the managing attorney's license to practice law." Affleck graduated from Georgetown University Law School in 1973. By 1975, he was the managing attorney of the GLSP office in Brunswick.

"I walked in," said Affleck, "and they said hello and handed me 150 open cases." GLSP offered free lawyers for poor people with civil—that is, noncriminal—legal problems. Founded in 1972 by a group within the Younger Lawyers Section of the State Bar of Georgia, and under the directorship first of Betty Care, then of John Cromartie, GLSP was designed to assist poor clients with divorces, land disputes, finance companies, disability, public housing, landlord/tenant problems, Social Security, unemployment compensation, food stamps, and welfare.

In the early 1970s, a staff of sixty-five people in eight cities served 154 rural counties. "We took in thousands of cases," said Affleck. "There weren't very good controls established back then in terms of how many cases would come in, and our office just got inundated. If somebody came in and needed help, we'd just take the case and open the file. Later on we realized this was not going to work, but by then we had I don't know how many thousands of open cases. But everybody was really enthusiastic, too, and wanted to take in as much as they could. It was exciting. It was wild. You'd have some lady come in with a paper bag filled with, you know, all her unpaid bills and part of her hamburger and dump it on your desk."

Affleck is today a partner with Affleck & Gordon in Decatur, Georgia; he has a thick brown mustache, and the rather startled expression and gangly carriage of the very tall. "I had one client," he remembered, "named Vasselonia. She came in and she'd been a maid all her life, and she was also a deacon of a church, which she had established, called the Firstborn Beloved Church of God. That's what it was called. And she wanted us to incorporate her church, basically. And what she was going to do, she was going to have ten members—including most of her family as most of the ten members—and she was going to turn her house into the church. And I'm sitting there, we were just having a little conversation; she had on kind of a bright gray sort of wiry kind of frizzy hair. It just expanded all over her head. She had one large tooth missing, and she had a very dark complexion and was kind of a little bit wild-eyed, but she was really engaging and pleasant. So we were having a little conversation and all of a sudden, at the top of her voice, she yelled, "HALLELUJAH!!" And my hair—it just took me totally by surprise—my hair stood straight up, and everybody around the whole office came running in. I mean I can't do it a tenth as loud as it was.

"And I said, 'What in the world was *that?*'

"And she said, 'I'm just praising the Lord for what you're doing for us today.'

"And so I said, 'Well, we'll look into it and see what we can do for you.'

"And then as she was leaving, she came up to me and she sort of turned her head and kind of looked aside and said, 'Here, take this.' I looked at her and she handed me a dollar.

"I said, 'What's the dollar for?'

"And she said, 'Little offering from the Lord, so maybe the job get done quicker.'

"I said, 'Keep your offering. We'll do the best we can.'

"I had another client," said Tom, "a woman who was five feet tall and weighed 280 pounds. And every document that came in about her condition—we were trying to get state disability benefits for her—they always used the same description about her personality: flat affect. You know, everybody said, 'flat affect,' and whether you knew what that meant or not, you could look at her and see it right away. She'd sit there basically just like a tree stump, with no expression, almost like she wasn't communicating with the outside world.

"And we did an appeals hearing for her and she—in a real monotonous tone of voice—she went through the whole exposition of what was wrong with her, and it was all flat and totally expressionless: 'Well, I've got aches and pains in my arm and I got the rheumatism in my feet and when I bend over my back hurts.' And all through the whole thing, no expression at all. And finally the judge looked at her and he said, 'Do you take any medications?' And that was the only time she smiled. Big smile appeared on her face and she pulled out this bag of medications. It was the size of a shopping bag; it had about forty years' worth of medications. It probably had 250 bottles in it. And that was the big smile. She said, 'Why, yes. I do.'

"And so the judge wrote an opinion on the case and he said: 'After listening to what seemed to be an endless litany of woes rivaling those set upon Job, it is the opinion of this Administrative Law Judge that the only trial yet to be experienced by this claimant is a plague of frogs.' It was, of course, totally inappropriate, but he awarded her the benefits. He actually put that language in the decision."

Mark Gorman, a 1974 law graduate of the University of Texas in Austin, is a squarely built, red-faced man with a bearish gait and good humor, who combines an equatorial slowness of movement and of speech with a sharp and quick mind. He is today on the staff of the Democratic Senatorial Campaign Committee in Washington, D.C. He had been recruited by VISTA (Volunteers in Service to America) at his law school in Austin: "VISTA initially said, 'We've got this program in Alabama that's doing this work building houses for people.' And I said, 'You understand I'm a lawyer? Find something lawyer related.' So they said they'd call back, and they did a few days later and said, 'We're going to send you to Georgia Legal Services.' When I got to Atlanta, I was told that I was going to Brunswick immediately. Basically, the way it was described to me was: 'We have this small office down on the coast, and one of the attorneys is getting ready to leave; and we need a body to throw into the breach, and you're it.'

"When I got to Brunswick, everybody in the office had water pistols. One of the lawyers' wives had visited her family in Miami and brought back a bunch of water guns shaped like porpoises and alligators. There were times, probably in response to stress, that water fights would break out in the office. Still, you'd try not to open the door and zap somebody while they had a client in there."

Most of the GLSP lawyers in the early years were in their twenties, freshly recruited top graduates from the nation's best law schools. Departing from turbulent campuses in the early 1970s, many of them veterans of antiwar and civil rights demonstrations, the young professionals felt encouraged—like the rural black people—by King and the Kennedys (though some were inspired, as well, by Gregory Peck in *To Kill a Mockingbird*). The law school graduates were attracted to Georgia on the promise of meager VISTA salaries of three thousand dollars a year or state-funded salaries not much higher. They were enthusiastic, bright, quixotic, and—once they passed the Georgia bar exam—undeniably litigious. They arrived prepared to work heroic hours. "The whole social conscience movement of the 1960s struck a deep chord in me for some reason," said Phyllis Holmen, a 1974 law graduate of the University of Chicago and the executive director of GLSP today. "I collected for UNICEF, I sold lemonade for charity, I visited senior centers; I thought for some time I would be a missionary. The only reason I went to law school was in order to perform public service. There was a sense in my generation that you could create social change."

"It was a great time to be in law school, unique in the history of this country," said David Walbert, one of that generation of GLSP attorneys, a 1973 graduate of Case Western Law School. "There was a small window there, a time when socially committed people went to law school," he said. "It had never happened before, and anyone talking like that today on a law school campus would be an isolate, an oddball. When I was in law school, we understood law to be self-evident truths about fundamental human rights. The question, we thought, was: How far can we take it?"

The new and unlicensed attorneys—male and female, black and white—drove south in their VW Beetles, their vans, their '57 Cadillacs; they moved their stereo systems, houseplants, crates of books, Earth shoes, batik wall hangings, and Chinese vegetable steamers from their student apartments in Boston, Ann Arbor, Washington, Madison, San Francisco, and Chicago. In Brunswick, Savannah, Augusta, Macon, Columbus, Albany, Dalton, and Gainesville, Georgia, the young lawyers roomed together, ate together, jogged together, and drank together. They furnished their apartments with secondhand furniture and with blonde wooden tea crates from the Savannah docks; their brick-and-plywood bookshelves were filled with red, white, and black paperbacks with angry titles, the political science reading of their undergraduate years.

The young lawyers set up shop in the small Georgia towns. They assumed the leases of padlocked storefronts in decrepit downtown areas, located amidst old brick churches, barbecue shacks, pawnshops, and luncheonettes, and then proceeded not to spruce them up much. The first offices of their careers were windowless, paint-peeling cubicles smelling of disinfectant, insecticide, and burnt coffee. They sat at battleship-gray metal desks with black rotary-dial phones and hundreds of manila folders spread out around them, each representing a client. Outside, elderly black men on bicycles bumped over the broken sidewalks, Spanish moss swung from the live oaks, and the warm air smelled of fried chicken from the propped-open alley doors of restaurant kitchens.

The female GLSP attorneys were invariably the first women lawyers to appear in the backcountry courthouses; state and superior court judges addressed them as "Miss" and "Honey." Phyllis Holmen remembers, "I walked into a county courthouse in Savannah, and a lawyer standing outside the courtroom said to me, 'Habeas corpus!' I said, 'Habeas corpus?' He said, 'I'd like to *have* that *body!*'" The black GLSP attorneys were the first black lawyers ever glimpsed in the backcountry, and some judges and local lawyers gave sarcastic, heavy emphasis to the *Mister* Bass, the *Miss* Henderson.

In the old downtown areas the young lawyers hung out their signs and marketed a very new commodity: Law. For the poor. In many towns it took upwards of a year for the local poor to see any benefit in it.

"There was an infamous justice of the peace in Waycross," said Mark Gorman, the Brunswick staff attorney who later became the first managing attorney of the Waycross GLSP office. "He was one of the worst examples of tyranny cloaked in the judicial mantle that you could ever possibly imagine. Poor people in that county were very much afraid of that guy. He was completely lawless. And then he had this constable, this huge gorilla who carried a gun. They'd go out and evict people without following the dispossessory procedures; they'd repossess cars without any effort to abide by the procedures. It took a long time after we established the office in Brunswick, and a long time after we established a branch office in Waycross, it took years and years and years of constant battles with this J.P. But we finally started hearing stories back from clients and even from the J.P. himself, in a rage, saying how tired he was of summonsing people and hearing them say, 'You don't have any power over me. I'm going to go get me one of those legal aid lawyers.'"

Over the years, GLSP grew into an ever more vocal, active, and prominent advocate for the poor as a class. Like brand-new doctors detecting symptoms of rare diseases in a common sneeze, the new lawyers descried constitutional issues in the slam of every door, the denial of every application. In several important class-action suits, the courts confirmed the lawyers' suspicions and altered existing laws or regulations in decisions sometimes costly to the state. State legislators were infuriated by the spate of class-action suits against Georgia arising from the state-funded program, and some country lawyers felt that GLSP was depriving them of their bread-and-butter divorce cases, so in 1976 the state legislature eliminated GLSP from the state budget, deducting $1 million from the program's operating budget of $1.3 million. After a shaky year, GLSP began to receive federal funding through the new Legal Services Corporation established by Congress, and the organization grew, mostly free of indebtedness to Georgia, from a 65-person, eight-city program to a federally funded, twenty-one-office, 325-person network with a budget of $7 million by the end of the decade. Still, with the poor population eligible for legal services estimated at around one-fifth of Georgia's population, even GLSP in its expanded and federally funded size was fantastically inadequate to the task set before it.

Given that money and personnel were limited—that each lawyer was, like Mark Gorman, more or less a body thrown into the breach—there were philosophical differences among the GLSP staff members. There were those who said, in essence, We are just lawyers and our clients happen to be poor; our role is service; we are not here to change the world; we will handle as many individual cases as we physically are capable of handling. And there were the political bomb throwers who said, in sum, We are the allies of the underclass, and it is our role to transform the system.

"I was always looking for the biggest bang for the buck," said David Walbert, an example of the latter type. "I wasn't into Band-Aid law." He was a backup expert in the GLSP central office in Atlanta, where lawyers, freed from their individual caseloads, attempted to look beyond the everyday cases and challenge them at their source. "When you think of five thousand dollars worth of overhead and lawyers' time being spent on a three-hundred-dollar debt case, you have to question that," said Walbert. "Just pay off the damn debt if that's all you're going to do."

In the regional offices, where demand was great and the

press of white and black clients was thick, however, there was no time to consider the larger sociopolitical arrangements. Phones were ringing off the hook; the waiting rooms—despite their soiled carpeting, their broken water coolers, and the presence of crickets, or worse, behind the file cabinets—were full; and the lawyers and paralegals worked ten- and twelve-hour days. "We didn't do much impact litigation in the Brunswick GLSP office," said Tom Affleck, "and we got criticized for that. But I think the people in the central office in Atlanta didn't really understand. There was always a kind of pressure to do the glamorous class-action type things, but we rarely had time to do that because we had so many cases."

"On one hand, we were sort of running a divorce mill," said Mark Gorman. "On the other hand, I never personally had a client who was more satisfied than a woman who was finally free. We used to schedule eight, nine, ten uncontested divorces at a time in some of the far-distant counties; we were generating this sense of hostility from the judges and the local lawyers; but those women were always very, very, very grateful and appreciative. I found that really important and satisfying. It was an important step for them.

"One day my car broke down; I was supposed to be over in Adel, and I couldn't get any farther than Lakeland. So I'm stranded thirty to forty miles away with my little Fiat convertible, and my client had been waiting for years to get a divorce. And it had been maybe a year since we filed it. And now the day had come and the hearing's scheduled and the lawyer can't get there. I called over there and told the clerk I wasn't sure I was going to make it. She found the client and told her what was happening; the client started crying and said, 'I'll get my neighbor to come and get him.' That's what they did. They found a car, drove to Lakeland, picked me up, took me to the courthouse, and got the divorce. They drove me back, and by then my car had been fixed.

I mean I understood what David Walbert meant, but that day-to-day role in the community was very important."

While political and funding battles raged in far-distant Atlanta, and clashes with local bar associations and state legislators continued in the county seats, the GLSP lawyers entered the rural Georgia countryside for the first time. The poverty of the deep South was a revelation to them.

"When you went into the really rural areas," said Mark Gorman—who had seen poverty in West Texas, but not like this—"or even into the black parts of the towns like Brunswick and Savannah, basically there were no city services and the streets weren't paved and people—black and white people—were living in Third World conditions. It was like James Agee's *Let Us Now Praise Famous Men* and Walker Evans's photographs, that degree of poverty. You could drive through the rural South and produce identical sets of photographs today in terms of living conditions. People's clothing has changed—blue jeans aren't as baggy—but the houses would be just as run-down, the plumbing just as absent. You didn't have to go very far off the main road to find it."

The young, upper-middle-class, mostly urban, mostly Yankee lawyers faced challenges akin to those of their friends who had joined the Peace Corps instead of VISTA and who now dwelled in Asian or African villages. The exoticism and foreignness of the surroundings were vivid, and they themselves were looked upon as bizarre implants. "We were in Glynn County State Court one time," said Tom Affleck. "I'd become friendly with one of the clerks there, and I was talking to her and I said, 'Now why do y'all think that we're so different from y'all?' And I was using y'all, y'all, y'all. And she said, 'Well, look at you.' And I looked at myself and I looked at Mike Froman, the managing attorney, and here we were both standing there with these huge beards and these totally different outfits we were wearing. I mean it was obvious. Obvious to everybody but us.

"And I remember the one time I was really comfortable, I went into Waycross one day and looked around and everybody had beards. And I thought, 'Well now there!' and I started to relax. Found out it was the Waycross centennial and everybody was dressed up."

The young white lawyers, far from home, were able to identify with the cause of the southern blacks in ways that would not have occurred back home, in Cleveland, for example, where David Walbert's family lived. "My father was a corporate president; there were family ties to be considered," admitted Walbert, who focused on voting rights and municipal services cases in Georgia. "I somehow can't see me throwing all the white guys out of the city council in Cleveland and putting in all black guys."

Stories were told by a generation of young white VISTA workers—community organizers, paralegals, and lawyers across Georgia and in Alabama, Mississippi, the Carolinas, and Virginia—of their warm acceptance by black communities, of a sort of obliviousness to their own color. "We got a flat tire on a rural road late at night," remembered one white woman, a community organizer in an impoverished majority-black county. "We were nervous every time a white carload passed us, and tried to flag down passing cars of black people. Finally a truck pulled over, and two white farmers got out. They were really nice and helped us change the tire and wished us luck and drove away. We stared after them a long time, then I said to my friend, 'You know, that's probably the greatest example of black–white cooperation in the history of Prince George County.' She agreed with me. We drove on and about ten miles down the road, it hit us: we were all white."

Another woman remembers visiting a close friend, a white

community organizer, and attending services at a rural black church with her. In the midst of the services the organizer turned to her friend and said, "How does it feel being the only white person in the room?"

"Well, but *you're* here," said the friend.

"Oh yeah, oh yeah," said the organizer.

All in all, the introduction of these confident, well-educated, middle-class, Constitution-intoxicated black and white young men and women, licensed to practice law, into the isolated, unspeakably poor black hamlets of rural Georgia had the potential to be an explosive combination. And nowhere was this truer than in McIntosh County, in the circuit-riding district of the Brunswick GLSP office.

2

Brunswick was a flat, hot, industrial little city, steaming with paper mills and crammed with fast-food joints, but adjacent to Georgia's "Golden Isles," including those millionaires' haunts, St. Simons Island, Jekyll Island, and Sea Island. Year-round housing on St. Simons was cheap then, so most of the Brunswick GLSP staff lived there in sunbleached wooden houses near the sand dunes. They lived strolling distance from the famous resort hotel called The King & Prince. They commuted across a causeway, over the salt marsh, and through a toll bridge to their work among the poor each day in sandy, palm-lined, smelly Brunswick.

"The Brunswick office was circuit riding to sixteen rural counties," said Michael Froman. "We had the largest circuit-riding assignment of any of the regional offices. Our office was responsible for over 4,000 square miles of territory, equivalent to more than half the state of Massachusetts. I used to get up at 5:45 A.M. to make a 9:00 calendar call in Adel." Froman, with an

M.S. from M.I.T. and a J.D. from Harvard, was the managing attorney of the Brunswick office from 1973—one year out of law school—until 1975. Today in private practice in Atlanta, he is a native Minnesotan with graying, curly hair and thick glasses, a computer whiz, and an amateur cartographer. "Most of our counties had populations of which more than 40 percent were below the poverty level, and therefore eligible for our services," he said. "Most of our cases were between people who, on one side, had never had a lawyer before, and on the other side, people for whom conforming to civil law was a novelty.

"People back then didn't bother with procedure. If they wanted something repossessed, they'd just call up their sheriff and he'd go and repossess it."

"We were circuit riding to places like Pearson and Waycross, Blackshear and Woodbine," said Mark Gorman. "At one point we had a staff of maybe two licensed lawyers and two paralegals trying to serve seventeen counties. It took over two hours to get to Cook County. Coffee County was ninety miles away. Froman had set up this insane schedule so he'd be in one of those little counties from, say, 9:30 to 11:00, thirty-minute drive to the next one, be there 11:30 to 1:00, thirty-minute drive to the next one, be there 2:00 to 4:00. Another staff attorney, Ed Zacker, used to go out there and just spend the night for five dollars. There were five-dollar motels out there in the hinterlands. The Eden Inn, I believe it was.

"The most, I guess, 'Faulknerian' place we went to was Charlton County," said Mark. "I mean half of Charlton County is in the Okefenokee Swamp, and it's a real small, real backward place, only two or three lawyers in the whole county. Folkston itself is virtually the area around the courthouse, with these enormous live oak trees filled with Spanish moss. Driving in there on a foggy morning was a very, very unusual experience. We felt like we were going back forty or fifty years in time. And in fact we were going back at least that far, if not further. Homerville, the county seat of Clinch County, had a segregated movie theater when I got there in the mid-1970s. Blacks went in a side door and sat in the balcony."

The Brunswick office consisted, in the summer of 1975, of three attorneys: Tom Affleck, managing attorney; Mark Gorman, the VISTA lawyer from Texas; and Ed Zacker, a 1975 graduate of the American University Law School, also a VISTA worker. Marian Smith departed that fall. Pat Bartlett, Jon Klawitter, and Don Samuel were the paralegals; and Veda Canon from Everett, Georgia, a large, funny, kind, black woman, mother of five, was the administrative secretary.

By day the lawyers and paralegals rode the circuit to the tiny towns in the Brunswick district. They filled up their backseats and car trunks with fresh manila folders, one for each open case. In the evening, back at the office, the folders rose like snowdrifts on the desks and tables. The lawyers consumed coffee and candy and carryout food and more coffee, often laboring till midnight, while support staff silently carried in more files like nurses carrying in clean stacks of folded sheets.

To the outside world they were a curious conglomerate. "We were certainly viewed as odd ducks, you know, by the local people," said Affleck. When for a few years there were two Jews in the office at the same time, local people treated them as indistinguishable, interchangeable. Donald F. Samuel, from White Plains, New York, and a 1975 graduate of Oberlin College, was a VISTA paralegal. (He later graduated from the University of Georgia Law School in 1980, and joined the firm of well-known criminal defense lawyer Edward T. M. Garland, in Atlanta.) Roy Sobelson, an Atlanta native and graduate of the University of Georgia Law School, arrived in Brunswick in 1976. (He later earned a postgraduate degree at Temple University and became a professor of law and the dean of students at Georgia State University in Atlanta.) Like Don, Roy was Jewish and of medium height, with curly dark hair, dark eyes, and a thick, full, curly beard. No introductions to the community were necessary when Roy arrived, because everyone assumed it was just Don: clients stopped to shake Roy's hand on the street and some embraced him with gratitude for his help even though he'd just arrived in town. Roy's initial impression of the poor community of Brunswick was one of unbelievable friendliness and warmth.

Veda constantly took phone calls from people saying, "Give me an appointment with that Jewish man."

"Which one?"

"One with a beard."

"Which one?"

"Name start with *s*."

"Which one?"

In one famous incident, Don and Ed Zacker walked to a bar across the street from the courthouse after work. They sat at a small table facing each other and ordered drinks. In the enthusiasm of an animated conversation, Don waved his hands and knocked his Bloody Mary into his lap. He stood up, dripping, and left to go home and change. Moments later Roy entered the bar, spotted Ed sitting there alone, and joined him, taking Don's chair. The same waitress appeared. Roy ordered a Bloody Mary. "Yeah?" snarled the waitress, who had just finished mopping up the last one. "You planning to drink it or wear it?"

The Brunswick GLSP lawyers and paralegals pursued a lone social life; they spent subdued Saturday nights in one another's apartments listening to music, playing Scrabble, and drinking. Their life was not without its pleasures and its humor. Some of them owned dogs, and the dogs sauntered along the St. Simons beaches in the windy, gray off-season weather. A lighthouse stood at one end of the island, and cruise ships passed by on the watery horizon. Once every few months one of the backup experts from the central office in Atlanta came to look in on things and savor the pleasures of the sea islands and the hospitality of the Brunswick staff. The solitary Brunswick group, grateful for company, wined and dined the guest: there were baskets of fried shrimp, fried catfish, and hush puppies at the Crab Trap on St. Simons, and late-night walks along the beach under the stars. In the office, Ed Zacker displayed his collection of "client art," chiefly the gifts of little old ladies expressing their appreciation to their free attorney by bestowing the works of their senior center's art projects on him. Client art—which decorated the offices of GLSP attorneys and paralegals across Georgia—included, but was not limited to, crocheted *TV Guide* covers, plaster ashtrays with raised duck-hunting images, chicken-shaped teapot warmers, and trash cans made of Styrofoam egg cartons standing on end, encircling an aluminum pie plate.

Pat Bartlett, the paralegal from Boston, was a wiry, suntanned, gray-haired woman in her forties, a mother of five. She lived in a windy, tall, wooden house on a sand street on St. Simons with plenty of ceiling fans, porch swings, ancient sofas, water-swelled old beach-house novels, a rickety black-and-white TV, gritty shower stalls, and thin, sandy towels. There was a goldfish pond set among lilies in the tiny side yard. Pat and her teenagers shared their home and their sailboats and their disgusting dog named T. Nasty (short for That Nasty Dog) with the isolated young men from the GLSP office. Pat's husband was an oceanographer–turned–deep sea fisherman; he was at sea for months at a time, but when he returned home with garbage sacks full of ice and fresh fish, the Bartletts and Tom, Mark, Ed, John, and Don feasted on fresh swordfish and tuna, cole slaw, and corn on the cob. They sat around the picnic table in Pat's kitchen under a heavy ceiling fan, passing back and forth a bottle of rum.

Within the group there was affection and high jinks. At the office, upon learning that Don's grandmother used to squeeze his cheek and call him her "little matzo ball," Veda—the administrative secretary—took to squeezing Don's cheek and calling him her little "muttsa ball."

"It's *matzo* ball, Veda," said Don. "Mah-tza."

"Muttsa," said Veda. "You my muttsa ball."

"Matza, Veda!" yelled Roy from behind the closed door of his office.

"Look, Roy," called Veda, fed up. "*I'm* not Jewish. I can't *pronounce* 'mutza' ball."

"Veda," yelled Roy through his office door. "I'm not *black,* but I can pronounce 'watermelon'."

Following exchanges such as this, the water fights would break out.

3

Sammie Pinkney was not the first person in McIntosh to call on the services of the legal aid lawyers. Sheriff Poppell was.

"I remember the first time I met Tom Poppell," said Tom Affleck, "though I didn't know at the time who he was. I was up in Hinesville, at the courthouse to do some divorces, and he came up to me: kind of a thin fellow wearing a polyester leisure suit. He didn't look like an intimidating or a hard-nosed guy at all. He came up and said to me, 'I understand you're from Legal Aid, and we got some folks over here in McIntosh need some divorces. Would you mind helping us out?' Very cordial and friendly.

"Then as we were up there more and more, we realized how powerful he was. We used to joke—and I don't know if this is true or not—we used to say he was the only sheriff in America who owned four houses, one with an airfield, and all on twelve thousand dollars a year."

As happened in most circuit-riding towns, a GLSP attorney—in this case, Marian Smith from Brunswick—borrowed the use of a cubicle at the welfare office in Darien and saw clients referred to her by welfare caseworkers. It was not the best method for getting at the true and large grievances in the poor community, but the twice-monthly appearances in town established a presence. Sammie Pinkney, well read and well traveled, probably the most well read and worldliest black man in McIntosh, assumed the legal aid lawyers would be capable of analyzing more complex cases than divorces and food stamps. But he was not one to sit on a folding chair in the steamy, crowded hallway of the welfare office among wet-bottomed babies and pregnant mothers and cane-wielding old ladies, waiting for a turn. In the middle of the summer of 1975, he phoned the GLSP office in Brunswick for an appointment with the managing attorney and invited Alston and Grovner—worn out and hoarse from the nightly church meetings—to take a ride with him down the coast.

"It had gotten so heated in Darien at that point, after Chatham Jones was let go," said Sammie, "that white folks felt they had to call in the Ku Klux Klan. They marched more than once. The last time they came, we came so close to having bloodshed it was unbelievable. They marched in Darien, then Thurnell Alston was shot at, at the Omega Club, by a particular individual driving by in a truck—shot the door out as Thurnell was going in. Most of them came from elsewhere. I believe there were two local people who robed up. We saw them; we took pictures of them; we knew who they worked for. It was so heated then, we were having nightly meetings.

"When I came back from New York, I already had two years of law studies, and I was very familiar with a lot of things I knew we could do. I was involved with a number of organizations in New York from Malcolm X all the way down; I met with him on two or three different occasions before he became nationally known. After seeing what was happening around me in McIntosh, I really began to get involved. One thing led to another. I contacted the legal aid office in Brunswick."

In the sloppy little building with sloping floors across from the Glynn County Courthouse, on a dusty side street shaded by gigantic live oaks, Pinkney, Alston, and Grovner seated themselves somewhat nervously at a long wooden table in the tiny office library. There they told a group of open-mouthed young white men—shaggy-haired, gangly, bearded, in mismatched socks—a great number of true stories from the backcountry. The rest of the staff, including Veda and the paralegals, slipped into the library to listen. Tom Affleck—exchanging occasional glances with Gorman and Zacker—began to jot notes on a yellow legal pad, one that was to become the first floor of a tower of yellow legal pads containing notes about McIntosh County. Mesmerized by the visitors, the Brunswick staff sent out for Cokes and coffee and sandwiches, and waited on their guests like some kind of exiled nobility from an unknown tidewater country.

Thus, the Brunswick GLSP office—perhaps the most conservative of all the regional offices in its interpretation of the lawyers' mandate to handle the divorces and other individual cases one, by one, by one—was introduced, by a trio of rural-dwelling black men, to the wider world of class-action suits and impact litigation.

Ten

The White Boys' Bible

1

Within weeks of their first appointment, Alston, Grovner, and Pinkney were driving to the Brunswick Legal Services office every day. In the backroom law library, maps of McIntosh County, population data, news clippings, and jury lists were spread on the tables, weighted in place by cold mugs of last night's coffee and Styrofoam boxes with the remains of yesterday's lunch. The McIntosh men shouted messages down the hall and from room to room like the lawyers did, sat at the desks to make phone calls, shared in the carryout food orders, and walked, occasionally, to lunch in "home-style" restaurants in downtown Brunswick, making public, with a shade too much jocularity, their racially integrated circle.

Back in the office, under the ceaseless barrage of the lawyers' questions, the Three Musketeers slowly built up a history and portrait of McIntosh County that could be presented in federal court. David Walbert flew down from Atlanta to listen to the McIntosh stories; he joined them at the long table with the maps, sitting back with his feet crossed on top of the table, relishing the sea air and the windy palm trees out the window and the fresh-fried seafood lunches that he ate out of a box in his lap.

Walbert was a hothead in those years, an affluent, superbly educated, fast-talking social revolutionary, the child of a conservative, Goldwater-Republican household in Cleveland, Ohio. He was a tall man with a pale, chiseled face and wavy, black hair, which he nervously wove his fingers through, curling back forelocks, as if it were more unruly and tousled than it really was. He swore probably more than anyone else in the state with the exception of Tom Poppell himself. In the mid- and late-1970s, David Walbert not only initiated fifteen voting rights suits across Georgia and helped redraw the voting districts in dozens of communities but also pursued a closely watched case arising from Burke County, Georgia, to the U.S. Supreme Court, and won. He was one of the leading proponents of the biggest-bang-for-the-buck theory in the GLSP central office.

"I just loved to go out and sue people," said David Walbert. To outsiders, he personified in every detail the sort of hip, cocksure, school-smart, nigger-loving carpetbagger detested by the rural politicians and landowners. Full of nervous energy, reclining one minute and jumping forward the next, talking fast, quoting law, jabbing with his fingers at his hair, and cursing, he caused Pinkney and Alston and Grovner to recoil in initial misgiving.

He looked upon law, upon the Constitution, as a series of fundamental truths about basic human rights. And he shared this love of abstract questions with the Three Musketeers in the manner he had with everyone else: speaking a-mile-a-minute simultaneously right at them and right over their heads, because, in part, he engaged in any conversation only insofar as what he had to say interested himself, and because he assumed any idiot who couldn't follow him ought to have the sense to stop him and ask questions. Sitting silently at first, nodding somewhat numbly, the McIntosh men understood plenty; and they appreciated his passion and intelligence, and drank in his rapid-fire, wide-ranging legal discourse. They came to honor Walbert and to count on him above any other white man they'd ever met.

Rebecca Alston, however, loved the Texan, Mark Gorman, because when he visited her house and spent the morning striding around the side yard deep in conversation with Thurnell and he got hungry, he simply came into the kitchen, made himself a sandwich, and kept on talking.

"What I remember about the summer of 1975," said Mark Gorman in his computer- and map-filled Washington, D.C., office of the Democratic Senatorial Campaign Committee, "is that these people from McIntosh County showed up in our office, and that suddenly there was a lot of commotion in our small office about the situation there, about the discharge of the black member of the school board by the grand jury. What the McIntosh people wanted the most was to get at the school board selection process. But it was such a Byzantine structure, we were having a really hard time figuring out what the legal remedy would be."

"We always met with the three of them, Sammie, Thurnell, and Nathaniel," said Tom Affleck. "They were all three equally involved and committed. They came to our office and we went up there a lot, too. In fact, I remember several times being followed by the police. I remember one time in particular. Mark Gorman and I went to Nathaniel's house, and a deputy's car just followed us the whole way. You know, talk about eerie shades of the Mississippi Freedom Riders and that sort of thing. But they didn't do anything. They just came up behind us, pulled alongside, and looked at us. I said, 'Can I help you?' and they just looked at me and then drove on.

"And we met with people in this little church—this tiny little church, like a one-room schoolhouse, that size building. We used to go out there at night, and we'd meet with people. And I remember every time the headlights from the deputys' cars would kind of go by and flash into the church, you'd sort of just step back a little from the open window. And you got a few of those feelings. But we never had any problems. Nobody ever actually roughed us up, but we thought about Poppell's reputation, and it created a certain amount of tension. But it was always reassuring to have Sammie along. He'd been a New York City police officer and detective, and he always carried a gun.

"I remember having to go out one time to interview a white woman who lived out in the country, and Mark and I went out there; and Sammie and Thurnell came with us to a certain point, and they said they'd be out of sight and kind of, you know, be there as a backup if we needed them. I don't remember exactly what her contribution was going to be to the case, but we went in and sat down to interview this woman. The first thing she did was take out a gun and put it on the table. She didn't say anything about it, but she had the gun right there. We finished in a hurry; and when we finished, we went out, but we didn't see Sammie and Thurnell. I had this little '69 Mustang convertible, which I still have. I remember just zipping down the road. We were anxious to get out of there. Thurnell and Sammie later—when they caught up to us—said they almost fell over because they saw the Mustang go by so fast on the road. They'd been sitting back down the driveway. That armed lady spooked us.

"But I loved it," said Affleck. "Oh, I loved it! What I loved was all the contact with the black community there. We were out there constantly, we were in the community. We weren't just sitting in our offices in Brunswick. We were out there doing things with them. We went to the functions they had, the political rallies. And we made sure they had good coverage as far as the normal services we provided in terms of welfare cases, Social Security, all that stuff. We made sure they had good backup there. I think that made a big difference to them, because I think it gave them some support."

"Our major problem was there was no simple way to get at the school board," said Gorman. "In McIntosh, as in many counties in Georgia at that time, the grand jury appointed the school board. And the local jury commissioners appointed the grand jury. And the local superior court clerk supervised the jury commissioners. You know—the head bone's connected to the neck bone. Where do you start?

"As we looked into it a little bit, what appeared, very clearly and simply, was a jury discrimination lawsuit: no black people had been on the grand jury in the last forty years. In fact, people couldn't remember a black person *ever* being on the grand jury and only rarely being on a trial jury. Since the grand jury chose the school board, the best vehicle seemed to be to go after the all-white grand jury, so that's what we recommended.

"I've thought about what might have happened differently," said Mark, "if Sammie and Thurnell and Reverend Grovner—ignited by the dismissal of this person from the school board—had contacted say, political organizers, the national NAACP or SNCC [Student Nonviolent Coordinating Committee]. There might have been a different approach to all this stuff. But they came to lawyers, you know, what can you do? As lawyers, we sit down, we say, 'We might try this, we might try that, and if you're interested in a lawsuit, here are some things we can recommend.'"

How do you prove in court that an electoral system is discriminatory? The standard at that time was "equal access." Was there "wholesale exclusion" of a minority population from the political process?

In McIntosh County, the proof was going to be tricky, if not impossible. Viewed from the outside, McIntosh County had the hallmarks of a county with a progressive and well-integrated electoral process. Deacon Curry and Deacon Thorpe apparently had represented the black community on the McIntosh County Commission since the late sixties, and another black man, the high school principal, Chester Devillers, sat on the city council. Also, since Sheriff Poppell relied on black votes to elect him—and to elect all the local, state, and national officials he told the blacks to vote for—black voter registration was high, in some years even 100 percent of the black voting-age population. This simply wasn't true anywhere else in the South.

Affleck, Gorman, and Walbert had a tough row to hoe if they were going to believe all the stories the black men told them: high black voter registration and the presence of black elected officials in a county in which they were supposed to prove to a federal judge wholesale discrimination against blacks. In fact, when the ACLU in Atlanta was approached about assisting with the case, the director wrote back: "The suit . . . presents some problems. As I understand it, there is presently one black on the board of commissioners. Have there been others in the past? Theoretically it should be possible to argue that at-large voting dilutes minority voting strength even though one black has been elected through the at-large system. However, as a practical matter, it is certainly inconsistent to argue that blacks can't get elected to office when blacks have gotten elected to office."

David Walbert said: "McIntosh was absolutely unusual in the South. In McIntosh County blacks were registered to vote. There was no history of violence in connection with registration. You compare this to testimony we received in other cases: in Warren County, I remember a black guy telling me that black folk got out of town when court was in session. The superior court judge had two sessions a year. And they would get out of town. He would leave the county. He wasn't a criminal; he'd just leave town when the judge came. Nothing good could come of it. It was just such a force, the white supremacy, and it could never be good, even down to being subpoenaed to go testify about something couldn't possibly end up being good."

"People *were* awfully well registered," said Mark Gorman. "At one point in the jury discrimination case, we needed a source list of community residents to use as a base list for potential jurors. I mean in lots and lots of places, now, you don't use the voters' list because so many people aren't registered to vote. They use all kinds of other lists. But we ended up using the voter registration list in McIntosh County. At one point the numbers we were looking at suggested that there were more black registered voters than the entire black population of the county—of any age. I mean it was very odd. It really was. It was very odd."

And the black men's explanations were complicated and far-fetched, stories that seemed stitched together of myth and archetype: a sheriff sitting in on the county commission meetings, appointing and dismissing black officeholders with a wave of his hand, vetoing county business issues with a slight shake of his head, collecting titles to black-held land by dropping criminal charges, and delivering county votes to statewide and national candidates. It was a very unusual case. But then, it was a very unusual county. David Walbert, Tom Affleck, and Mark Gorman believed the black men's stories.

Their research the summer and fall of 1975 disclosed the following:

According to the 1970 census, the total population of McIntosh County was 7,371, of which 50 percent were black and 50 percent white, 51 percent female and 49 percent male.

The voting-age population in McIntosh was 4,251, of which 45 percent were white and 54 percent black, 53 percent female and 47 percent male.

The registered-voter lists (from which trial jury and grand jury members were supposed to be chosen) were 56 percent white and 44 percent black, 52 percent female and 48 percent male.

But the 1973 biennial traverse jury list—the list created by the McIntosh County jury commissioners from the voter-registration rolls—contained the names of only 398 persons, of which 87 percent were white and 13 percent black, 92 percent male and 8 percent female.

And the 1973 grand jury list, also compiled by the jury commissioners from the voter-registration rolls, contained only 156 names, of which 90 percent were white and 10 percent black, 92 percent male and 8 percent female.

In short, a lawsuit would contend that the McIntosh County Board of Education had been appointed by an unlawfully composed grand jury, one nonrepresentative of the population and non-randomly drawn from the voting lists.

2

For Thurnell Alston, the surprising thing that summer was not learning that the all-white, all-male grand jury that had replaced a black man with a white man was improperly composed. Any fool could see that, and the data unearthed by the research simply confirmed it. These were the facts as he had always known them.

The amazing thing, to Thurnell, was how quickly and easily the young white lawyers had named the ill health of the county; how they had listened as the three McIntosh men tumbled out their tales of poverty, underemployment, and a sense of being the untouchables in McIntosh's caste system; how the lawyers had nodded, made notes on their yellow pads, exchanged glances with one another over the heads of the black men, and thumbed through green leather-bound law books; how—when the McIntosh men had finished speaking—the lawyers had pronounced the recent events to be the results of "discrimination" and "a violation of due process" as proudly as a toddler shown a picture of a cow says, "Moo." Then they planned to affix *his* name to their cleverness. This whole process amazed him.

It was as if he'd come to them delirious, a feverish child, and they had smoothed his hair, laid a cold cloth on his forehead, and explained to him that he had the mumps and this was the cherry syrup he must sip from a spoon to be all better. The tangled, dark, secret politics of the county were fearlessly and confidently examined by the young white men, as if they drew from a chest strands of colored yarn, rather than the coiled poisonous snakes the three black men told them lay within.

Was such knowledge, then, harvested in books, taught in northern universities? What did it mean that itinerant outsiders could so calmly and quickly quantify and express the events of his life—"the continuing effect of past and present race and sex discrimination against adult black and adult female residents of McIntosh County"—so that a federal judge would be moved to pronounce *him* victimized? He had a sensation like a country boy in homemade coveralls trying on a factory-made suit for the first time and learning that a mass-produced commodity slipped on as easily as the pinned and tucked creations of his own mother. It all meant to him simply that it had happened before, and had happened elsewhere, and that the wrath and indulgence, the manipulation and familiarity that the McIntosh blacks and the McIntosh whites generated toward each other were common commodities. The revelation was that the justice he and the others instinctively had longed for and fought for across many years—relying on the Bible, relying on their own embattled sense of manhood, of personhood—in the meantime, elsewhere, had become federal law: the law of the land.

And he knew that the white men who had befriended him—the first white friends of his life—were not part of any local power structure or even any local community, were not reaching down to him from the vantage point of illustrious social, professional, or political niches, but were outsiders, hippies, idealists, Yankees. He was forced to appraise them in the midst of their somewhat shabby, somewhat outcast surroundings; coming from nowhere, uneducated, a skilled laborer, Alston had to judge the reliability and worth of their characters and of their scholarship.

And this Constitution of which they were so fond, with which they felt so intimately acquainted! Housed in distant Washington, under glass, indecipherable script fading from parchment, it spoke to the black people, for the black people, and would protect the black people, according to the lawyers. The Constitution, Thurnell was promised, had something to say about the miserably low status of *his* small community on the Georgia coast. In similar soothing, promising tones, Rev. Grovner told the sick and the angry that God loved them, too. The Constitution, the black men came to understand, was the white boys' Bible; and the lawyers quoted it often, chapter and verse, taking secular pleasure in its ornate language every bit as much as the rural people relished the antiquated resonance of biblical thou shalts and wherefores and cometh and goeths. But was this religion, or was this fact? Were they to trust the lawyers?

When Affleck and Gorman and Walbert promised the protection of the Constitution, was it similar or dissimilar to Rev. Nathaniel Grovner assuring parishioners of the love of Jesus? Was this protection available in the real, everyday world of McIntosh County when people's homes, jobs, and lives were threatened in response to the lawsuit they would bring? Or was the protection available only on some elevated plain, some secular heaven, whatever that would be—for example, the lasting esteem of a handful of American civil rights lawyers?

Nevertheless, Alston threw himself, his family, and his community upon the law. He entered the sanctuary of the law. The law spoke to him—as it did to Walbert—of fundamental truths. The law echoed the truth he had carved from his own life: Men were born equal and should be treated equally.

Even if the law were not able to protect him tooth and nail from local adversaries—and on this point he had profound doubts, despite the lawyers' frequent assurances—he still would cast his lot with the law. If the law failed in McIntosh County, he would go down *with* the law. He was not about to start *now* choosing moral principles on the basis of which ones were likely to come out on top.

The law sounded God-given to him. He opted to trust the white lawyers.

3

"We will bring suit in federal court," said Thomas Affleck, adding that federal court meant not in or from McIntosh County, meant appearing before a federal judge, one not owing his position to Sheriff Poppell.

First, said the lawyers, try once more to negotiate, try to work it out with your officials. "That's what we tried to do," said Pinkney, "to show them we weren't so naive or so blunt-headed that we couldn't sit down to try to work things out. They just turned a deaf ear, acted as though we didn't exist. They didn't believe we had the expertise or the knowledge to take it any further. We asked them for some blacks to be appointed to some boards. We asked again for a black to be on the school board. We turned in names. None of them were appointed. They appointed everybody *but* them."

Then—like the Wizard of Oz sending Dorothy and her friends back repeatedly into the countryside for more proofs of their sincerity—the lawyers required something else. They required plaintiffs, local people who would sign their names to the lawsuit. The Three Musketeers as plaintiffs were a good start, but many more were needed, including women, to represent a strong cross section of the types of people excluded from political participation in the county.

The three black men drove home to McIntosh with the heavy responsibility of recruiting volunteers willing to sue, in U.S. district court in Brunswick, not only A. S. Poppell—chairman of the jury commission and the sheriff's brother—but also the board of education members, employees of the board of education, and George Gardner, member-elect. It was one thing to appear en masse before the authorities, submerging one's own voice in the larger clamor of other voices, and quite another to sign one's name to a legal paper. Even the three leaders were nervous.

So one more assembly was called in a hot, throbbing little church on U.S. 17, and this time Brother Alston was looking for more than amens from the crowd. He was going to have to ask them to accept, as their allies, a few young white men from out of town, quoting a piece of parchment a thousand miles away.

Gorman and Affleck drove north out of Glynn County, through Darien, and up into the northern half of McIntosh to be introduced to the community and to speak about the lawsuit and the need for plaintiffs. For a while they saw nothing ahead or behind but the old highway slicing through darkening pine forest. Then there was a clearing on their right, and bare light bulbs dangled from tree branches to illumine the sand parking lot—filled with cars—of the Calvary Baptist Fundamental Independent Missionary Church.

If it was 95 degrees in the parking lot, it was 120 degrees in the whitewashed wooden church. Every pew was filled with dressed-up adults and children, and the singing people crowding the aisles parted to make room for the pale young men carrying briefcases. Tom Affleck and Mark Gorman sat quietly in the front row, where space had been reserved for them, the only whites for many miles around. Dressed in gray and navy and white amid the tumultuous singing, clapping crowd, they looked like a black-and-white photograph tucked into the corner of the screen of a large sound-and-color movie.

Green-robed, scarlet-robed, and purple-robed choirs sang, succeeding one another with great pomp on the wooden bleachers; gigantic pumpkin-shaped choir women delicately descended with tiny black-slippered feet, pearls of perspiration dotting their great faces and necks; and preachers made benedictions and closed their eyes and cried out, their hands raised, their faces squeezed shut around their open mouths as if the gospel words arose out of great pain within. The hour grew late and a slim moon sailed past the open windows. Tom and Mark compared wristwatches and wondered when the church service would be over and how many people were likely to stay for a late meeting afterwards. Thurnell specifically had invited them to the meeting here, tonight, but it appeared that there had been a scheduling conflict.

As the rows upon rows of chanting people worked into a more and more frenzied pitch, it slowly occurred to the two lawyers that this *was* the meeting—they were attending the meeting. The people didn't need to have the facts laid before them (and the lawyers laid aside the pages from which they'd intended to speak, outlining the history of discrimination in McIntosh County). This was the meeting. The people had packed the church to pray to God for the courage to proceed. In McIntosh County, God—Deliverer of Sheetrock—also was invited to meetings.

Affleck and Gorman stood when finally introduced, and each quietly spoke a few words, thin-voiced and secular, while the congregation ponderously sat down and vigorously waved their fans, the choir members caught their breath, and mothers rocked babies on their shoulders. The white men addressed several issues of special concern: Could the black McIntosh County citizens who signed the complaint be arrested for suing the county and the jury commissioners? Could the plaintiffs be fired from their jobs? Could they be harassed? Could they be evicted from their homes? Could their welfare or disability payments be terminated? Could they be expelled from the county? .

The answer to all these questions, obviously, was: Legally, no; it was within the people's rights as citizens to bring suit. And the sweating, heaving crowd, fanning and swaying, received their words warmly and appreciatively, saying "That's right, that's right."

Many, however, had misgivings: in that time and that place, the idea that law might inhibit the actions of powerful local white men was a novel idea indeed. And even if the black people were to accept the notion, who was to say that the local whites would? Who was educating *them?*

Alston, Pinkney, and Grovner—the only three plaintiffs at this point—were economically untouchable: Alston received worker's compensation, Pinkney received a police pension, and Grovner had his church. Still, no one would deny that the economic independence of the three men was backed up by raw physical courage. And now the three—and their lawyers—were asking the community to come forward with their own names and sign.

Thurnell Alston was the first to stand and face the suddenly subdued crowd. Wearing formal attire—a green suit with diagonally cut pockets and lapels trimmed in dark-green velvet, and a light-green shirt with a frilly front—he stood as calmly as it was possible for him to stand, shifting his weight from foot to foot and trying his hands in this or that decorative pocket. Sammie Pinkney walked heavily to the front and stood beside Alston. The Reverend Nathaniel Grovner hurried up front beside Sammie and broke into smile upon smile, then drew his lips down over his long front teeth to reflect the gravity of the situation.

Minutes passed, during which choirs of crickets could be heard from the bushes below the windows, happy there, as if all the world, human and arthropod alike, had gathered together to greet the new moon with song. Then pews creaked and skidded as the first volunteers made their way across their rows to the aisle and walked down front to stand beside the three men: Louise Goodman, a fine, throaty, serious woman, a childhood friend of the Three Musketeers and one of the organizers since the beginning; Teretha Skipper, Becca's humble, plump, sad-faced friend, the daughter of Miss Fanny; Edgar Timmons, Jr., a fiery young minister; Sadie and James Littles; John Henry Young; Ola Mae

Reed; Naomi Parham; and Abe James, Jr.—strong and poor middle-aged Christian people from deep in the county.

A dozen people stood unsmilingly in a line facing the congregation. The minister of the church exploded, "We thank you, Jesus!" and the church pianist hit a few beautiful chords as the choir started up again in a final hymn. The congregation stood and allowed the plaintiffs to exit first. The mood was precariously between that of a wedding and that of a funeral—no one knew know whether to sob or applaud.

Several nights later, Gorman and Affleck drove to Darien to meet with the twelve plaintiffs. They met at Club 17, a black-owned juke joint on a gravel parking lot on U.S. 17 near the Alstons' house. Thurnell unlocked the door and turned on the lights, then everyone entered and circled the pool table, where the lawyers set their briefcases and then arranged legal papers on the green felt.

"It was a cinder-block building with a pool table," said Mark Gorman, many years later. "That complaint was signed on a pool table.

"We met the name plaintiffs there; there was no one else there, but they were nervous about actually signing their names on that piece of paper. We had told them, and we told them again, it was their right, there won't be any reprisals. If there was anything like that, they could be protected. But I remember how really anxious the clients were, and how radical a step this was, to be suing, to be going into court and actually suing the sheriff's brother and the jury commissioners."

They all signed, gravely, feeling as if they were signing criminal confessions and were about to be led away and incarcerated. The lawyers thanked them, shook their hands, assured them that they'd be in touch, and snapped closed the gold buckles of their briefcases.

"They were so damn courageous," said Mark, "being willing to go forward with lawsuits and confront the county. They had to *live* there. I wasn't living day and night in that community. Thurnell and Sammie and Reverend Grovner, I think, were really genuinely committed to trying to improve the living standard and living conditions, and they really believed that their activism might be able to impact the quality of life up there."

"I admired them very much," said Tom. "I was very leery of Sheriff Poppell, because here you had a guy that was accused of being involved with prostitution rings, drug smuggling, gambling operations; and constant rumors of murders and of drugs coming in on the shrimp boats, and Poppell sanctioning it, all of it. So the whites had that air about them—I don't really think they would have resorted to violence unless they were really put in a position of feeling desperate. But there were a few there that could certainly have hurt one of us or hurt somebody in the black community. I think the black community was in greater danger than we were. They were pretty matter-of-fact about it, but Thurnell had a lot of guts; so did Sammie, so did Nathaniel. I think they definitely took serious risks. Thurnell, I thought, was the lightning rod. We took courage from them."

The lawyers drove back down the narrow, dark highway in subdued silence, feeling now that the signed document riding inside the briefcase between them on the seat—the document they'd earlier tossed into the car trunk after work—was a priceless thing, almost a holy thing.

4

They filed suit in U.S. District Court in Brunswick on September 9, 1975:

> This action arises under 42 U.S.C. Sec. 1983, the Sixth Amendment and the Equal Protection and Due Process Claims of the Fourteenth Amendment to the United States Constitution. . . . This is an action for injunctive and declaratory relief to secure the right of qualified adult Black residents and adult female residents of McIntosh County, Georgia, to be fairly chosen for Grand Jury and traverse jury service in McIntosh County, Georgia, without discrimination as to race or sex.

"I guess we were more or less prepared for it," said the Darien city attorney, Charles Stebbins. "It seemed to be happening in other places. Suddenly it was like, 'Well, here *we* are. *We* got one coming now,' or something like that."

He sat in his law office in Darien, with furnishings that must have been elegant and handsome in the 1940s, with plenty of dark wood tables and floor-to-ceiling bookshelves, but that appeared not to have been rearranged or dusted since then. The shabby yellow-walled office, with its shifting piles of coffee-stained papers and full ashtrays, and the brusque, unkempt manner of the red-faced, white-haired, carelessly shaved lawyer bespoke a certain gentility in decay.

"I guess I'm just a typical southern person," said Charles Stebbins. "My relationships with black people have hardly changed over the years. I hardly ever had any occasion to deal with black lawyers. There are none here. There might possibly be one in Brunswick; I think there is. I haven't dealt with him. I spoke to a black woman dentist on one occasion, I've forgotten what about, but that's been my only contact with the black professional.

"The schools were separate when I grew up, but we played with black children all the time, sandlot football, you know. There were three or four hundred black folk who lived in the quarters around the turpentine plants, and I knew all of them by name practically and they knew me, and we'd holler at each other when we met. We always had perfectly happy relationships with them, from my standpoint. Of course, I don't know what they were feeling, but there didn't seem to be any constraint. I guess in a way we were—I hate to use the word—but we were the power structure, I guess you'd say, and they were the other folks, and we all worked together.

"The first job I ever had I worked in the sawmill, sixteen years old and had black folks all around me and we were good friends. I mean we were on the job, we did the same work. I see them now and they come up and hug me and shake my hand and all that. I mean I feel they are lifelong friends. I'd go in their house, eat sweet potato pie or whatever. I realize they didn't come to my house and do the same thing.

"Of course, I knew all the time that I was going to college. When I went to work in the sawmill at sixteen, it was the middle of the Depression and my sister was off at school and my parents couldn't possibly have afforded to send me to college. So I worked for a year and then I went to college. I never had any idea that I was going to work at a sawmill or turpentine camp all my life. From the standpoint of a white person, it was a very orderly, very systematic existence."

"The day the first suit was filed, I felt a little timid, a little nervous," said Sammie Pinkney. "We didn't know how the courts would react. I had no conversation with the sheriff during that period."

"Sheriff Poppell was very calm during the lawsuits," said a Darien lawyer. "He would handle everything just as cool and brilliant—just country brilliance is all I know how to describe it. He probably saw the lawsuits as, 'It doesn't really matter if we like it or not. It's going to be the law.'"

"I'm not sure the racial aspect was the biggest thing with Poppell," said Tom Affleck. "I think the bottom line with Poppell was that he just didn't want anyone tampering with his county. If you challenged his operation and his power and his control, he didn't care what color you were, but you were in trouble.

"The first deposition I ever took in my life was of the senior judge of the Atlantic judicial circuit in connection with this lawsuit," said Affleck. "We were trying to be friendly about the suit. Of course, they never were rude to us or anything in the sense of overt hostility. But I'd call the judge's office and say, 'Judge Caswell, we'd like to take your deposition. Would y'all mind us coming down?' He'd say, 'No, no, come on, come on, I'll be there.' And then he'd refuse to do it. So we had to go back and give him notice and bring in the senior judge and sit Judge Caswell down in his own courtroom to ask him questions about how the jury commissioners were selected. As I say, it was my first deposition, which was a little intimidating. And Sheriff Poppell tried to come in. I'll never forget it. He came in and we said, 'Sheriff, sorry, but you're going to have to leave because we're in a deposition.' And he kind of looked around and he couldn't believe it."

David Walbert said: "Precisely what happened is this: A number of black non-plaintiff folks came to the deposition of Judge Caswell to watch. Dan White, the McIntosh county attorney, objected to their being there. He asked, 'Are these plaintiffs in the case?'

"We said, 'No, they're not.'

"'All right, I want them out of here.' He had the right to ask for sequestration, and we had to ask these people to leave.

"A few minutes later, Sheriff Poppell came in. I didn't know who he was and I naturally asked, 'Is he a defendant?'

"'No,' Dan White said, 'he's not.'

"'Well he's going to have to leave.' The sheriff looked over at Dan White, but Dan White had been boxed in by his own previous request that *our* observers leave, and he had to tell the sheriff to leave. Sheriff Poppell went off in a bit of a huff and I remember him saying, 'Thrown out of my own damn courtroom!'"

"Then Judge Caswell had to answer the questions," said Tom Affleck. "It was amazing. He didn't remember a thing. Couldn't remember anything, as I recall, when you'd try to pin him down on details on how they were selected and who they were and what race they were. Not one thing."

Dan White, the county attorney, who died in 1989 after a long struggle with cancer, negotiated with the GLSP attorneys. Until then the lawyers had not had a good look at the McIntosh County white community, other than furtively, out of doorways and windows when uniformed deputies slowly and meaningfully drove past. So they were startled by Dan White's kindness, openness, and fairness.

"It has occurred to me, since then," said Tom Affleck, "that we never put much effort into trying to find out what the white community was thinking. But we had a lot of contact with Dan White, the county attorney, and he was a very nice guy. He did a lot of the negotiating. And he was not—I did not find him to be—all that hostile. I never found him to be hostile at all. In fact, years later he referred cases to me."

"This was not a difficult case to litigate," said Mark Gorman. "We presented the statistical claim, the underrepresentation, the almost complete nonrepresentation of blacks and women on the lists compiled by the jury commissioners. U.S. District Judge Anthony Alaimo told the county the law was clear on this and there wasn't any point in fighting the case. He told everyone to reach an agreement and he would sign a consent order. So there were a couple of conferences with Dan White, Tom, and me with the McIntosh County superior court judge. That first meeting was one of my most amazing things ever: here's these two real young kids talking to the county attorney and the superior court judge about, you know, 'What are you going to do about this situation in McIntosh County?'

"They were polite, of course. Dan White was always extremely pleasant. We informed them that if we didn't get a satisfactory resolution, we were going to sue the judge as well. As a result of that meeting, they agreed that if leaders of the black citizens would go to the next grand jury meeting with a list of four potential nominees for the board of education, that somebody black would be selected. Even though the board was full at that point, they would see to it that somebody would resign to create a vacancy."

Judge Anthony Alaimo's consent order, signed in May 1976, ordered that McIntosh County grand and traverse jurors were to be chosen at random, and the meaning of *random* was laid out step by step, lest there be some mistake: "The defendant jury commissioners shall place the voters' list in an identifiable order, alphabetical or otherwise, and shall choose a name as a starting point. The defendant jury commissioners will select every third name . . ." and so forth. Random selection was a new approach in McIntosh County.

So the black community won its first lawsuit without ever going to trial.

5

While this civilized jousting went forth in court, garbed in legalese, conducted by soft-spoken white attorneys for both sides, a fiercer, ungloved confrontation began at the home front.

At the end of the summer of 1975, shortly after the lawsuit was filed, Thurnell Alston ran for county commissioner again. He personally solicited the support of the sheriff. "The sheriff didn't like Walter Fisher, the boy I was running against," he said. "He told me point-blank, 'Alston, I rather have you for a commissioner than that goddamn Indigo.' (He called Fisher an Indigo because his father was of Native American descent.)

"I said, 'All right, sir, I really appreciate that sir, but now you going to give me support?'

"He say, 'Yessir, we going to support you.' He get on the phone, call all his guys, tell them to go into the different districts and get the votes. He told them he didn't want no bullshitting; he wanted it *done.* Go out and do it.'

"Then it came up time for the election, Tom disappear. The day of the election, Tom disappear. Say he was down in Florida. And he sent a whole lot of Mailgrams, to all his goons: Sheriff wanted Walter Fisher elected instead of me. Walter Fisher beat me by three votes.

"But the hurting thing that day was this: Before I went to Darien to find out what the final vote was, I went back home and there was five guys sitting around my table. They were sitting around, had a bottle of whiskey. I said, 'What's happening fellas? Everything all right for you guys?'

"They say, 'No.'

"I say, 'Now wait a minute guys, don't mean to tell me, sitting down at my table, *with* whiskey, at *my* table, and you ain't even going to vote today?'

"Say, 'No, we ain't going to vote.'

"'What if we lose by five votes?'

"And sure enough I went to bed that night and God knows I was bitter that night. I lost by three votes."

Tom Affleck, Mark Gorman, and David Walbert also were not happy with the loss of a countywide election by three votes. But Thurnell Alston's explanation of why he had lost—five men drinking whiskey at his kitchen table, and Sheriff Poppell changing his mind—did not satisfy them. In a county with a majority-black voting age population, it ought to be possible to elect a black man even *if* the sheriff mailed postcards from out of town endorsing his opposition. They also felt that in a county with a long and lurid history of official fraud, a county currently embroiled in litigation initiated by candidate Alston, loss of an at-large election by three votes was, at best, extremely suspicious.

Tom Affleck learned that 137 black voters had been turned away from the polls that day as having been improperly registered, and that absentee votes had poured in for Fisher. "There were some improprieties," said Affleck. "It wasn't like they had gone out to the cemetery and registered 150 voters; they actually *had* live people who voted, but there were some problems." He filed an election contest, but no evidence of fraud was found. "The actions of the registrar in removing the names from the list, although improper, was done in good faith," the court found.

"It *was* an awfully technical matter," said Affleck, "and the judge was very fair, but he declined to rule in our favor. We were probably on pretty shaky ground with the challenge. Still, a lot of people came to the hearing, and I think some good came of it. It put people on notice that they were being watched and they were going to be challenged."

Would it be possible, all fraud aside, for Thurnell Alston

ever to be elected to the county commission? Probably not, said the black leaders, and this was deeply troubling to the lawyers. "You run the election at-large," said Mark Gorman. "You lose by three votes. There's some evidence of voting irregularities. You go through the state-prescribed procedure to get redress there and you lose. There's nothing else you can do within the existing electoral system to try and break out of it. At that point, your only remedy becomes, 'Is there something in federal law? Is there something in constitutional law we can turn to?' And that is where the discussion went."

The attorneys began to consider the legal alternatives. They were starting to approach what would become their legal centerpiece, the flagship of their efforts to rearrange the distribution of power in McIntosh County: two lawsuits aimed at carving Darien and McIntosh County into voting districts, including majority-black districts, so that independent black community leaders could be freely nominated and elected. It would mean the end of the sheriff's ability to anoint frail, elderly black men of his own choosing for countywide office and call that representative government.

Eleven

The Boycott

1

January 1976

Meanwhile, on the home front—far from the Constitution, chapter and verse, far from the courtrooms and the softly modulated voices of well-educated men—good old-fashioned power struggles continued. Mayor Gene Sumner of Darien was sworn into office, and he immediately fired the seven blacks—six sanitation workers and a police officer—employed by the city. This occurred while the jury discrimination case was pending and all jury trials in McIntosh had been suspended awaiting that decision, and following the failure of Alston's election challenge. "There was a sense in the black community that there was a retaliatory aspect to the firings," said Mark Gorman.

The official language was that the blacks were "not rehired" by the new city administration. They were given neither notice nor severance pay. For the GLSP lawyers watching from Brunswick, it was as if all the attorneys played chess at a polished table with ornate pieces, while outside, their clients—plaintiffs and defendants—scuffled in the dirt. It was as if the lawyers were referees at a boxing match; but while they conferred quietly with each other over the rules, the boxers slugged it out illegally, with low blows and hits to the face, breaking each other's noses.

"Gene Sumner was elected mayor," said Sammie Pinkney, "and he fired every black on the city payroll, every last *one* of them. He had made promises to some folk, his backers, before he got elected. Of course, we didn't know that, and a lot of black people supported him. After he got elected, he fired the entire city department, all the blacks, said he was going to hire new folks completely. He thought it was just that easy that he could do that. Somebody had told him he could fire anybody he wanted because, you know, 'You *there* now.'"

Thurnell Alston learned of it by a phone call, and then neighbors and friends converged on his yard, filling his driveway with their cars. He stood listening, and staring past the angry group down the highway. He appeared to the people, as he increasingly did, as a man grasping for the response that would be not only emotionally true, but historically and politically true.

And *he* was thinking that the blows were starting to fall, the blows in response to his jury discrimination lawsuit and his election challenge, but they fell on other men. One could gauge the force of one's threat by the force of the blows that fell in return. The reaction told him, for the first time, that he *had* made an impact. It was like a test-your-strength carnival game in which he had swung his mallet and brought it lustily crashing down: he had sent the lawsuit, like a silver ball, shooting up the highway toward Darien; and now, months later, the sound of the bell was heard, and it was a huge gong powerfully chiming, coating the countryside with its resonance.

Four hundred people streamed into a cool and dusty church in Crescent the Thursday night after the firings. They prayed, they sang, they clapped, and they voted to boycott the white businesses of Darien.

Thurnell made his way up the crowded middle aisle, pausing frequently to shake hands. Old men in loose-fitting brown suits fondly thwacked him with their newspapers. Young men in T-shirts lined the walls like lieutenants, at once surly and attentive, radiating with their slouched posture the message that they had not planned to be at Thursday night church service with their mamas, but Thurnell and Sammie had asked them to be there.

Beneath the high, dim light bulbs inside, Alston spoke to the crowds: since they'd already sued the county, and since this act of Mayor Sumner's was an act of retribution, there really was no turning back; being docile and meek was really no longer even a choice. He thought maybe they ought to boycott the white-owned stores and businesses of Darien. This meant all the businesses of Darien except one black-owned gas station.

The idea had come to him instinctively rather than vengefully, as, years before, he had refused to bend and sip the warm water from the black drinking fountain at Babcock & Wilcox. He had felt a growing incapacity to walk one more time into local stores that refused to let a black girl be cashier or a black boy be stock manager, a growing reluctance to pay money to white shop-owners who refused to let members of the 50 percent–black population sit on civic boards or serve on juries.

Outside the church deputies slowly drove back and forth on Highway 17; inside, speakers succeeded one another at the microphone—"Someday I want to walk into a black mayor's office in Darien!" said one; and by the end of the evening the people had voted to boycott.

"It started," said Thurnell Alston, "because we drew up a list of different things that was going on in the county that we really felt we should have a share of. We presented it to the commissioners, and tell them these are our demands. We didn't use the word *demands*—we had some other words for it—but, I mean, they *were* demands. We wanted quality people to have quality positions. We didn't have anybody black running a single cash register in a single store. We made that emphasis point-blank. We came out with a whole list and let them know.

"We also told them if some of these things weren't going to change, well, we give them a date. Then we come up with the selective-buying campaign: 'Buy only at places where blacks have positions of responsibility.' And there weren't any."

2

"We had elected Sumner with our vote; and as soon as he got there, he fired everybody," said Sammie Pinkney, who had lived in New York during the Ed Finch disaster and the Chatham Jones disaster, but was home for this one. "I liked him, and his wife, she was a good cook. Then we got him in there and that's the way he did. That brought *everybody* out. Within about two days or less, we took over City Hall."

Again.

The evening after the meeting in the Crescent church, hundreds of people drove into Darien and pushed into City Hall, as they had done four years earlier for Ed Finch, to demand that the jobs be restored to the seven fired men. It was felt to be the third great offense, and the people once again rose to the occasion.

"The worst part of it was the mayor said to me, 'Sammie, you know I'm not a mean person or a hard person to get along with. You know I used to do things for you.'

"I said, 'Yeah, that's why I know you. But what you did was wrong. There's no excuse for that. Who told you you just going to literally force every black off the job and tell them, "Child, you don't have a job no more"? That's not going to work.'

"Sumner said to me, 'Sammie, I been knowing you all your life.'

"I said, 'Yeah, I been knowing you too, but I'm not the same Sammie you used to know. I'm a different person now, my thoughts are different. I was a young boy at that time. I'm a man now.'

"He said, 'You were a cop up in New York.'

"And I said, 'Yeah. But I'm home now.'"

Viewing the scene from across the street—for it was a city tumult again, not directly implicating the county—Sheriff Poppell was overheard to remark: 'Goddamn Sumner's gone and let the monkeys out of the cage again.'

The monkeys surely were out of the cage again, but with a difference: this time they had their lawyers with them.

For Mark Gorman and David Walbert, the scene in City Hall was nothing like a courtroom, nothing like anything they'd ever seen before. Here they were spectators rather than participants, invited to sit back and watch as the black community demonstrated its own strength and cunning. This, the blacks seemed to say to their lawyers as they thronged into the room and faced down the officials again, is how the game is played *here;* this is what *we* have learned; this is what we are capable of when facing powerful whites who do not set such great store by the Constitution as you do.

Said Walbert, who flew down from Atlanta and drove up from Brunswick for the event, "What I always remember first about McIntosh County—not that it was the first time I was there, but it was so dramatic that I always think of it first—was the tremendous uproar when the city council fired the black workers. For those white folks sitting at those tables up front, surrounded by all those black guys, I think it must have felt like the revolution of the Mau Maus."

Mark Gorman said: "The excuse of the city council was that everybody who worked for the city had their jobs completely at the pleasure of the mayor and the city council and that after the election they declined to rehire the employees of the previous administration. But they'd been steady jobs, and everybody who was not rehired was black. A few whites who should have been in the same category *were* rehired, so the racial slant to this action was pretty clear and the black community was aroused. It was a very dramatic moment for me. A huge number of people came out."

"Oh my God," said Sammie, "everybody was there. This was doing something special for them because they never have anybody stand up to this Scotchman before. They sat back and accepted what was given to them. But after Finch, and after getting started with class-action suits and all that stuff, people had other avenues that they had found. They were able to challenge."

"I'll never forget that meeting and that night," said Mark. "David and I drove up there. I still had the VISTA car, the government car, very identifiable, and we went into this meeting room maybe thirty by forty feet, you know, the combination City Hall and fire station. Mayor Sumner was there, and the members of the city council—three whites and the one black, Chester Devillers—and Charlie Stebbins, the city attorney. And then this room was full. You couldn't get another person into the room. There must have been more than 100 people there, all black men and women. The only thing they wanted to talk about was this personnel action that had taken place.

"David and I were introduced to the city council as the citizens' lawyers, but I don't remember that David or I said a word. All the talk was between the elected officials and the members of the community. And there were a lot of people from the community who wanted to have their say. The talk and the emotions were very high. Mr. Devillers gave a very eloquent speech about what's right and what's fair, speaking against the council's actions. But he wasn't alone. Everybody spoke well. My perception of David's and my role was that we were sort of the six-guns strapped in the belt of the black community: 'Our lawyers have already filed this one suit on the jury, and they're here and they'll take whatever action is necessary.' But neither of us said a word that night. It didn't fit the dynamic of what was going on there.

"At that point the city council declared an adjournment. They went into this very small room in the back. And the people, all the rest of the citizens who had come at this point—nobody's left in the room who's white except David and me—and they start singing 'We Shall Overcome' and they start singing hymns, gospel hymns, and there's really no way out of the building for the city council. I've often thought about what those people in Darien, who as white people in this very small town had never experienced anything like this before, what they must have been thinking to be in this little room in the back with very high passions going on, then to have this group to start to sing these anthems of civil rights. They must have thought the end of the world was coming, or something equally dire.

"Then they came back and reconvened the meeting and announced that they were going to reconsider their action of dismissing these people."

Pinkney remembered: "They said, 'Well, we'll do it, give us a week. And we said, 'No, no, no. These people go back to work *today*.' And they did it. They called them all in, they did it—they put everybody back on payroll. I mean he had canned *everybody*."

"That was the end of the meeting," said Gorman. "Directly across the highway from City Hall was a gas station owned by a black man. That's where David and I went with Sammie, Reverend Grovner, Thurnell, and most of the men. This was a strictly 'men only' meeting in the gas station over there. We were having a couple of drinks, celebrating our victory, when we noticed out the window that the sheriff's department was slowly, very slowly cruising up and down U.S. 17, back and forth in front of this gas station. By now it's around eleven at night.

"And to my distress, our friends started taking guns out of their pockets and out of the holsters under their coats. And I realized that all the men at the meeting, with the exception of myself and David, had been armed."

"We were having a whiskey at the gas station," Walbert remembered, "when everybody pulls out their guns and lays them down. I hadn't realized they were armed. Those white folks had to have known they were all armed; I suddenly remembered hearing Sammie say he would never go anywhere without his rod. Because of all the corruption in the county, people would get cut up and killed from time to time. I don't know that it was race related so much as this was just a very dangerous county to be in."

"I came to realize," said Mark, "during my years in south Georgia, that one of the principal reasons for relative peace between the races was that both were equally armed and each side knew it. Particularly the whites knew that the blacks all had guns; they all had shotguns and handguns. They carried them around with them in their cars, and their homes were all armed. You really had here a condition of deterrence that prevailed.

"After that meeting, when it was time for David and me to get back to Brunswick, they gave us an escort. Thurnell and Reverend Grovner and the rest were sufficiently concerned that they convoyed us to the river back into Glynn County. There was at least one car in front and one car behind, and we were in the middle. It was getting foggy that night, and we're up there in the swamps of McIntosh County in the night, when the fog's coming down, and you know you don't have to be up there very long to hear about what life is like in the Poppell kingdom. So I felt very relieved that our people were taking care of us enough to guarantee our safe conduct out of the county. *They* were armed, but David and I certainly were not."

The lawyers never forgot that night, and they left with two great impressions: one, of the relative timidity and thin-bloodedness of their own approach, the quiet midnight library work, the polite flurry of interrogatories; and two, of the strange and deep and powerful black community that had seized on them as allies but did not, in the last resort, rely on them exclusively.

"When I saw all those guns," said Walbert, "I remember thinking, 'Jesus Christ, no wonder the city council rescinded.'"

3

The capitulation of Mayor Sumner and the city council did not avert the boycott. The black community now was stirred up over more than the firings, and the rehiring of the black workers had become simply the first item on a long, long list of grievances. Furthermore, the city hedged at the last minute, after the crowds in City Hall dispersed, by clarifying their position: "The rehired workers would serve a thirty-day probation period," the officials said, "under observation, while an evaluation is made of their work." The community leaders simply added this to their list of grievances.

The boycott commenced January 21, 1976. This was to be the community's counterpunch (without excessive reference to the Constitution, chapter and verse) to the unfair firings.

The list of the people's demands, or "objectives," was typed up by Grovner, photocopied in Brunswick, and distributed to the *Darien News,* to city and county offices, to black churches, and to any white citizens who would take one. It read:

WE THE BLACK CITIZENS WOULD LIKE TO PRESENT THE FOLLOWING OBJECTIVES. WE REQUEST THAT THEY BE CONSIDERED IMMEDIATELY:

1. We hereby recommend that the Mayor, City Councilmen, City Attorney, and all concerned officials put forth every effort to change the existing City Charter regarding hiring and firing of city employees to one that is more equitable.
2. We further recommend that during the thirty day probationary period now in effect every effort be made by city officials to determine the efficiency or inefficiency of all City employees regardless of race. . . .
3. We urge public officials to utilize local talent in our community before going outside the community to fill vacancies in city and county offices and departments.
4. We further urge that whenever any persons are hired for city or county positions, black people share proportionally such positions.
5. We appreciate the interest shown to date by the Darien Bank toward the employment of black people. We recommend that the present ratio of minority employees be increased as soon as possible.
6. We recommend that there be an input of black citizens whenever appointments to boards or commissions are made.
7. We want more blacks hired in businesses in McIntosh County:
    a. Banks
    b. Supermarkets
    c. Offices
    d. Cafes
    e. Motels
    f. More black managers
8. We recommend that the City Council and the County Commission appoint a biracial committee, consisting of five competent white and five competent black citizens, to serve as a liaison committee between the community and the city and county governments. We further recommend that the black

> representatives of this committee be chosen from a list prepared by the McIntosh County Branch NAACP and McIntosh County Civic Improvement Organization.

It was like harvest time eighty years ago, or like the semi-mythical semi-African harvest time the old rheumy-eyed half-mad ones said they recollected, back when neighbor helped neighbor, and rejoiced together when the work was finished. Wasn't it like *this?* the younger people seemed to ask the elders. In high spirits they shared eggs and flour, butter and sugar, from house to house. The fishermen and their wives and children drove slowly down U.S. 17 in trucks and handed out plastic bags filled with ice and fresh shrimp. Parents withdrew their children from the public schools, and their own people—trained schoolteachers among them—taught the children in a one-room church. Stout ladies in flowery dresses and straw hats rode forward-facing, three abreast, six to a car, north to Savannah to the Oglethorpe Mall, or south to Brunswick for groceries, shoes, and children's clothing. U.S. 17 stayed lit up past midnight; seen from above it was a long, skinny wire of yellow porch lights slung between Brunswick and Savannah. Crowds stayed in the dirt yards chatting, and children played Witch Hazel and hide-and-seek, screaming in mock terror.

The people had a good feeling about the boycott. It felt like church. It felt like church in the morning, church in the afternoon, church at night, not only because they did gather, by the hundreds, in their churches every night of the boycott, but because the boycott lifted them out of themselves, made them a part of a larger and important thing. They could see the reason for the boycott, the pattern in the fabric, even as they felt themselves to be the small stitches embroidering the whole.

The boycott felt right and consistent with the Bible as they understood it. They had prayed to God for leaders, and He had shown them, from out of their midst, Nathaniel Grovner, Sammie Pinkney, and Thurnell Alston. Thurnell taught them: "The Bible teaches that the bottom will rise to the top. Justice will prevail. The only thing you've got to do is do the thing that is right and pleasing in the sight of God, and He'll make everything all right for you." The people prayed alongside him, urging him ahead with their amens and their glorious songs, and they stayed away from Darien.

Participation was high, maybe three-quarters of the community, maybe higher. And there was something about the boycott that made it very different from the two demonstrations at City Hall—the one for Ed Finch in 1972 and the one for the fired workers the week before. In a demonstration, one served by being present, and the effect was finite and stationary: one was present, say, from 10:00 A.M. until 11:00; a certain number of whites witnessed the event; and one was seen to be participating.

In a boycott, though, one served by absence. The effect could not be ascribed to certain hours, and the impact seemed almost infinite: If I do not shop in your store, Heaven knows how many things I am refraining from buying; Heaven knows how many visiting friends and out-of-town relatives I may have brought with me today; Heaven knows what savings account I may have depleted in order to make additional purchases. The boycott, even more than the demonstrations, became an affair of the imagination. Oh, the handbags, the fancy shoes, the radial tires, the strollers, the towels and sheets, and the refrigerators the black people did not buy in Darien in those two weeks! In this way, imaginatively as well as actually, nearly everyone bought into the boycott. And the elderly, the feeble, the very young, and those with a so-so political commitment all could participate magnificently, 100 percent, simply by *not shopping in Darien.* The people milled together, cooked and ate and prayed after supper together all through those weeks. The communal presence kept morale high. Also, everyone secretly wanted to keep an eye on everyone else: if you are *here,* their approving nods and greetings seemed to say, through smiling teeth, we know you are not *there*—in town, shopping.

Alston said: "Our organization furnished the car, plus the gas and the driver to go shopping in Brunswick. People let us know wherever they want to shop, somebody be there to take them. We raised money by raffling off TVs and guns, and by charging NAACP dues, and some people made pledges for fifty dollars or a hundred dollars.

"There was a lot of people that didn't even want to be bothered, now. We find a lot of people stuck in their ways, you know. They have already gotten themselves used to being dictated to, or being taught or being told. The volume we got, the biggest result, was from the people that knows better. We got ready to talk to Deacon Thorpe—he wouldn't talk to us. It was something new that the old didn't want to adjust to or didn't want or didn't want to believe. A lot of them sit back and wait, see what going to develop first. Then if you achieve something, they get on the bandwagon. But then if you fall, they haul off. Then they say, 'I knew it was going to happen all the time. That he couldn't do it.'"

The boycott put people like the Thorpes—who wanted chiefly to please and not to irritate—in the uncomfortably visible position of having to irritate one side or the other. They tried to soft-pedal by buying just a couple of little things in Darien, not as much as usual.

After three weeks of boycotting, the black community received a response: "AN OPEN LETTER TO THE BLACK CITIZENS OF MCINTOSH COUNTY: WE APPRECIATE AND NEED YOU" appeared on the first page of the *Darien News*, signed by the chamber of commerce:

"The merchants here like to believe that they have contributed much over the years for the good of all citizens here," the letter began. "We *had* thought we were appreciated by *all* our citizens. . . . The objectives of the Blacks against the merchants in the hiring of more blacks is *hurt* rather than helped when buying in stores is stopped. Businessmen here are not politicians, nor are they public officials against whom Blacks have made their complaint. If the boycott continues longer, sensible businessmen will be forced to discharge their present employees, Black and White alike, because they have no need for their help to serve a portion of the public who is refusing to buy from them."

In interviews with the *Savannah Morning News,* business leaders in McIntosh insisted that a tremendous chasm existed between white political leaders and white business owners. One would have thought, hearing their denials, that few men of commerce were actually on speaking terms with local officeholders or that the businessmen saw themselves as an estranged group subject, like the blacks, to the whims and peccadillos of the men in power.

The chamber of commerce was trying "to get blacks to differentiate between business and politics," the chamber president told the *Savannah Morning News,* "to try to let the blacks know that business will try to resolve business issues, but that businesses cannot be expected to resolve political issues." The chamber president reported that different businesses were being hurt on different levels, but none had been hurt "severely" thus far. He felt his "open letter" to the black citizens was being well received.

Thurnell Alston, however, was quoted in the Savannah paper as saying, "The chamber's letter indicates to me, personally, that they're kicking up a lot of smoke but they don't have any answers."

Meanwhile, in the provinces, they were belly-laughing, stripping green beans, and passing the shrimp sauce.

Twelve

"Got to Go Vote for My Little Thurnell"

Georgia story: A black man with a Harvard law degree comes home to Georgia to vote in an election.

"Boy," says the registrar, "you have got to take a reading test first."

"No problem," says the lawyer.

They give him a section of the state constitution to read. He takes it, reads it aloud, and interprets it for them. So they give him a section of the U.S. Constitution, and he breezes through that too and recites the Bill of Rights by heart, just for the hell of it. So they get together and whisper for a few minutes and then they give him a section of the Chinese constitution to read, written in Chinese.

"Can you read this one, boy?"

"Yep, sure can," says the lawyer.

"Oh yeah? What's it say?"

"The black man holds the paper out in front of him and states, 'It says, Ain't no black man gonna vote in this here election.'"

1

August 1977

"Black people have controlled the politics in McIntosh County for all of my life," Charles Williamson, *Darien News* publisher, had said. "There's never been a time that the black people didn't control the elections. We are practically fifty/fifty. Voting as a bloc is what makes it powerful."

"Oh yes," David Walbert had said, "and tell me the good of controlling the vote if your choice is between two arch-segregationists?"

And if a black candidate ran for office in opposition to the wishes of Sheriff Poppell, the whites would bloc vote as well, against the attempt.

So much for controlling the politics, the GLSP lawyers thought.

"The white perception of black power is always greatly exaggerated," said David Walbert, in irritation. "Before 1946, you have to remember, the blacks had no role in politics at all; then, suddenly, they had some role. The whites saw this as vastly more significant just because it was compared to a vacuum. The idea of dealing with blacks as a political entity was so strange that what power the black vote *did* have was perceived as much greater than it really was.

"But in terms of what the blacks really needed, if you looked at the blacks and asked, 'What do they really want and need, and what is in their interest politically?' what they got by their 'balance-of-power' voting role was negligible and nonreflective of their real desires. For example, in Albany, Georgia, you could say they were the balance of power. So, that's cool. They have their choice between one segregationist and another. They had no capacity to elect a guy who was opposed to segregation. I think that typifies it."

Would it be possible, wondered the lawyers, to carve McIntosh and Darien into majority-white and majority-black districts so that freely chosen candidates might arise and be elected from within each, so that the blacks really might control the politics in a single district?

The boycott of the Darien stores had been suspended after three weeks when the county commission agreed to the black community's request for a biracial committee to oversee affirmative action hiring in the county. A year and a half passed with virtually no progress before the black community unveiled its greatest weapons: two voting rights suits prepared by the GLSP lawyers—*The NAACP v. The City of Darien* and *The NAACP v. McIntosh County.* The suits alleged that the at-large electoral system for electing city and county officers diluted the votes of black citizens.

"The only plaintiff this time around was the NAACP," said Mark Gorman. "People were anxious about having their names as individuals on these two. This was perceived as a much bigger, bolder step than the suit against the jury commissioners. I think they felt, and rightly so, that to bring a lawsuit against the city council and against the county commission was attempting to strike right at the heart of the power structure."

Dot Googe, owner of the Keystone Motel and city clerk since 1966, was a pale, sweet, black-haired woman. She was of that degree of blue-veined thinness that when she wore a wide-brimmed white Easter hat, it made her positively top-heavy; when, on a special occasion, she donned a corsage, it made her little face look even smaller by comparison; and when she attempted eye makeup, it somehow looked too blue or too green, like colored chalk on a sidewalk, but you immediately forgave her for it. She had been a tall, bony, shy, giggly sort of girl from Mississippi, and her friends in Darien gently chided her for being so soft-spoken. "They used to say I had to hire neighbors to holler at my children for me," she laughed. She was a warm, fluttery presence in her brown-paneled cubicle in City Hall, the rug of which smelled of the old cigarette smoke of years of city council meetings, but the air of which smelled of Dot's sweet perfumes and hair-sprays and the moist, velvety fresh flowers she brought in from her garden at home. Her only window opened inward, into the large, dark, stained, old council meeting hall, cluttered with disarranged, heavy wooden armchairs. After twenty-five years as city clerk, Dot was still just as friendly and accommodating as could be, full of little tidbits of news, little grocery-store-aisle snippets of gossip and none of it harmful; and she counted many lovely black people along with the many lovely white people who were her dearest friends and acquaintances.

"Now in 1966 when my husband and I moved here to open a motel," she said, "Darien did have a reputation for being kind of clannish. If you didn't wash your diapers in the Altamaha, you know! And some of my friends in Jacksonville, Georgia, where we lived then, said, 'You know, you may not *like* [pronounced "lock"] Darien. You like people and you like going out. You may not like Darien. Are you *sure* ["show"] you want to move there?'

"And I said, 'Well, ever' place I've ever been, I found out that people treat you like you treat them.'"

Dot Googe has been happy in Darien, and she raised her three children here while running the Keystone Motel. She has sat in her dim little cubicle day after day after day, happy to chat, engaging in a sort of ongoing monologue that people were free to wander in and listen to, then wander out. "My oldest son's thirty-three; and my only daughter is twenty-six, and she trains employees for a motel chain—where she grew up, in a motel! But anyway, first she was a beautician, and that was not her thing. She found out she really did like office work and being with people, so she trains office managers and bookkeepers. She has a baby that's only three; and when he was born, she didn't work for a long time. Now she's kind of getting back into it. Anyway, my youngest son is a hair stylist in Tampa, Florida, and he won third in the Florida state competition. I *would* have to get that in!"

Dot Googe was clerk in August 1977 when the McIntosh County NAACP sued Darien and McIntosh County. She felt flustered and angry remembering it:

"We had not heard *anything*. We had not heard one complaint. We had not heard anybody state an objection or have anything to say about city elections. Then one day a federal marshal just *walked* in the door, and he served all of us, all the councilmen, subpoenas. It wasn't against me directly, because I'm appointed, not elected; it was against the mayor and councilmen. They were saying that the city election diluted the black vote. And we *had* a black councilman at the time, Mr. Chester Devillers. I worked with him for several years. And there probably would have been more, too, if they'd have come forth and qualified, you know, offered themselves for council.

"But they wanted four districts in this little tiny town! And the council, we were just in shock that there was any complaint about it. The suit was brought by Sammie Pinkney, Thurnell Alston, and Reverend Grovner, those three people representing, I guess, the NAACP. And they had this attorney out of Atlanta: David Walbert. I think he just dropped everything else to work on this. And there was a law that was amended some way so that if the defendants lost, we would have to pay all these big settlement fees, attorneys' fees, everything like that.

"Anyway, this David Walbert also had the assistance of the Georgia Legal Aid Services out of Brunswick. And they and he came in here and set up shop. It was the most lack of courtesy and common respect I have ever seen from anybody. They propped their feet up on the council table out there, in the middle of our meeting room; they ate their lunch there and left their chicken bones for *me* to clean up! I mean I realize that it's a dinky little building, not a real elaborate thing, but still I felt like there was just total lack of respect. But he did get a little upset when I said I was going to call up Judge Alaimo.

"I tell you really, really, it really broke my heart. I'll tell you what: I feel like elected officials are elected by the majority of the people, and they *deserve* a certain amount of respect and courtesy. And they came in here and they had a little court reporter with them that came in to take our depositions. Now these people that work here are probably the most underpaid people in the world, the people that work in the public works department and in here, but we like our jobs; we like them because we're dealing with our people here.

"But they brought this little court reporter in to take my deposition on payroll day. I said, 'Okay now, I have to do the payroll. This is their pay day; they need their money.' So, 'Oh, it won't take long!' They finally used, I guess, their third tape up on me, and this little girl had the filthiest mouth I have ever heard. She was using some four-letter words that I think I've heard and probably will hear again, but not in this office. Not in any public office. I finally said, 'Look, I know I don't have to sit still for this. I'm going to call Judge Alaimo.' And I went over to call Judge Alaimo, I was so upset with them, I said, 'You don't talk that way to me!' And I offered to wash her mouth out with green soap after I got through calling Judge Alaimo.

"And David Walbert walked over and said, 'You know, she's just upset.'

"And I said, 'You talk about upset! *I'm* upset because I'm not able to do the payroll for these poor people in here who work, and the majority of them are black. I want them to have their money. Most of them have a one-family paycheck.' And I said, 'I'm upset too, I just feel like the lack of respect that's shown here, I have never!"

Dan White represented the county; Charles Stebbins, the city. "Dan's approach, as always, was 'We can work something out here,'" said Mark. "So the courses of these two lawsuits immediately went in two completely different directions. With Dan White, it was, 'Bring your maps down and we'll start talking.' The county lawsuit was resolved with a consent order, and McIntosh County was divided into five voting precincts."

The city, on the other hand, didn't want to settle. "I was the city attorney," said Charles Stebbins. "I, of course, answered the suit, denying that we were discriminating, alleging that our system was fair and there actually was no intentional discrimination, which I don't think there was. Never have thought there was in this county. I mean, I couldn't be accurate historically, but the fact is that in this county, as far as I know, there's never been any concerted effort to keep black voters from voting. They voted ever since I can remember. And we had black councilmen. It just depended on the man. If he was popular, he got elected."

The presence of a black man, Chester A. Devillers, as mayor pro tem and city councilman, was the chief stumbling block in the litigation.

The retired high school principal, a stocky man in his late 70s, was born in McIntosh County, and was a graduate of the first black ninth-grade class. He lived in a pretty brick ranch home beside the school playground. "Years ago," he said in a husky, tired voice, "education was provided to black children as far as the seventh grade; for whites till the eleventh. But Professor James L. Grant started a junior high school in 1933. He paid part of his salary to bring a teacher here from Savannah. Our parents paid a fellow to drive us to school in an automobile: the girls got transportation both ways; the boys got transportation *there,* so we'd be on time, but we had to walk home. There was transportation for white children at that time, but there was none for us.

"I graduated ninth grade, then went to Savannah to school. I was the oldest child in my family; my parents wanted me to get that education. I was the first in my family to finish college, the first to get a masters degree." Devillers returned to McIntosh in 1937 and became the principal, teacher, bus driver, and janitor of a small black elementary school. His salary was $80 a month. "I drove that bus for two years," he said, "and I had this in mind: I knew if I ever got them started furnishing transportation to black children, they couldn't just stop."

Devillers was the principal of Todd-Grant High School for 39 years and he served as mayor pro-tem for eight years. "My first term of office was about six months," he said. "A councilman had moved out of the Darien district and they had to replace him. Mayor Gene Sumner said they felt it was time to appoint a black to serve on the City Council. 'Can you suggest someone?' he asked me. A few days later he came back and said, 'We've been talking about it. What about you?'

"I said, 'I'll talk to my wife about it and if she agrees, I'll try.' I was appointed to serve those six months, and for four straight years I was elected. The first time I ran, I received more votes than the mayor. This is how I became mayor pro-tem."

"The city tried to hide behind Mr. Devillers in the lawsuit," said Mark Gorman. "Basically, they were saying, 'This black guy *did* get elected, so obviously there's no discrimination here; whites will vote for blacks.' And that really wasn't so. They would vote for *him* because he was special. They wouldn't vote for anybody else black. When we looked at the historical returns by precinct, the racial bloc voting of whites voting for white candidates whenever a black was running against them, well—to use David's exact words—'It came through. It was clear as a damn bell.'

"After the first day in court they asked for a settlement of like ten thousand dollars!" said Dot Googe. "It was a fourth of our tax digest! Mayor Sumner asked, 'Why didn't you all come and sit down and talk to us? We want people to be served fairly. There's no prejudice in this office.' Anyway, the county had settled out of court, but the city didn't have the money to settle out of court. Besides, if it had been divided into four districts, it would have been a real costly process. You would have had four little election districts. In this little tiny hamlet? And no complaints had been made! Nobody thought about it. They said to us, 'Well, you *should* have thought about it.' But nobody really did think about it because nobody was thinking racially one way or the other.

"We really felt, Why hadn't they come forth and just said, 'We feel like this system is wrong. We feel like our vote is diluted. We feel like we're not well represented, so we'd like you to consider dividing it into four districts.' And I really and truly think that what happened in the end could have happened right then, without the expense of this lawsuit."

In court, the GLSP lawyers ran into trouble. The critical piece of evidence in these types of cases was "depressed minority voter registration." In other words, if 50 percent to 60 percent of a county's residents were black, black voter registration of, say, 10 percent was considered compelling evidence of discrimination in an at-large voting system. And what percentage of black voters were registered in McIntosh County? It had been a finding of fact in the jury discrimination case that the population of McIntosh County, Georgia, aged eighteen or over, at the last census was 4,251. And according to the July 1974 voter registration rolls, how many registered voters were in the county? Why, darn if it wasn't 4,251.

Of course, no one who knew McIntosh would have been surprised if it had been 4,252. It could have been 5,251 and no one would have batted an eye.

"There was something very unusual about McIntosh," said

Mark Gorman. "And Judge Alaimo was troubled by the fact that we couldn't make that element out in our case. I mean he was really bothered by it. And I'm not sure *we* ever figured out exactly what had been going on."

Unable to establish depressed minority registration, the GLSP lawyers argued that there were two basic models of white establishment response to civil rights activism, and both were evidence of problems with an at-large system: One was the Thorpe/Curry approach, where the whites just *picked* somebody to run. And the other was the Devillers approach—the election of a black person only if he or she had credentials vastly superior to those of other local people, black or white. "Our analysis was that in an at-large system that's infected by racial discrimination, the black voters are going to be submerged and their legitimate political demands are not going to be met, despite the presence of one or two black officials," said Mark.

However, the presence of C. W. Devillers as mayor pro tem, the high black voter registration, the fact that the only requirement for getting on the ballot was the payment of a reasonable qualifying fee, the lack of "slating" of candidates, and the dearth of evidence attesting to harassment of voters or reprisals against candidates all greatly troubled Judge Alaimo of the Southern District, and he dismissed the suit.

The GLSP lawyers appealed their loss. On October 19, 1979, the U.S. Court of Appeals for the Fifth Circuit reversed and remanded the district court decision. The circuit court cited evidence "that blacks in Darien are on the average less well-educated and poorer than whites"; evidence of the purge of 137 voters, all black, from the rolls in 1976; and evidence that a forty-dollar qualifying fee might be a hindrance to poor potential candidates. The circuit court was concerned by evidence introduced by the plaintiffs "that a small group of whites act as an informal slating organization that exercises considerable control over city politics. . . . If such a group exists and wields its power to aid only white candidates, it is strong evidence of denial of access. . . . Nor did the [district] court discuss testimony . . . that some potential black candidates were deterred from office by fear of economic reprisals and that some black citizens in Darien had been intimidated in their expression of political views by fear of economic reprisal by whites.

"The effects of past racial discrimination may persist for many years after the discrimination has ended," the court concluded.

In sum, the circuit court reversed; attorneys for both sides met; and Darien, like McIntosh County before it, was sliced into districts, including a majority-black district.

"What happened was that *we* won," said Dot Googe. "But after we won the case, they were going to appeal it. And the appeal was to be held in New Orleans. And we couldn't afford to travel way over there to argue. So the council said, 'Well, if we didn't have so *many* little districts. We object to four, but they might as well go ahead and divide it in half.' And that's what they did. So now we have a south ward and a north ward."

2

August 28, 1978

By late summer the buzzing of the dog-day cicadas is of such ubiquity and volume there might be a bug firmly attached to the underside of every leaf in the county, each with a kazoo in its mouth—wide eyed, upside down, and blowing mightily. The woods vibrate with ten thousand Bronx cheers. The ratchety noise goes all summer, day and night, a diminutive Hallelujah Chorus. It seems the third part—with the heat and the humidity—of the Georgia summer, as if it would be less intense and lush without the cicada tympany. (It's not the heat, it's the sonority.) Then it stops, and one realizes one quiet evening, going back inside for a light sweater, that it is November.

An old cinder-block toolshed sat deep in the tintinnabulary woods. Woody vines twirled slowly down out of the branches above the clearing and looped along the ground like old garden hoses. The toolshed had been emptied out and swept in preparation for that August day, and two voting machines driven down a gravel road in the back of a pickup truck were installed inside. Now it was a voting place for the Crescent district, and at 6:50 A.M. candidate Alston, age forty-one—running for county commissioner for the fourth time, but this time under the court order that had created the majority-black Crescent district—was invited inside to inspect the voting machines and to see for himself that the ballot box stood empty. A poll worker, a white woman, had demonstrated to him how a stub was to be torn off the ballot and deposited separately, registering a single, anonymous vote—as if that were a new concept, he thought to himself, smiling. One thin black woman in a pantsuit busied herself among the others, and her eyes had met his once, noncommittally. Then he retreated to a weedy clearing 250 yards down the gravel service road to await and greet the carloads of voters.

At about the same time across town, a shopkeeper in Darien stood on a stool in his parking lot, rearranging the letters on the Tastee-Freez sign to read: "All you honkies get out and vote!"

Thurnell Alston had left home that morning in anxiety and impatience. The boys had sat kicking in their chairs, playing with their toast, while the sink had rung with pots and clattering water. Becca, in a ripped housedress, with her hair stuck out sideways, had set down a plate of scrambled eggs and sausage. And suddenly there they all were: the baby under the table, the steaming food, the sloppy little boys, and not an appetite in the house. Thurn, the oldest, was pleading, 'Daddy, do I *got* to go to school today?' and Anthony, the second, was smacking himself in the forehead, saying, 'Oh man, he think he get to go with Daddy!' but raising his eyebrows hopefully just in case. And the house, as usual, was as stuffy and swarming as a nest, with crumpled potato-chip bags springing out of the garbage can and tiny socks, eyeless bears, combs, BB pellets, and Wiffle balls strewn over the counter and underfoot. And the third boy, Van, tipped over his glass of Tang, then giggled. The lawn mower lay disemboweled in the side yard, the rubber welcome mat rested halfway down the driveway, chickens pecked in the weeds, and a stack of newspapers swelled on a kitchen chair.

"I'm going," he had said, standing and leaving his full plate; and she, with her back turned, elbow-deep in dishwater, scrubbing last night's frying pans, had said, "All right then."

He had kissed the boys goodbye on top of their heads and left, then had yelled back, "You bring them when you come," and she, musically, "Okay!" Then he had slipped under the steering wheel, not seeing the house or road or trees; and she, as he drove off, had left the faucet streaming and, winding a towel around her hands, had sat at the table to correct a boy or two. Would their lives change today? Was this what the morning was like of a day that changed your life? Was this the sort of house, the sort of breakfast that county commissioners had, and ate? But Thurnell, in the car, less optimistic, recalled a local saying referring to voting fraud: "Even dead white folks vote in McIntosh County."

He stood in the buzzing clearing down the road from the poll site, with cicadas screeching in the trees all around him, and began checking off the arriving black carloads against his memory and against his list of registered voters. At eight o'clock he walked down the road and voted for himself. His opponent was a white man, the sheriff's choice, so there would be bloc voting on both sides today. Numbers alone would not tell the entire story—there would be some crossover voting: a few whites had phoned him at home, and one man had pulled into his driveway one day after work to talk, aspiring to casualness but obviously nervous, keeping the truck door open, the engine running, and one foot on the running board. So he knew he'd gain a few white votes, lose a few black—but numbers would tell most of the story.

At 10:00 A.M. Rebecca's skinny, wild, youngest sister, Joey, came yawning and slapping through the roadside weeds in her thongs and stretch pants. She directed Thurnell to bring beach chairs from her car trunk; and she walked up the road to the convenience store and returned with an ice cream sandwich and a cherry soda. She plopped into her seat, crossed her legs, and made herself at home like a fan settling in at a football game. He stood mute and serious and buttoned up to the collar in his long-sleeve business shirt beside her, appearing—to her—rather ridiculously formal for a man who stood knee-deep in weeds and had crickets crawling on his pant legs. A line of trucks and cars dug off the main road, crunching onto the gravel, and moved in second gear past Thurnell in the clearing. White men with hard hats on their seats, balancing Styrofoam cups of coffee on their truck dashboards, looked him over as they passed. Some said, "Morning, Alston." Black men in overalls slowed and bent through their windows to clasp his hand. "All right, all right brother," he said, squinting and smiling and nervous. He checked names off his mental list. As soon as they freed his hand, he searched the road, looking for more.

Some whites, lurching forward in pickup trucks or idling past in air-conditioned sedans, ignored him. Thin, straight-backed, copper-haired women in navy or black dresses chose the moment of passing him to look out to their right, to peer into the drainage ditch on that side.

"Is this the day? Is this the day?" cried Fanny Palmer when

a neighbor came to fetch her. "Carry me on! Carry me on! I got to go vote for my little Thurnell."

By noon 200 people had driven by to vote, and the sky was white with heat; the clearing whined insanely with flies and mosquitoes. Joey pressed a soda bottle to her forehead. Black workmen in white overalls, on their lunch hour, jammed the ancient brick convenience store. They shoved together deep into the ice cream cooler, for the day's only moment of relief was in bending to root for a Popsicle, icy air clinging to their arms. Then, with up-ended Coke bottles, the men sauntered toward Thurnell's clearing.

"How's it going, man?"

"All right, all right," he said, jittery, not hungry or thirsty until Joey handed him a sandwich and a Coke and he finished them in a bite and a gulp. "Man," he said, "ain't seen your mother and stepfather this morning."

"They be here, Thurnell, they be here after work."

"Rodney, where your brother?"

"In Atlanta, Thurnell."

"Good afternoon, good afternoon," said Thurnell, the charmer, to the slow-passing cars crunching along the gravel.

Back at the house, the kitchen table was heaped high with food. With sleeves rolled, hair pinned, and shoes off, Becca's sisters, neighbors, and friends, some pregnant, some shouldering babies, ganged together in the small space, kindling burners under huge pots, rolling freshly killed chicken parts in flour, and icing cakes. Whether it was to be a celebration or a wake, there would be plenty of food for everyone that evening. Golden chicken pieces drained into glistening paper towels. Toddlers were handed one hot piece in a paper napkin and were shooed back outside. They sat together on the woodpile in the hot sun, nibbling and marveling at their good fortune, attracting cats. A truck jolted off the highway and pulled up all the way to the kitchen door, and a hearty, round man—one of Thurnell's brothers—filled the doorway.

"Ooooh ladies! What y'all done did?"

"You get out, T.J., this for tonight!" they cried.

"You vote yet?" called aproned Becca from the stove, her hair white with flour.

"Yes ma'am, first thing this morning."

"Well, go get you one piece, but don't tell nobody."

And they shared with one another a piece of local folklore: "You might as well vote white, because they're lynching the nigger tonight."

The clearing was crowded by late afternoon. A flock of teenagers perched on car hoods, listening to their radios, singing, flirting, and littering the clearing with bottles, ice cream wrappers, and cigarette butts. They hailed and applauded every black carload.

When Nathaniel Grovner's silver Cadillac eased onto the gravel, the teenagers grew appreciatively quiet. He stopped, solemnly lowered the electric windows, and chirped, "Hi, y'all!" in his cricket voice, with his little squinting face and long teeth and narrow black eyeglasses. He made dozens of trips that day, ferrying elderly voters from the far reaches of the district. Once, from the depths of the dove-gray leather upholstery, came a shy, young, pleased, and guilty glance; and the teenagers, spotting one of their own, mobbed the car.

"What you doing in that car, boy?"

"Yo' *Mama* can't bring you down here? Got to make *Preacher* stop for you?"

"What wrong with your *feets* boy?"

"Oh him, he just want to ride in the reverend's fancy car."

"Damn straight," said the young man, who regally leaned back, murmured, "I'm ready, Rev," and electronically raised his window.

"Oh, Reverend Grovner, let me ride!" cried the girls.

"That man going to let me *drive* that car one of these days," said Joey.

At 6:58 P.M. the last carload crept off the highway; bland, tired, smiling faces pulled up for a chat. "You better get on up there and not let those polls close," everyone yelled. The car went crackling over the gravel into the woods. By seven Thurnell was half-blinded by the all-day dose of white sky and white light flashing off the car chrome, and numbed by all the damp, merry, reflecting faces. What he felt chiefly, at this moment, was rage that all this was so difficult, that it had taken so long to get here, that he was so hot and exhausted; and he felt anticipatory rage in case something went wrong again, denying him victory. He rolled the list of voters under his arm and walked stiff-legged, with pain in his back, toward the poll site. The friends and brothers and sisters-in-law and teenagers followed at a distance, rather funereally, trying to reflect, at this last moment, that they comprehended the day's seriousness.

The sun, by 7:30, was an orange globe. The cinder-block building was buried in chirping greenery when Thurnell and his group arrived; and a group of whites stood leaning against their cars parked on the mown weeds nearby. Officious humming filled the neon-lit place. The pine trees at dusk cast the clearing in navy-green darkness. Mosquitoes dropped out of the air onto everyone's arms and legs like fine nets, like delicate lace, falling lightly everywhere at once, before placing their burning, minuscule pockmarks. The blacks and whites stood silently in separate groups, eyeing each other.

A vigil. Nathaniel Grovner and a few of the teenagers drew close to the light and bustle visible through the doorway.

"Rev, when you going to let me drive your car?" asked Joey.

"No time."

"I can drive *good.*"

"No ma'am."

Thurnell watched the sky grow ragged and dark with clouds. The whites, too, were silent; farm people, fishing people, they crossed their arms over their stomachs. Alston knew that some of them, when they thought of him, thought "nigger"; but he also knew that others were tired of Poppell's dynasty and would even vote for a black to pit against it.

Then Grovner and one of the white men were invited inside to witness the final count. The bony minister, all in black, scampered to comply. He vanished inside; then ducked back out once—leaning out into the gray evening, he bounced his eyebrows up and down, up and down like Groucho Marx—then withdrew back inside. "Now what the hell do *that* suppose to mean?" muttered the young men, exhaling in impatience and flicking their glowing cigarettes. They sighed and looked up over the rough branches into the oval of silver sky above the clearing.

Then Grovner sang, "Whoop!" and dashed out of the doorway like a black colt tangled in his own legs, carrying his flat hand over his mouth. He did a jig in the grass while the others surrounded him. He lowered his hand, his eyes wide, his high voice breaking. "We got it!" He danced another jig and enjoyed, out of his long and complicated life, a moment of true and simple happiness.

No shout rose from the group, though their arms lifted in surprise, as if from a sudden, heavy gust of wind, and Louise murmured, "Well, praise God." Two of the teenage girls squeezed each other's hands and laughed, and Grovner shook Alston's hand: "Congratulations, Commissioner."

That afternoon Thurnell and his white opponent had waved affably at each other, and he had called, "I think I got you this time!" Then it had been like a game, like that was the thing one said in a democratic county to one's fair opponent. The ballots now lay in the ballot box and had been counted under the eyes of two black witnesses, the lady in the pantsuit and Nathaniel, and he had won.

Louise, in pearls and a plaid-slacks outfit, put her arm around his back to escort him from the clearing. He walked stiffly beside her. His first reaction was a gasp of shock and relief. Thank God. Thank God this fight is over, thank God this day is over. The rage he had felt since morning, the anticipatory rage if the election were stolen from him, disappeared, leaving him surprised and grateful. He believed in democracy at that moment, he believed in the Constitution, he believed in litigation and the rule of law; he believed that he could be an intelligent and good civil servant and leader. In pain from his back, he walked with Louise out of the little clearing full of momentous concepts, with a sudden feeling about his own place in American history.

Before heading back up the service road toward the car, which he'd parked at the convenience store at 6:30 A.M., he looked over at the clutch of white people also departing the polling site. A sunburned woman in a green sleeveless blouse scooted off the hood of her Mustang, threw open her door, slammed it to, and backed out with the tires furiously throwing gravel. A group of men stood beside their cars. He saw one shake his opponent's hand. And that glimpse brought him around immediately from his meditation on America and justice. The sight of them reminded him—within the first minutes of winning—that there was no such thing, in this fight for racial equality, as clear and permanent victory.

What if the election turned out to be a fraud? he suddenly

thought. What if the office of county commissioner was something the blacks had been taught to crave so the whites could give it up with pomp and regret as if it were a thing of great value? What if the sheriff had larger plans, for the protection of which he sacrificed the whites in Thurnell's district, believing that would satiate the blacks? What if the plump, pale, round-faced men were simply going to close their portfolios and withdraw to another chamber one more door removed?

There was no simple happiness in winning. He could not share Nathaniel Grovner's quick tango in the grass. He had won nothing yet, done nothing yet. Better, instead, to prepare himself for a fight. He would like to show the whites that filing the lawsuits and carrying this election arose from a powerful sense of history that they refused to understand; that everything that had happened so far was just Thurnell Alston rolling up his sleeves.

3

Half the black county gathered at Club 17—the cinder-block bar on U.S. 17—on election night and shouldered into the single, red-lit, deafening room. The rest stood out in their dirt yards and on their front porches miles away and felt the throbbing bass notes coming to them across cropland and forests. It was a clear night, the country sky was fuzzy with stars, and everyone knew: they were celebrating at the club.

Curled and perfumed teenagers arrived from the far reaches of the county, from the cabins and trailers in the woods, like moths attracted to high-wattage lights. Young men had stood burning in showers till their shoulders seemed to swell and then had worked bare-chested, draped with a towel, ironing their dress shirts on kitchen tables. Their mothers had talked while the sons had ironed and buttoned and tucked themselves in, paying their mothers no mind: "Now you be sure to tell Thurnell we'll be to his house tomorrow," or, "You tell Rebecca that I'm bringing that sour cream cake to the church." The sons were eager to be off; the mothers were sorry to see them go.

In their homes, the young ladies, with tiny waists and platform shoes and purple eyeshadow and puffed-up hair, ran from the dens—where younger kids lay on their stomachs in front of the TV—down their dirt driveways to the waiting cars when they heard the toot of a car horn. The cars spun onto the green, buzzing backwoods roads and zoomed from all directions toward Club 17.

Club 17 served, on Sunday mornings, as the local icon of Sin. On Sunday mornings church families paraded along the highway: heavy-chested women with handbags and fans, thin husbands in pointed shoes, and dainty, lemon-smelling old ladies beneath umbrellas opened against the sun. They walked along the roadside, ignoring the gross trucks horning through their midst, and trooped righteously across the club parking lot. Club 17 was strictly snubbed—on Sunday mornings.

On election night, though, the church ladies—friends of Becca and Louise and Teretha, supporters of Thurnell—walked with heads held high but with ankles uncertain across the gravel parking lot and entered the dim, beery hall where teenagers and young adults convulsed together on the dance floor. They put gloved hands over their ears and ducked and made their way through the room as if dodging shrapnel. Seats were offered to them in booths along the side wall, and they placed their pocketbooks primly at their feet, folded their plump hands on the wet tables, and smiled bravely. Some ladies peeked in, holding a freshly iced cake on a plate, unsure where to put it. When invited in, they picked their way through the sweating, rhythmic crowd and placed their dessert on the bar.

No one had pictured this: through the protests and petitions and lawsuits, no one's imagination had carried them this far, to a victory celebration. Certainly not Thurnell: he had spent the long day nursing the beginnings of tremendous rage, anticipating that the election would be stolen from him; and, as the numbers of black voters climbed, assuring his victory, he had become more angry and bitter about the extent of theft and fraud that would probably be perpetrated to defeat him. So the ladies did what they usually did in times of joy and sorrow: they baked. And the men did what they likewise did at those times: they drank. But he had won—they all had won. Now the young people required a tremendous, deafening volume to their music to help them shout, See what we've done! See what we've done! They twisted and pushed and pulled on the dance floor, glistening with sweat; it was for them a night of strenuous happiness.

Blasted by music, reeling with alcohol, they conspired, by shoving together on the dark floor, to raise a sound like roaring; it sounded like they all pumped in the furious red darkness to stomp something underfoot. Some staggered out to the parking lot for air, and the glowing sky swirled around them. Cars sailing past on the cool highway slowed, and passengers turned in their seats to glimpse the carousal. And sheriff's department vehicles drove back and forth, back and forth; but the young men, feeling invulnerable, screamed ecstatic insults and made foul gestures at the brown cars' taillights.

Workmen inside wedged tight at the bar. They'd come to Club 17, as always, to mull over the news of the day and because the Club, when they sat at the bar drinking, gave the only breathing space for a hundred miles. They hadn't expected to be invaded by hundreds of teenagers and choir members. The first brown tinge of whiskey darkened their minds as they stood. They accommodated the bartender and the crowd by dispensing beer mugs to the throngs behind them. They turned occasionally to watch the young women in blue jeans and hoop earrings dance with closed eyes. When the middle-aged men turned back to the bar, they seemed to hunker down together. They slid their glasses through pools of ice water standing on the polished wood. The bottles behind the bar looked chrome and copper in the half light, with labels like foreign flags or royal seals. They moved, each alone, and with the music exploding around them, toward the soft interior explosions of liquor in the bloodstream. The image of Alston as a suave, self-possessed black man seating himself at the county commission table grew on them.

"Hey nigger!" they called when they saw him. "Come here man," and they opened a place for him at the bar as he made his way through the crowd, working the crowd like a true politician with handshakes and embraces, a stupid, happy grin on his face. He swam through the mob toward them, and they shook his hand when he arrived. He was breathing hard; they could see he was lit up. He stood holding onto the counter. They saw him through a brown fog, with the fiery, leaping figures in the background.

Their hands hungered: this Thurnell understood by their silence and their steady drinking. Red-eyed, with muscles like granite under their T-shirts, they would be up before dawn stamping into boots, preparing for their day labor. They would come home caked with cement, deafened by the scream of machinery in their brains, or saturated with the reek of fish or garbage or sewage. Not one of them filled his days with loved work: they worked for wages. They worked for white men. All their lives they had understood it was far better than no work, but it was not work freely chosen; it was at times brutal work, performed while white foremen watched from air-conditioned trailers. Getting Thurnell Alston downtown was one thing: the lid of the pot that compressed them lifted, a little. But meanwhile, they were getting older, and their hands hungered, and it was only another lousy drunken Tuesday night.

Thurnell was about half sober, and the anguished, hurling music and the rejoicing of the crowd kept him unsettled, like a swimmer in a lake with no beach. He left the men at the bar and paddled back through the crowd. At the door he stood watching. Church ladies, ready to escape from the bath of music and heat, having confirmed their suspicions about what exactly went on in here, hoisted their pocketbooks and wobbled toward the door. They stopped to squeeze Thurnell's hands before hurrying away. Thurnell watched the young people hopping on the packed dance floor.

"Dance with us, man!" they called.

He waved and slipped out. He walked across the parking lot and down U.S. 17 toward his house. The cool air assailed him. The driver of a passing car gave a friendly honk. Alone, his head was a cannonball, heavy and flying. He headed home, where Becca waited for him in rooms filled with the cakes and pies dropped off all day long. The party behind him reddened the night sky. He flew along, savoring the solitude and feeling at once exalted and humble. The brief sense of elation he had experienced on learning the election results, the sense of history and America and justice converging on that spot, that weedy buzzy clearing, still was with him, but he tempered it with what he knew was true: that the black community had taken really only a very tiny step forward. The leaping and dancing in Club 17 behind him was fine for the the young people, but for him it was either too little—the banal, ear-splitting dance music too silly to capture this moment of destiny and power—or too much. The joyous, perspiring celebrants placed too much faith in the election of one inexperienced man to a seat on the county commission of a poor and forgotten county. He was a serious man, and from the start he measured his pleasure in winning against the likelihood that the winning wasn't worth much.

Meanwhile, he hoped to be of service. The minimum he hoped for, for whatever length of time they let him stay in office, was to get a few simple things accomplished.

Thus it was that a new principle was about to enter county politics, the principle that if a person is freezing to death in the winter, she shouldn't have to pray for sheetrock. Municipal services ought to provide her with some.

Thirteen

The Old Fox Gets Away Again

1

The U.S. Constitution had entered McIntosh County in the company of the talkative young GLSP lawyers, with their uneven haircuts, secondhand suits, and backseats full of law books. Within three years of making the acquaintance of Pinkney, Alston, and Grovner, they had helped revise the jury selection system for grand juries and trial juries, and the selection procedures for the board of education members; they had redrawn the city and county voting districts; and they had seen the election of a freely chosen black man to countywide office—and all because the document they loved and quoted was a heavyweight and took precedence every time over local tradition, tribal custom. For the first time ever, the followers of Sheriff Poppell found themselves to be, like the title of the play, children of a lesser god.

However, the friendly GLSP lawyers, chewing on fast-food hamburgers as they cruised up the coast out of Brunswick, were not the only Constitution-wielding invaders of McIntosh County in those years. By the late 1970s the little county was crisscrossed daily by white and light-blue GSA (Government Services Administration) vehicles out of Savannah, Brunswick, and Hinesville.

The VISTA lawyers drove them; FBI and GBI staff people drove them; U.S. Customs agents drove them; and IRS field staff drove them. GSA sedans lined up at the Darien gas stations, and the drivers poked government credit cards out their lowered windows.

What the GLSP lawyers and the NAACP leaders did not know, when they began their lawsuits, was that within a year or two of their first courageous attacks on the "courthouse gang," in the same weeks and months in which they fought the sheriff and the white establishment over racial equality, the Poppell family was beset by law enforcement agents descending from all corners.

"The coast was the last stronghold of the political bosses in the state of Georgia," said Chief Bill Kicklighter.

Sheriff Poppell and a few other leaders in nearby counties ruled like despots until the 1970s, when a combination of factors, especially the civil rights movement, the migration of outsiders into the counties, law enforcement agencies' increasing reliance on federal grand juries and federal judges, the bypassing of the little fiefdoms by modern interstates, and their own aging—exposed the last generation of powerful High Sheriffs and other politicians to public and legal scrutiny. "They got indicted for things," said Savannah attorney Clarence Martin, "that their families had done for years."

From the day the McIntosh County black people stormed City Hall in the Ed Finch incident and refused to disperse when so ordered by Poppell's deputy, the balance of power between the black and white communities began to tip. But Poppell was fighting for his professional life on all sides, not only in relation to the blacks—a battle being lost by his colleagues across the state.

Sheriff Jewel Futch, for example, of Towns County, was indicted in 1974 on fifty counts of taking gambling protection payoffs, misusing public funds, and committing theft by conversion. When Sheriff Futch was questioned at his trial about the speed traps and other illegal activities in his county, he gave an answer worthy of a Poppell: "Times was rough," said Futch. "I had deputies to feed."

2

Sheriff Poppell's most famous escapade still lives in story and song along the southern Atlantic coast. It is referred to as "The Night on the Marshes," or as "The Great Sapelo Bust."

The essential story places on the marshes under a full moon in August 1975 the following assemblage: Sheriff Poppell, waiting with his deputies at water's edge; a crew of marijuana smugglers on a shrimp boat, puttering across the silvery lagoons toward a dock; and a team of Savannah-based Drug Enforcement Administration (DEA) agents and U.S. Customs agents, who had received a tip that a "drop" was to occur that night.

The federal agents patroled the numberless green inlets in search of the drug smugglers and whoever was awaiting them. The sheriff was on the lookout for the smugglers, too, probably in order to signal them into port. And the smugglers were looking for safe harbor and probably had an eye out for Poppell and his men, unaware that an informer in their midst had radioed ahead to U.S. Customs agents that they were coming.

The DEA agents—undercover agents in blue jeans, long hair, and beards—suddenly came upon the sheriff. Poppell, startled, assumed they were drug pirates out to intercept his shipment. He opened fire. The DEA agents, taken by surprise, shot back. With the shrimp boat in the distance, a shower of bullets fell on all the law enforcement agents. Coming closer to the sheriff, the federals identified themselves to their assailants as DEA and Customs. The drug boat hove into view, and Sheriff Poppell smoothly shifted his aim toward the drug boat, calling out to the DEA, "Thank God you boys got here in time."

This story, fast becoming coastal folklore, has been given a number of interpretations, depending where on the spectrum of guilt and innocence the teller chooses to place Sheriff Poppell.

Vic Waters, a local rhythm-and-blues musician and composer in his early 40s, believes in Poppell's innocence and contends that the High Sheriff was in the marshes that night for the same reason as the customs agents: to catch smugglers. Waters lives in a modern log home at the edge of Roscoe's Creek, which runs into the yellow marshland. Long haired and bearded with graying red hair, dressed in blue jeans, boots, and a blue-jean jacket, he practiced his guitar in a den while a football game lit up a portable TV.

He faults the federal agents for not advising local law enforcement of their intentions ahead of time, and he certainly forgives the sheriff for making a mistake and shooting at them. "The sheriff wasn't escorting the boat," said Vic. "A lot of people would like you to believe that, but that wasn't the truth."

Vic Waters wrote and recorded a song about that night, called "The Saga of the Great Sapelo Bust." It appears on his album, *Highwater Britches.*

There was a full moon a-shining on the river
When the boat came in with the goods.
High Sheriff was hiding in the marsh grass
While the customs agents waited in the woods.
Well, Sheriff didn't know about no customs man
And they didn't know about the Sheriff
And the shrimp boat didn't know about nobody
And when the lights came on it scared them half to death.

They were running through the woods
Trying to figure out a way

To get out of this mess
They had all done got into
Looking for some cover
Shooting at each other
Bumping into each other
And calling for their mother.
Yoo-hooo! Yoo-hooo!

Tag line: *I know that's what they were doing cause everybody's running through the woods saying Motherrrr!*

Well the boys commenced to unload the trawler
When the law moved in and grabbed them fast
It's pretty damn hard to conceal the evidence
You just can't eat 18 tons of grass.

They were running through the woods
Trying to figure out a way
To get out of this mess
They had all done got into
Looking for some cover
Shooting at each other
Bumping into each other
And calling for their mother.
Yoo-hooo! Yoo-hooo! Yoo-hooo!

Doug Moss, among others, is less moved by the notion of the sheriff's innocence—in fact, he gives it no credence whatsoever. "Old Tom was smuggling drugs back before it was fashionable to do that. He was sort of a pioneer, I guess you'd say, in his way," said the former Brunswick police detective. "It was common knowledge that Tom was in the gunrunning and pot-smuggling business. That night Tom was in the woods, he was there to supervise the off-loading of the cargo. When the DEA jumped up, Tom got to his car and called for help, saying he had a suspected drug boat coming in and there were all kinds of druggies in the woods with guns.

"Having known Tom, there's no doubt in my mind at all that he was there to help unload the drugs. But he smelled a rat. Word was that Tom was incensed that the whole thing was set up to catch him. Among coastal law enforcement, it was kind of the best joke to come along in a long time."

The incident generated a blizzard of baffled and frustrated paperwork in the GBI, DEA, FBI and U.S. Customs offices, which had been monitoring the drug situation in McIntosh for a few years already. They knew, for example, that from December 1972 through February 1973, four thousand pounds of marijuana had been smuggled into McIntosh, valued at $600,000. They knew that in April 1973 a large shipment of marijuana originating in Colombia had entered the United States through McIntosh County, and they believed that Poppell had divvied up $450,000 with the crew.

In early 1975, U.S. Customs agents arrested over forty people and seized twelve tons of marijuana at Shellman's Bluff in McIntosh, just ten miles from the S&S Truck Stop. In August 1975 there were twenty arrests and eighteen tons of marijuana seized during a smuggling operation into McIntosh County, the one that came to be known as the Great Sapelo Bust.

A federal grand jury convened in Savannah in August 1976 to consider DEA evidence of smuggling and payoffs to Sheriff Poppell and his closest associates. Several indictments resulted from this investigation, charging six individuals with conspiracy, intent to distribute, and importation of marijuana. The charges against Poppell's closest friend later were dismissed as the result of a plea-bargain agreement, and insufficient evidence existed to charge Sheriff Poppell.

What the DEA later said was: "The old fox got away again."

3

Tom Poppell had succeeded his father to the office of sheriff in 1948, and by 1952 the FBI was fielding complaints regarding clip joints, gambling houses, and brothels operating in the county "with the knowledge and blessings of Sheriff Poppell." According to FBI field reports regarding the "operation of pecan centers in McIntosh County": "It was common knowledge that Poppell was receiving kickbacks to allow the gambling joints and houses of prostitution to exist. Further review . . . indicates that Sheriff Poppell owns numerous pieces of real estate in McIntosh County on which restaurants, gambling joints and houses of prostitution are located."

By 1975, nearly every FBI and GBI memo and report contained the warning: "AS POPPELL IS KNOWN TO CARRY FIREARMS AND HAS MADE THREATENING STATEMENTS IN THE PAST CONCERNING LAW ENFORCEMENT OFFICERS, HE SHOULD BE CONSIDERED ARMED AND DANGEROUS." Sometimes this warning regarding McIntosh County's chief law enforcement officer was abbreviated to "ARMED AND DANGEROUS," and stamped across the bottom of every report.

For many years, attempts by state law enforcement personnel to prosecute were thwarted by the sheriff through his manipulation of county grand juries and the superior court judges: nobody in McIntosh would indict him. In the early sixties the IRS was inspired to charge Sheriff Poppell and his wife, Nell, with failure to pay taxes stemming from undeclared illegal income from the clip joints. The IRS collected $27,434.62 in taxes, fraud penalties, and interest assessed against the Poppells for filing false income tax returns for 1957, 1958, 1959, 1960, and 1961. The Poppells appealed and went to trial, seeking recovery of their money. The government contended that Poppell had been paid by clip-joint operators to allow them to keep their illicit businesses open. The former wife of a clip-joint operator swore in U.S. district court that her husband had paid Sheriff Poppell $300 a week in payoffs for being allowed to stay in operation. But the Poppells testified that their financial worth included $18,000 worth of loans received from Poppell's mother (the jailer) and cash gifts of $32,000 from Poppell's millionaire friend, the late R. J. Reynolds, who had had a vacation home in the county, and that these gifts should not be considered income.

A jury deliberated two and a half hours before finding in favor of the Poppells. The IRS had to pay them back.

Because of the impossibility of obtaining indictments—much less convictions—at a local level against the sheriff, the FBI and GBI decided in 1975 to concentrate on *federal* law and the commitment of *federal* crimes, so that the sheriff might be indicted and tried by a federal justice system beyond his control. "Past experience has clearly shown that successful prosecution cannot be anticipated within the Georgia Atlantic Judicial Circuit," wrote FBI special agents. Thereafter, the investigations focused on gathering evidence of federal violations of the Interstate Transportation in Aid of Racketeering—Prostitution (ITAR—P) and Racketeer Influenced Corrupt Organizations (RICO) Act.

The FBI and the GBI, under Bill Kicklighter, raided the S&S several times in the mid-1970s. They netted hundreds of crates of material, including suitcases full of drugs and file drawers full of trick cards and prostitution receipts. Several prostitutes were arrested. Federal indictments led to the conviction of two men for illegally possessing marijuana, amphetamines, and barbiturates with intent to distribute. But Tom Poppell, as usual, was unscathed.

A *Savannah Morning News* report, on October 21, 1975, of one of the raids read:

> Poppell, sheriff here for almost 30 years since his father died holding the same office, was not informed of the impending federal–state look into possible activities in the coastal county.
>
> The Sheriff, who said he was out of town at the time of the raid, told one reporter that although county law enforcement was his responsibility, it was beginning to 'look like a federal job.'

Poppell was quoted as saying he was "ready to step down anytime they ask me to." "Why in the hell," the sheriff stated, "don't the federals take *over* the sheriff's office if they want it.'"

4

Semitrailers were being relieved of their cargoes regularly in McIntosh County through the mid-1970s. Some trucks stopped along U.S. 17 as a result of the normal mishaps of heavy interstate traffic; others suffered a loosened bolt, a deflated tire, or a siphoning-off of gas while parked at the S&S or at one of the clip joints. When they were laid up further down the road and the driver hiked off in search of help, the sheriff and the local citizens alighted at the scene. The sudden gift to the populace of the spoils of another truck was a random and delightful experience, like winning a lottery, and such occurrences earned the sheriff ever-widening circles of supporters.

Only once did criminal indictments follow the stripping of a truck in McIntosh County. Trouble followed the only truck in the history of the county to be looted by a crew *other* than the sheriff's department; and when the indictments were issued, Sheriff Poppell stood back and watched it happen.

Mayor Gene Sumner of Darien took office in 1976. In the spring of 1977, an opportunity presented itself to the mayor: a food truck crashed and burned inside the city limits of Darien. The Georgia Department of Agriculture dispatched a man named A. B. Beckum to inspect the cargo—which, as it turned out, was thousands of Snickers bars—and Beckum condemned the load as fire damaged. He asked Mayor Sumner to dispose of it. The mayor assigned the city sanitation department to the truck site, and the Snickers disappeared—but only briefly.

Within days, every truck stop, diner, and gas station on a 150-mile stretch between Savannah and Jacksonville was showcasing Snickers. Purloined Snickers lined the racks and shelves of stores in McIntosh and filled the freezers and refrigerators of county residents. Folks who once had served their guests a slice of pound cake now presented, rather unappetizingly, a cold slab of Snickers on a plate, with its wrapper conveniently folded down. Brown, crumpled Snickers wrappers littered the side of Highway 17 until it appeared the county was experiencing an early autumn. For two weeks Snickers was the dessert of choice for hundreds, perhaps thousands, of people. "I remember Tom Affleck showing me a freezer full of Snickers," said Michael Froman. Then the craze faded.

In June 1977, Mayor Sumner was indicted for theft by taking, and for offering adulterated food for sale to stores in Georgia. Beckum was indicted as a codefendant.

"The mayor was a person," said Thurnell Alston, "that him and the sheriff didn't get along too good. That was one of the main reasons he got indicted. He was a pretty good person for a mayor. I mean he did some things wrong, but he had been a pretty good mayor."

Mayor Sumner was defeated for reelection that fall and left office still under indictment, though never tried.

Snickergate.

5

Between 1973 and 1975, the last links of I-95, the four-lane interstate, were completed through McIntosh. Ten miles west of U.S. 17, it arched over the county like a suspension bridge. Sterile, bald, and white, I-95 scooped up the southbound high-speed cars in Boston, New York, and Hartford and shot them straight into Florida. If the cars can be imagined as silver balls on a pinball machine, and the new highway a fast chute on the far left, then the ledge labeled "Darien, 10 points," illustrated by a shrimp boat, no longer rang its bell, no longer bounced the cars along their way.

The U.S. 17 motel owners doused their establishments with pink or lime-green paint; they set out geraniums along their white gravel driveways and installed satellite dishes. The State Tourism Department posted signs that urged, "Stay and See Georgia." But the coast listed toward Disneyworld, the quarters and half-dollars rolling thataway; the lawns yellowed; the yard flamingos toppled over and rusted. Women in the nickel postcards wore ponytails and ankle-length skirts and perkily waved, "Greetings from Darien!" and the aging waitresses leaned on their damp sponges and reminisced. The only guest at the Old South Manor was a shrimp or lumber businessman who ate the diet lunch and left after one night, or an all-but-forgotten former resident down to bury an old relative and claim an inheritance. The NOs in NO VACANCY signs shorted out and fell off.

The northern families and their station wagons were serviced efficiently by the national chains at the exit ramps: they bought peanut brittle at Stuckeys; drank Ho-Jo Cola at a Howard Johnson; and selected postcards, in the cool, carpeted lobbies of Holiday Inns, of the shrimp boats and herons they never saw.

"Well, it was different," said Archie Davis, owner of Archie's Restaurant, in his slow, easy drawl. "Business dropped off overnight. We went into a remission-type situation. It's hard to get people off the interstate. If I'm not familiar with the place, I'm not going to get off the highway and wander around either. For every carload that comes in now, 500 never stop. I'll just say it was different."

The old highway became a long, hot daydream of Florida. At night the motel owners dreamed about the late-model cars hissing south on the interstate, their transience like the sound of distant surf, and the vigil continued with daylight. Finally, the owners sold their motels or abandoned them, and they moved to trailer homes in Fort Lauderdale where they could study the reddened beach crowds firsthand. Archie Davis himself went to Miami once to have a look around; he shrugged his shoulders and came back. "I couldn't really see what all the fuss was about," he said. He began cooking for the locals.

"In the beginning it was drastic," said Dot Googe, the city clerk and owner, with her husband, of the Keystone Motel since 1966. "But I think people will begin to realize there's a Darien here. When we looked at that motel to think about buying it, the more we came and looked at it, the more we liked Darien, the more we liked the area, the atmosphere. Tourism is just one of the cleanest industries there is. It's just a little hamlet where people, you know, care about you, care about each other. It's just a whole different world from what I came from. Here you get to feeling sleepy during the day because you're not used to this coastal atmosphere. I think there's just fewer and fewer places like we are.

"I mean, just look at the assets we've got: freshwater fish and we've got saltwater fish. I mean you're close to the Golden Isles, yet you're here, and it's a little hamlet where people care about you, care about each other. And, too, I think more retired people are beginning to travel. And they don't have to go that pace. They don't have to drive sixty-five and seventy miles an hour. I think they like to get off and travel the secondary roads. And it's more economical to stay in a small motel than one where everything is, you know, more elaborate. And then the elderly people, once they stay, a lot of them, they feel secure there. And then we get sportsmen. So you can still make a living doing it. You don't get rich or anything, but you can make a living doing it. And then, too, you can walk across the road without fear of your life."

Along U.S. 17 in the mid- to late-1970s, the carnival medley of shops and diners and motels and gas stations began to dry up. The clip-joint owners were hurt too, and they drifted into less tourist-oriented crime like drug smuggling and gunrunning. In time, only junkyards and flea markets remained on the old highway, offering an infinite reshuffling of the same tired neighborhood possessions. The timberland was felled by paper companies, and technology and pollution thinned the shrimp crop and slowed the canning factories. Two hundred miles of coastal pine trees raked the dry sky.

Yet the county holds.

Part Three

Be not deceived; God is not mocked: for whatsoever a man soweth, that shall he also reap.

—The Epistle of Paul to the Galatians

Fourteen

Commissioner Alston

1

Thurnell Alston presented himself at the door of the meeting room of the county commission, where two long, metal-legged tables stood end-to-end, and white men in short-sleeve shirts and ties sat with Styrofoam cups of coffee and blank legal pads in front of them. In the first hours, days, and months of Alston's decade as a county commissioner, no matter what the typewritten, mimeographed agenda—the zoning requests, licensing requests, county hiring decisions, landfill problems, the industrial authority—the unspoken agenda in that room was for the body politic to absorb the intruder.

He wore his bridegroom outfit—his white satin, velvet-trimmed nightclub outfit, his patent leather boots, his ruffled shirt; he was as frilly as a signer of the Declaration of Independence. And the skin of his face and hands—straight from Africa, unsullied in his family line by the laying-on of master's hands—was as black as the circles of steaming coffee that filled the white cups; and his hair was a grizzly, upright mane. Half of the white men pointedly did not even look up. They found him distasteful; they found him gaudy; they thought him greedy. They who had relaxed, and talked as if among themselves, with Deacon Curry or Deacon Thorpe in the room, now had a true observer and listener, a spy in their midst. And he, with his mix of humility and anger, greeted them in his high, nervous voice, with his grimace of a smile, "Good evening! Good evening!" and never, not once in ten years, ever yielded a point, ever compromised, or ever voted with the group for the sake of unanimity. On his guard perpetually, he never trusted them, never became a team player, never shared in the exasperation, the sarcasm, the chuckles, the snacks, and the in-jokes that allow boards to function without withering of boredom. In the careful way he moved and dressed, and the excited way he spoke, and in the things he said, he felt he expressed, with dignity, "I am a man"; while to the white commissioners, it felt as if he never ceased shouting, "Negro, Negro, Negro! Black, Black, Black!" at them.

The county commissioners ruled an underdeveloped county whose riches had vanished with slavery, a forgotten county needy in every way. The white commissioners attempted to address serious matters such as the necessity of attracting industry and of paving roads. But Alston, unwittingly or not, trumped them every time with demands that the sparse budget be dedicated to shortages even more fundamental. When the other commissioners spoke of business licenses, he spoke of hunger; and when they spoke of fostering development near I-95, he spoke of water. In his decade in office, ignoring, defying the sheriff at every turn, taking the issues to the public, he oversaw the creation of a hospital authority and a physician-staffed medical building deep in the county. He brought plumbing and water to settlements where people used outhouses and wells. He arranged for a renovation assistance program that aided homeowners in adding bathrooms to their cabins. He saw that a multipurpose building was built for the antebellum black community on Sapelo Island. He attracted a grant to build a mental health facility out in the county. None of this endeared him to the other commissioners, nor to the sheriff, who made a point of exaggerated affability toward Thurnell, the joke of which—the insincerity of which—was lost on no one.

"The sheriff could read the handwriting on the wall," said a white Darien lawyer, "and he said, basically, we can either like it or not like it. For his day, you'd have to say he was enlightened. He could have stolen the black people blind of the land they got from Civil War days. But he pretty much helped usher in civil rights. He just stayed very calm."

When Thurnell's high-pitched voice filled the meeting room and broke into stammers with the justice and righteousness of his entreaties, it irked them all: he was a hysteric; nobody's that goddamn noble. When he finished speaking, the response was most often silence, then yawns, stretches, the cracking of joints, sighs, and a good-natured, "Let's go get us some lunch."

"I irritate people," Thurnell Alston said, rather sadly, after his public life was over. "I do. I just irritate both black and white. I have a tendency of irritating, but I'm not going to lie for them. It's just every darn day people want something that I'm not going to give, or they want me to do something that I know is wrong." This was his inheritance from poor Deacon Thorpe. "And if I can't do it for the blacks, why would I do it for the whites and put my neck on the line? Here comes a guy, say, 'Hey I need this and you do this for me.' I say, 'No, I can't do that,' point-blank. And he goes to one of the other commissioners, and he may sneak around and get it to work for him, you know? So then, hey, I got me an enemy. And it works the same with the blacks, too. It was a no-win situation. You losing all the time. But I had more fights with whites than I did with blacks.

"I always been very polite. I respected everybody. I always told them if you want respect, you've got to give respect: 'You don't respect me, I have none for you.' So they gave me respect until I leave and they get by themselves, real buddy-buddy. But I don't care about that as long as I get respect in front of my face, in front of the public. That's all that matters to me.

"But things had to change for them with me on the commission. And they wouldn't dare call a meeting without me. They couldn't pull the deals that they want to pull by me being there. I mean, guys go out there and spend $8,000, $9,000 to be a commissioner, a position that pays $24,000 a year? What they spending their money for? How somebody going to get their money back? After I got there, I cut out all the deals. I want to see the bills, the monthly bills. Policemen used to go buy groceries for the jail, nothing about what it cost; I want to see a copy of the receipt on my desk. Two-thousand-dollar telephone bill a month? I want to see it in front of me, period. I don't want to hear, 'We spent $800.' Give me the receipt. Let me see that you paid that. You know guys buy a tractor for the county and instead of buying one, they buy two? Carry one home with them. I got all that junk cut out. A lot of people that want to run for the commission won't run now because they feel it would be *hard* for them to get their money back. Buy a pickup truck and get one for the county and one for you."

Sammie Pinkney said: "The sheriff used to sit at the corner of the table at commission meetings, which he had no right to be at in the first place. No decision that had any meaning was made until they got the signal from him. When Thurnell got elected, that changed entirely around, that change the entire thing."

Off the main road and far from money, the chop and scrape and chomp of natural life continued. People married (some married badly) and had babies (some had them too young), raised chickens, grew thin or grew heavy and complained about it either way, tied their hair up in kerchiefs, and paced off the mud of their side yards, planning the extra room they would build if they had the wood. Children stood up, wavered, and stomped across the floor for the first time, waving their arms for balance while their mothers clapped; and they raised their slight eyebrows at the sound of "juice" or "no" or "cookie." Some people never learned to cook but stood night after night in a square room of smoke that fled, in a blue stream, when someone came in and opened the window. Others found they had a knack with a brush, a chicken, and a bowl of sauce, and friends gathered in their yards on Saturday nights, drinking beer, smacking mosquitoes, gazing down into the barbecue pit, and setting up folding chairs with the twinkle of fireflies in the dry hedges all around. And some of the very old perched quietly on the uneven folding chairs in the dirt yards and watched the babies sitting straight-legged on the ground, patting the dirt, and discerned in one the angle of her great-grandmother's eyes and heard coming from another the chuckle of his great-grandfather.

The black people, the people in the cabins and the trailers under the pine trees, went quietly back to their lives, laying aside their boycott and their demonstrations and their lawsuits forever. They left the rest of the work to Thurnell, who apparently wanted it. In a strange collapse of vision, the election of Thurnell Alston to the county commission now appeared to everyone to be the chief thing they had worked for, the ultimate victory. They had surged up like a tidal wave and had placed one swimmer on the beach; now, their public energies dissipated, the community organizers drifted apart, watched TV in the evenings, caught up on sleep, and planned for the weddings of their children or for the new kitchens they would install. The maids returned to their cleaning rags, the gardeners to their trowels, the drinkers to their hootch.

It was damaging to Thurnell that the rich and close-knit black community lost interest in him, and in his struggles with the white commissioners. He became, to the black people, simply the Commissioner; not the Barber, not the Undertaker, not the Preacher, but the Commissioner, as if the larger community had no more vested interest in his daily work than in anyone else's. People's lives do not consist, on the whole, of politics and large ideals, but of children and groceries and laundry and paychecks.

So everyone praised Thurnell Alston highly—if his name came up—and asked him for help in time of trouble, but the great battles for equality that had begun so short a time before were deserted. Everyone except Thurnell Alston returned to normal life.

"Thurnell was a black Moses," said Nathaniel Grovner. "He's always done an outstanding job as county commissioner, helped make McIntosh County a better place to live in, being a pioneer in seeking district voting. He was the first to reap the benefits of district voting. He was a much younger man than Deacon Curry or Deacon Thorpe. I don't take anything from them, in their day and time they were good; but quite naturally, a much younger person would be able to surpass an older, mentality-wise. Thurnell has always been for things for the young people. He wasn't afraid to stand up and speak out on an issue."

"Thurnell would stand up—that's all I know how to express it is, he would stand up," said Louise Rasheed (formerly Goodman). "If we have to go before any office, he could get up and express it. He wanted things better, and he knew that we were behind him. I think he just wanted things better than what he had come up with. Because he came up in very poor surroundings, and they wouldn't ever let him live; he just wanted to *live*."

"Well, he was pretty smart all right, all right," said Deacon Thorpe. "He fought for his race all right and so forth. He even fought me. Oh, he fought me something fierce to get on that board. And the only way he could get on that board was they had to cut up the county, cut it up in districts. At the at-large voting, *I* get the biggest crowd."

"We always did like Thurnell," added Belle Thorpe in sweet non sequitor.

"Thurnell is one of my former students and I'm proud of him, very proud," said Chester Devillers, the retired principal. "Three of our young men worked together very beautifully—Thurnell, Sammie, and Reverend Grovner; these young men are responsible for getting district voting in McIntosh County and in Darien. Thurnell had the opportunity to do certain things that I didn't have. The old adage back in those days was that they treat you all right as long as you stay in your place."

"I got two sons and one of them used to be down here all the time," said Lois Reed, in her fifties, from deep in the county, "and Thurnell used to always get on them. He say, 'Now y'all boys, y'all growing up now, y'all learn to stay out the street and stay out from trouble. Don't you bother with no drugs.' He say, 'I rather see you with a can of beer than to get hooked on drugs. Because if you drink, you can always do without, but once you get hooked on them drugs, they going to be hard for you to get off of, and it ain't going to do nothing but worry your mama and daddy to death behind you.' He talk good talk. Every young person come to his house, he always tell them that."

"I used to go around Thurnell a lot, I ever did like to be around him," said Florine Pinkney, the Holiness church member. "Thurnell has done some wonderful things for this county, he has fight some good battles for us, he look out for the white as well as the black."

"Thurnell was a commissioner," said Sammie, "that looked out for his constituents. He was a thorn in some of the other commissioners' sides. He had an attitude they didn't like. They felt he was arrogant. Naturally, if they don't like your attitude, they'll do everything they can not to help you. He felt there were little small personal vendettas against him, though they would never admit it. Deacon Thorpe was more to their style. He did probably the best that he could do at his time—which wasn't much. He was a token. He was a good person, but he didn't know what was going on; he just did *not know* what was going on. Most of the time Deacon Thorpe seconded a motion. He probably never made a motion of anything important.

"I supported Thurnell 100 percent," said Sammie. "When I lived in his district, I voted for him. He was one of the best commissioners that has ever been elected. He was a strong commissioner from the day he was elected to the present time. He was a brave man, very much so, and he looked after his area. I'd vote for him today if need be."

The white people were more skeptical; they put up with Thurnell as commissioner, but they weren't impressed by him. Some thought him as corrupt as the rest, as easily bought as a Thorpe, and others mightily resented his one-focus, one-constituency politics. They appraised him as being too small minded to vote for some vague "good of the county," always nitpicking, always promoting his own cause. The white public tired of the impression they, too, had of Thurnell shouting, Black, Black, Black! at everybody all the time. "Thurnell had a good mother and a good father," said a lawyer, "hard-working people that everyone respected. But he was a nothing, had nothing to show for himself."

"When Mr. Alston made actions and votes that benefited this community, for black and white, I was grateful for that," said Charles Williamson. "When Mr. Alston determined that he was going to be a powerhouse politically, he was, but only because he represented one precinct of the county that was predominantly black; and he could do anything he wanted to do, and he thought he was assured of reelection."

"You're always going to have people that are smart in a certain way, cunning," said a scholarly, elderly white man. "But they always outreach themselves and get into trouble."

"He was as good a county commissioner as any," said Gay Jacobs, the Direct Descendant who runs the shrimp dock. "Of course, we don't ask very much of them. We are kind of self-sufficient in this county. We pay our taxes and go about our business. Thurnell was not all that unpopular, though. I think he saw himself as a thorn in the side of the white establishment.

Because I can remember reading back in some of the commission's minutes, he would invariably vote against what the others voted for, almost as if, at times, he was going out of his way to vote no. Maybe he thought he had a problem with respect and that he had to get their respect. I don't know what the deal was."

"Thurnell was probably the first black commissioner that was concerned with the rights of black people," said David Earl Lane, the redheaded chairman of the county commission. "I don't say that in a derogatory sense to Dan Thorpe or Deacon Curry, but I think Thurnell brought black rights, civil rights if you want to call them that, to the county commission.

"Thurnell was a good district commissioner, I've always said that," Lane said. "He looked out for the people in his district, and that's who put him in office. He had the time to do the job, got the district in good shape; somebody in that district needed some help, he tried to help them. We had our differences as far as issues that involved the entire board; I think whites *and* blacks would say they didn't like him, but as far as trying to help the people in his district, I'd say he was a really good commissioner."

"This is the Crescent district," said Vic Waters in his modern log cabin overlooking Roscoe's Creek. "Thurnell used to come by. I'd see him every two years when it would come to election time. I couldn't believe the people in this county voted for him; of course they just bought into the black-and-white deal: all the blacks were voting for Thurnell and all the whites were voting for whoever was running against him, and the whites don't have enough votes.

"And he'd come by here and say, 'Hey, I'd like to solicit your vote if I can. You know we're going to try and pave this road.' And I just laughed in his face. And I said, 'Man, they been going to pave this road since I was a little boy, they going to pave this road since I was born, and they going to pave it every election.' The dust problem is just incredible when it is dry—and in the rain, it's just a giant mudhole. And now, evidently, we got us a new election coming up, because there's heavy equipment out there now; they been hauling in all this dirt and dredging it out—it's a mess. No, Thurnell never got my road paved. I never saw a road he got paved, I can't think of a one. And I've lived here, like I say, most all my life. And I can't think of a single road. He didn't get Highway 99 paved, and that's the only paved road in Crescent. I can't think of one thing Thurnell ever did."

2

On a summer Sunday afternoon, off the road and far from controversy, Rebecca Alston—her hands and dress front plastered with flour, her wide, pumpkin-colored face glistening with sweat—shouted directions at children across a yellow pile of fish she prepared for frying. Thurnell did the odd errand around the house. He puttered under the sink, spreading newspaper neatly over the dark linoleum before stretching out across it; then wandered out to the yard, into the blast of overhead sunlight, and hosed off the car; and then Becca came outside to stand with crossed arms to watch him.

The youngest boy, Keith, cried "Mama!" and came hurrying over with his round little belly to climb on her as she sat down on a kitchen chair in the dirt yard. He patted her lap with sticky hands and said, knowledgeably, "*Mama.*" He'd tried to drink some juice with his big brothers, and a dust-sprinkled stain of purple circled his lips and cheeks.

"Come here, disgusting thing," said Becca, and hoisted the toddler over her shoulder, and he slid back down to sit comfortably on the bench of her bent forearm. From there he peered proudly around.

"My cousin call and say, 'Come get this son of yours!'" said Becca, about Keith.

"And I say, 'What he done did?'

"She say, 'You know I call Thurnell's name and that boy say, "That not my daddy." And I say, "Who your daddy, boy?" And he say, "*Mister* Thurnell Alston."'"

Rebecca, jiggling him higher until he hugged her neck like a bear cub clamping a tree, said, "Who your daddy?"

"No it ain't," said Keith shyly.

"Who your daddy, boy!"

"Mister Thurnell Alston," he whispered and mashed his face into her neck.

"And who your mama?"

"Becca," he said.

"What?" she cried. "How bout *Miss* Becca?"

"Becca!" he cried, catching the joke.

"What?" she said again. "No, that ain't your mama."

"Yeah it is."

"Who your mama?"

"Ain't got no mama!" he shouted, full of himself, leaning backward to grin proudly up at her.

"You ain't got no mama, boy?" He giggled. "You sure ain't," she shrugged. "You ain't my baby."

"Yeah it is!" he hollered, alarmed.

"Oh no, *oh* no. You ain't my baby. *Van's* my baby."

"I'm your baby! I'm your baby! Mama! Mama!" he cried, wide-eyed.

"Yeah, yeah, you my baby, you bad thing," said Becca, wrapping her arms around him again. "This here's a wild child," she said, rocking him.

Inside the house, the foster girls strutted between the rooms in their slips, with pins between their teeth, proud to be sewing dance dresses whose slinkiness Thurnell was going to outlaw, which they were going to wear anyway when they snuck out of the house later that night. They would slip out the front door and scurry down U.S. 17 to Club 17; there they would lean against the sides of cars in the parking lot, with the arms of young boyfriends around their waists, and laugh, drawing fire and fun from the hot summer night, electrified by the same sultry heat which exhausted their elders.

In 1971, the foster children had been living alone in a house just down 17 from the Alstons. "They been abandoned by their family," said Rebecca. "The kids were running back and forth over there. I was feeding them their meals, so we finally just opened our home as a foster home to them."

"We contacted the welfare office," said Thurnell, "and they say they want to check it out. So Rebecca and I fill out some papers and all, that we taking responsibility for the kids. Rebecca wanted it. I wasn't too set on it because I thought, you know, kids like that, parents leaving them, been messing with the kids for years. That's why I told Rebecca, 'No, I don't know if we ready to even deal with that.' But she want the kids.

"I say, 'You want them, okay, we'll see what we can do for them.' So we did.

"They were not nice kids. Been in foster homes all their lives. All was anemic. We had to take them back to the clinic every week to get shots. And that's saying nothing about the two oldest girls, fourteen and thirteen, because you set most girls in foster homes, all kinds of things going to happen. So we started chatting with them, and you'd be amazed at the stories those girls told us. Abused sexually and every which way you could name, like every time they go to take a bath. And every one of them knew about it. All four of them knew about it. Rebecca and I would just sit there and look at each other.

"But they was very good kids. I mean, they stubborn in their own way, like a person who really need some good guidance. The second girl, she was real smart. The boy, he was smart. But then the oldest one, she been back and forth to where she just didn't care anymore. And the baby girl, she was just too stubborn for anything; she loved to holler.

"But we survived it, because we know the problem. They

would never have make it. They had parents, they had people here, their aunt, their first cousins never stepped in to give them anything. After we got them and got them looking like something, gained weight, start dressing them like something, their people want to use them to mop their floors or pick up around their yard and I wouldn't let them do that."

The Alstons attended foster-parent meetings for five years, and Thurnell became vice-chairman of the Foster Parents Association in Brunswick. "Rebecca really fell in love with those kids," said Thurnell. "My children loved them, loved those girls and boy. We had those kids for a long time."

Thurnell strung a hammock between two pine trees in the side yard and lay in it, looking like a pointed cigar. Becca handed him his whiskey and ice in a paper cup and set out a bag of potato chips for the children. Cousins and neighbors tooted their horns at him when they passed on the road, seeing him suspended there between two trees, and later they drove onto his front yard, parked, and pulled up kitchen chairs near the hammock. The teenagers flirted with each other and engaged him in their banter, pretty girls in rounded, tight jeans and pink toenails dusty on their rubber thongs.

"Thurnell." Their warm, pouting voices.

"Yeah baby."

"Make Rodney quit it."

"What he said?"

"Call me and Tricia two fat little pigs."

"They *is* two fat little pigs—look at her, Thurnell!"

And Thurnell, straining to lift his head out of the netting, would look, then fall back. "No man, I ain't going to touch that. No way."

He floated in the hammock as if it were a bateau in the warm air. He stuck his hand out and waved tolerantly when the fuzzy-headed old woman from a cabin behind the house picked her way through the bushes to come sit at a picnic table in the yard and wait for Becca to bring out a paper plate of Sunday dinner to her. "Thank you, sweetheart," said the old woman when Becca flopped a plate before her. And she ate, there in the yard, fried chicken, a slice of ham, green beans with ham, fresh corn, two slices of white bread, and gravy, then tiptoed home with her leftovers, shielding them with her hand. It was the meal that saw her through the week.

Thurnell drained his paper cup and lay sucking on the ice. The sun was a hot sponge on his forehead. The oak trees were thick with light. An occasional breeze made the heavy leaves hiss and stir, the branches tossing their manes like horses. The children organized a softball game and begged him to umpire; he watched them through the rope mesh of his hammock with half-open eyes.

They used a plastic bat and Wiffle ball, but one of the foster girls—dressed in shorts and a T-shirt, her hair in curlers—belted the ball into a stand of pine trees at the edge of the property. The high school boys had to crash through fallen branches and thorn-bushes to look for it, while the laughing girl wheeled around the baseline barefoot, kicking up dust, and the girls' team shrieked for her. "Foul!" screamed the older boys from the woods; "Foul! Foul!" cried the younger boys, wringing their hands. "Thurnell, ain't it foul!?"

"Foul, Daddy," said Keith, the youngest, poking him with a stick through the hammock, urgently, with not much insight into what a foul was.

"Okay, foul!" called Thurnell, supine.

Then the girls' team surrounded him: "And you flat on your back? How you call that foul, Thurnell?"

"I said *foul,*" said Thurnell, lifting his head up at the word, then falling back. "Ain't I'm the umpire?"

"It *ain't* foul," they said, and girls took hold of one side of the hammock and began to lift. The prospect of dust and pine needles on his hot arms and clothes repelled him. "You better get back out there and play now," he said sternly, threateningly, or with as much threat as he could muster from a forty-five-degree angle above the dirt.

"I'm up!" cried Becca, bursting out of the kitchen door, untying and flinging the apron behind her. She whacked the ball, first swing, and sent it skidding past her second son, the shortstop, as she went rolling and laughing toward the base. She tagged up but overshot, and Anthony leaped on her.

"You're out, Mama!"

"No I ain't out, you fool thing. This here ain't football."

"Daddy! Ain't Mama is out?"

"Yeah, she out," called Thurnell, who had not seen the play, chuckling. And so it went.

By nine o'clock at night twilight muffled the yard as if a tarpaulin had been dragged overhead. Frogs sailed out of the woodpile. Thurnell shoved split firewood up into the grill and laid the pink and white ribs sideways on the grizzled metal bars. Uncles and friends carried a picnic table around from the back and spread newspapers over it, and women came out of the screen door with paper plates, long bags of Wonder bread, bowls of coleslaw and Jello, quart bottles of cola, and platters of chocolate cake. Children hopped like crickets in the dirt yard, leaping to catch lightning bugs. Becca saw, in the distance, the silhouette of two girls, one behind the other, pussyfooting down U.S. 17 toward Club 17.

Thurnell and Becca broke and tossed pine needles into the fire, and took turns holding little Keith, who was worn out and half-asleep on their shoulders, his smudgy thumb jammed into his sweet face. The neighbors' far windows quivered yellow across the fields. The heat of the day had lifted and moved on a little, across the road, across the county line; then a block of cooler air, which had spent its day over the Atlantic, settled over McIntosh. All the families who had stayed for dinner without being asked—without having to be asked—passed around plates and bowls and spooned out children's portions. And it felt, in the firelight, like a pioneer homestead, like a settlement at the edge of great wilderness. These were the benign years for the Alstons, the years of the childhoods of their four sons.

When Thurnell Alston became involved with the NAACP, Georgia Legal Services, the lawsuits, the boycott, and the county commission, the local Department of Family and Children's Services began threatening to remove his four foster children from his home. The warning notices began by speaking of inadequate square footage in the bedrooms and came around to stating, rather plainly, that the political atmosphere in the home was inappropriate for children. The threats clearly were intended to strike back at Thurnell for the NAACP lawsuits and his election to the county commission. But Thurnell Alston at that point was many years beyond the reach of coercion. He told the caseworkers to go to hell, and they came and took the children, basing their administrative decision on inadequate square footage in the Alston home.

"I figured out all their games," said Thurnell. "They came up and said the kids' family wanted them, but there wasn't no family wanted no kids. They just trying to manipulate me. The welfare got them out of my house and didn't give one of them a dime. They never went to school a day after they left my house. I felt like if they let the kids stay, the kids would wind up being more what they really wanted to be in life. Rebecca grieved a long time about it."

Thurnell stood silently, and Becca and the Alston boys and their foster siblings pleaded and whimpered, when caseworkers arrived and carried the foster children's folded clothing and shoes out the door to a waiting car. "Hush now," was all Thurnell said. "They're gone and you hush."

3

As Thurnell Alston's power was increasing, Sheriff Poppell's influence was declining and his health was failing. In 1977 he began a series of hospitalizations for blood disease, eventually diagnosed as leukemia, and underwent treatment at St. Joseph's Hospital in Savannah, at Emory University Hospital in Atlanta, and at a Texas clinic.

"Efforts to reach the sheriff by telephone were consistently unsuccessful," reported David Nordan in a profile of Poppell in the *Atlanta Journal* in 1977. "And when his wife Nell finally came on the line, the questioner was dressed down for having the audacity to inquire about something as personal as a man's health.

"She stated in no uncertain terms that Poppell and McIntosh County have had enough of inquiring reporters over the past thirty years—'It never appears exactly like we tell it.'

"Then she added sharply: 'He's not going to tell you any more than I'm going to tell you.'

"Mrs. Poppell even refused to divulge her husband's age.

"'I understand he is 59. Is that right?'

"'No,' she said. 'He's not 59.'

"'Is he older than 59?'

"'No, he's not older than 59.'

"'Then he's younger than 59?'

"'Yes. He's younger than 59,' she admitted. 'Why do you want to know, anyway?'

"Other, more definitive, reports have it that the silver-haired Poppell is 56. Regardless of his age or his physical condition, the second-generation sheriff presides over the day-to-day affairs of his county and its 9,000 citizens with an authority that may well be unmatched in any political subdivision in the United States."

Even from his sickbed at home, propped on pillows, looking yellow and wan, he ran the county and dispatched deputies on errands to and from his bedroom. The summer of 1979, on his deathbed, Sheriff Poppell sent for Thurnell Alston.

Thurnell Alston declined to go.

Alston said: "The sheriff's deputy come over there and told me Sheriff said he wanted to see me," said Alston. "I said no, I'm not going."

"He said, 'Now don't be scared.'

"I said, 'No, it's not that I'm being scared. I'm not coming, okay?'

"He got hot with me, say, 'Mr. Alston, the sheriff may have something for you.'

"I said, 'Yes. I'd be happy to have it. Send it by deputy, because I'm not going.'

"I wasn't curious enough to go, let's put it that way. So the next time he sent for me—he was real sick that morning—deputy say, 'The sheriff still say he want to see you.'

"I say, 'I might go after I get out of this meeting.' Then we learn that he in bad shape, man's going to take him in the car to the hospital. Before we got out of the county commission meeting that day, they call back and say he passed.

"He'd have shot me," said Thurnell, in explanation. "You can't never tell what that man was thinking about. He know *he* going anyway, maybe he could have got rid of the white problems and take me with him before he go. Everybody talking, 'Man, you crazy!' I say, 'You can't always tell what a man be thinking about, and I'm not going to give him the opportunity."

Sheriff Poppell, dying, had sent for Sammie Pinkney as well, and Sammie, unflappable, appeared at his bedside.

Pinkney said: "He called, said, 'Sam, I need to talk to you.'

So I went. He told me, says 'Sam, you're a damn good man.' He always cussed. 'You're a damn good man.'

"I said, 'Well, thank you sir, because I try to be.'

"He say, 'I want you to remember something. Goddamn this old sickness of mine, I ain't going to be around here much longer. But I want you to look out for my goddamn Indians.'

"I say, 'What you mean?'

"He say, 'Ah, you know, Abe and Dan and all them fellas. Look out for them boys.'

"He was talking about his little deputies. I couldn't understand how he meant. I thought, 'Why is he telling *me* this?' I guess maybe he didn't want to see them get hurt in the long run, or that a new sheriff might try to get rid of them.

"I said, 'Well, I'll do the best that I can. That's all I can say.'

"I had no reason to have any fear of him. I can case a place. I look for certain signs. If you're going to have trouble, there's always something that's going to stand out different than normal. So I went and stayed there a good forty minutes. He was talking. I enjoyed it. He went from one place to another. He said, 'Y'all say I used to run the commission!'

"And I say, 'Well, Sheriff, you didn't run the commission, but you had your influence.' He couldn't do anything but laugh.

"He said, 'Aw, them some good old boys. They just try to do it and do what's right.'

"'Watch out for my goddamn Indians!'"

Thomas Hardwick Poppell died on August 15, 1979, at the age of 58. As a county commissioner, Thurnell Alston stood as an honorary pallbearer at Sheriff Poppell's funeral. It is said the GBI infiltrated the mourners to get a close look at the casket and make sure the man was really dead.

At the next commission meeting, the commissioners voted to make Nell Poppell, Tom's widow, the interim sheriff, displacing the county coroner, who became sheriff by law at Poppell's death. A former county commissioner introduced a petition of 781 names calling for Mrs. Poppell to be honored in this way. "We owe her this appointment out of courtesy and because she has done such a fine job for the county these past several years," the former commissioner was quoted by the *Savannah Morning News.* "Mrs. Poppell would like the job so that she will have a chance to get the office in order before a new sheriff takes over."

Sammie Pinkney also was quoted by the Savannah paper: "There's a time for courtesy and being nice but this is not it. The lady is not qualified for the position."

It would have been unanimous on the commission, except for one vote: Thurnell Alston voted in opposition.

"Everyone felt Tom was Mr. Big, so they wouldn't cross him," said GBI agent Harry Coursey. "They didn't see his violent side. Since his death, McIntosh County has come out of the Dark Ages. We have an open door with the current sheriff, Lamar Echols. The working relationship is totally different."

"Tom was sheriff when he died and if he hadn't died, he'd probably still be sheriff," said Doug Moss. "With his death, the people saw an opportunity to come out from under the good old boy system and upgrade. The people were ready for a change, ready to join the twentieth century. His death was the end of an era."

"What I notice in this county is a lack of achievement on merit," said a local hotelier, remaining anonymous. "This population, having played so many roles of pandering to special privilege, has lost the ability to know, to a certain extent, how to achieve on merit. This was a county in which the rules were not played by the rules of the outside world. That is the sheriff's legacy."

But Vic Waters said, "There's only one thing wrong with McIntosh County today. Sheriff Poppell died and didn't appoint an heir."

Sheriff Thomas H. Poppell was dead, and Thurnell Alston sat on the county commission. Like playmates on a seesaw, one came down and the other went up. Good old boy politics and black power could not coexist. The sheriff's hegemony began to fail the day the white police chief overstepped the bounds of even segregationist etiquette and shot Ed Finch in the face because the man annoyed him, evoking a black response that was sudden, bitter, and communal. That harnessed anger culminated, over the years, in the election of Thurnell Alston. In the same years, U.S. 17 was bypassed, and federal agents swarmed around the sheriff like wasps—although—as many were quick to point out—he died unindicted. Now, with Alston's election and Poppell's death, the great forces in the county were temporarily at rest.

Fifteen

"Through the Ocean of the Sea for Her Child"

1

It would have been a dramatic and satisfying truce: the first were last, the last were first. It would have been a simple, happy ending for the black community and for the members of the white community eager to lay aside racial differences and corruption and to embark on modern times. Alston might have become a people's commissioner, rising above race, a model for future local politicians. But life dragged on, towing this story and the people in it toward a finale more muddy and confusing.

First, in mid-1982, Thurnell had his terrible nightmare.

"Thurnell got out of the bed one night and started walking around the room," said Becca, who was already awake with their twin daughters, Margo and Michelle, who had been born in October 1981.

"He said, 'Rebecca, I'm going to ask you something.'

"I said, 'What it is?'

"He said, 'Everything I have, you can have it.'

"I say, 'What you talking about?'

"He say, 'I don't know what it is, but I feel like I need to just get away from around here.'

"During that time we was down, we didn't know what the next day was going to be. Because only thing he was getting was

$158 disability. You know that wasn't no money to take care of no home.

"I say, 'Thurnell, I know we under a lot of pressure, but the Lord going to *make* a way.'

"And I told him, I say, 'Thurnell, God's got us this far, He'll take care of us all the way.' So he laughed again and he went to crying. I could tell he was crying because he went to the bathroom, kept blowing his nose. And he cry, he cry, he cry."

"I laid there one night," said Thurnell, "and I had one of the worst dreams in the world. In that dream I left my home. It was a place, when I looked at it, I never been there before. I found a great big house, a two-story building with a carport, and stairs all the way around. I was interested in fixing one part of it at a time. That was the upstairs. I said I'd fix the upstairs and then later on we can fix the downstairs. I never could remember if I had my family with me. But then I had to have somebody, because I was talking with them. We looked out the back door, and there was some more big old houses back out the window. Look like there were clotheslines—nice clotheslines, all real long. It seemed like I'd been to that house before. But some people ask me, 'You going to stay here?'

"And I say, 'Yes, I not never coming home. I'm going to stay here. I have no reason to go back.'

"In the dream I trying to explain the place to Rebecca, but I said, 'Is this the place up on the hill? There's no houses there. Where did I get the money to acquire that building?' And then somebody died. And it seemed like somebody was saying to us about who's fault, or my fault. Then later I left there and everybody wondering why I left. I said, 'Something came up and I couldn't get it resolved. So I think the best thing for me to do is to leave.' Then I found out the place I was living was really a place for prisoners. That's it. Then I woke up. I dreamed about prison. And I dreamed about somebody dying."

"I got up after him," said Rebecca, who followed him into

the bathroom. "I say, 'Is there something I did? You mean to tell me you going to walk out of here and leave me with these two babies? You know I'm not well.'

"He say, 'No, it's not the way you think.'

"And I say, 'Something I did?'

"He say, 'No, you can't be a better wife. I don't think nobody can have a better wife than I have, honey.'

"So he come back, we sit down on the bed and talk, and I say, 'Well, what you want to do? You want to go someplace and be away awhile just to think?'

"He say, 'No, I'm going to leave and I don't want to come back.'

"'Alone, not the whole family? And Thurn nothing but sixteen years old and Margo and Michelle not a year old?' I got up and I went to cleaning up. It had *been* clean up, but I had to do something. My nerves just be working me. I ran and woke up Thurn. And I told Thurn, I say, 'Thurn, something wrong with your daddy. Get up and go talk to him, because he talking about leaving home.'

"He saying, 'All I tried to help people, look like I get the worse end of it.'

"I told him, 'Well, if you want to go someplace, let me know where you want to go at. If I have to borrow money, me and the boys get together and borrow the money and let you go and be off for awhile by yourself.'

"All six of the children awake, all my children crying, that be like two in the morning. Margo and Michelle lying up there in the bed wide awake. Thurnell talk to the children and get them calm down. The next morning I went down the road to my friend Geneva's house, and I call Thurnell's sister in Atlanta and call his mama too. It was like he just didn't have nobody to turn to. And saying all the different things he wanted to get and the bills is getting behind. During that time I been going to work myself. Be at work at 6:00 A.M., back home at 10:30, back at work at 3:30 in the afternoon, and work until 1:00 or 2:00 at night. This big old restaurant on Jekyll Island only big-shot people come in—different groups come in. And if they have a party, you can't put the people out until they're ready to leave. We got to sit around and wait till they get through, to clean up the tables and stack them. I used to be so wear out, come home to two little babies, get home, everybody's in the bed sleeping.

"Things never did get back on track from the night he's depressed. But he didn't never leave us. I told all the children I wanted to talk to them. I say, 'Now your daddy gone down the road, but I want to talk to y'all alone now. The doctor told me your daddy is on the edge, he's about to fold, and it's going to take all of us to bring him back from the edge. Now I want y'all to help: a lot of time when he raise his voice, you know, take it in love and grin. Right now he's fighting to pay light bill, phone bill, trying to keep groceries in the house. You all be old enough here to realize you never have been in this position before, and you all don't really know how hard it is.' But we start working, and he start coming back and he start going back to church."

Thurnell leaned hardest for support on his youngest son. Keith was a second-grader now, a round-faced, neatly-groomed, smart, and happy boy. Through the child's adoring eyes Thurnell still saw the man he had meant to be, the man he had started out being: tall, brave, and invulnerable, unbroken by economics, unwearied by political backbiting and trickery, inexperienced in the temptations of bribery, unafraid of the future. Keith's first complete baby sentence had been, "My father name *Mister* Thurnell Alston," and now, at eight, he was his daddy's frequent companion. He was groomed like a young prince for fine and noble things;

his intelligence and boldness were nurtured; Thurnell shook out his dreams like a quilt for the little boy to play on. Keith was, in Thurnell's eyes, a future leader, a future torchbearer for his people. When the father felt himself flagging, slipping, drinking, and felt himself more hesitant each time to say no when various little business-as-usual payoffs were proffered—his poverty so extreme, the house either damp with heat or icy with cold, the wife and six children squeezed into too-tight somebody-else's-cast-off clothing—he had only to lift his eyes from his glass of bourbon to Keith, playing on the floor with his baby sisters, to feel that out of his endless work and worry there was good springing up, a pure, brave soul with his mother's gurgling laugh and snaggle teeth. The father paid the son his highest compliment: "McIntosh County not even *ready* for Keith."

"I used to take him to commission meetings with me," Thurnell said. "Different places I go, like they have a banquet or something and the commissioners extend an invitation, Rebecca say, 'I'm not going.'

"I say, 'Don't worry about me; Keith will go.'

"And we go to banquets and different things like that together. He was very smart. He start up a whole conversation with *anybody.* He didn't care who they were. And don't say nothing about his daddy! He was that type of person.

"If something was wrong, he didn't care—he's not going to just bear it out. He'll get up and say, 'What you told me yesterday, that was *wrong,*' or 'Mama, you said such-and-such a thing yesterday and it wasn't like that.' That's why I always tell him, 'Whatever I tell you, Keith, I'm going to tell you right.' That's why I always tell Rebecca, 'McIntosh County not ready for Keith.'

"He used to say, 'I'm going to grow up to be your lawyer, Daddy.'"

And Becca, tolerant but superior, would say, "Keith was more closer to me than Thurnell. Now a father is good—child need the father and all that—but a mother is different. A mother will go through the ocean of the sea for her child."

It did not last, even this did not last. With four good-looking boys growing up, and plump, gussied-up twin baby girls learning to toddle, and Thurnell wrestling with commission issues, but willing to change into a T-shirt some evenings and shoot baskets with the kids at a hoop nailed to a pine tree on the hard-dirt side yard, the Alstons were at the tail end of their happy family life. They were poor, but so was everybody else. The boys were good students and brought home good reports from their teachers; the friends of the four boys chose the Alstons' house as their hangout and devoured the Alston's cookies, bread, sandwich meats, and sodas; and the spoiled, fat little babies were thriving and bossy.

On December 6, 1983, Keith ran into the house after school, kissed his mother at the sink, and gleefully hugged the rotund baby sisters who spent their afternoons waiting for him to hop off the school bus.

"Keith, go change your clothes and take Auntie some fish," said Rebecca, who was cleaning fish on the counter and separating it into bags of ice.

"Okay, Mama," said Keith. "But when I come back, can I go and get me and Margo and 'Chelle a Moon Pie? I have three cents, but I need a quarter."

"Okay," said Becca, "I'll give you a quarter." And he relayed the great news to the babies. Their tutor and champion, he instructed them in the finer things of life, like sweet, chocolatey Moon Pies, to be acquired from a convenience store just across Highway 17 and then relished on the front stoop together after school on a mild December afternoon, him in his khaki pants and school shoes, and the girls happily smearing themselves and their clothes with melting chocolate. "Child, look at those children!"

Becca would scream. "Keith, you going to have to *wash* them children. I not having no part of them." And Keith would call, "Okay, Mama!" regarding the delighted, filthy babies with hilarity.

"When he come back from taking the neighbor some fish, he came in the house, washed his hands, and I gave him a quarter," said Becca. "And he went on out to get those Moon Pies. I kept on putting the fish in the bag, and I came and sit down in the chair in the living room.

"Then the phone ring, it was my backyard neighbor. She call and say, 'Something got hit.'

"I say, 'What?'

"She say, 'Something just got hit on the state road. I heard it.'

"I say, 'Oh my God, Keith!'

"I sling the phone, jump up, and ran to the door. When I ran to the door, I see my insurance man and the neighbor from across the street coming up the road running, saying, 'Keith got hit!' I remember picking up my girls and handing my girls to them."

A white woman driving south from Savannah, who'd recently swallowed a few prescription drugs, failed to slow or to swerve when a schoolchild stepped onto U.S. 17, hurrying back to his house, carrying a paper sack with three Moon Pies in it.

"I went to running," said Rebecca, "and when I got upside my mailbox, it felt like something just lift me up and when I come down, I come down on top of Keith. I was in burgundy house slippers. You know, I ain't find them house slippers yet today; seem like something just lift me up out of them and when I came down, look like I came right down in the road on my baby and I commence to pray. I ask the Lord, 'Don't take him away from me now.'

"While I was on the road, a cousin of mine came down the street to find out where I was; I remember looking up, tell him,

'Run down the road and get Thurnell!' Then the emergency squad got there with Dr. Christian, and he was checking him on the road; Thurnell got in the ambulance and took him to the hospital, I was in the station wagon behind with Thurnell's first cousin."

"One of the foster kids had come out on a visit that evening," said Thurnell, "and brought some fish to put in the freezer. So I put the fish in the car and I was going to take them to the club and put them in the freezer. But I told Rebecca before I do this, I'm going to take the fish out and send some to Ruby and send some to Purnell May and have some for Dorothy, take some out for ourselves and put the rest of them in the freezer. So that's what I did. And I went down there to take the fish to the freezer and I drove by the funeral house, a place where I always stop by a friend of mine. And the same guy that sent the fish to us says, 'Help me take this door off. I can't get this door off.' He was getting a door off an old car. So I helped him take the door off and put it in the back of his car. And a car came up there and told me my son got hit. I never got that fish down in the freezer. When I got back up there I saw: Keith was lying in the street. He was dead.

"I knew he was dead. I didn't tell Rebecca that, but I knew he was dead. And the doctors and all came from the medical center, and I rode in there with them. I knew he was dead, but they didn't let Rebecca know that. They waited to get to the hospital to say he died at the hospital. But he was dead when we got him in the ambulance."

"We got to the hospital about the same time the ambulance did," said Rebecca. "We went on in; they took us in some kind of little room, the pastor's room or some kind of little thing. I remember saying to myself, I was asking the Lord, 'Don't let him suffer and don't let him be a vegetable.' Within myself I knew my baby was already dead, I knew it as soon as I saw him on the road. After I heard my sister scream, I got up out of the chair and went to walk out the door. Doctor came in and soon as I saw Thurnell turn around, I knew he was gone. All I remember is, I passed out.

"I had just cut his hair the day before. Now you know this was a sweet child. He was a good student in school, never gave the teachers no problem. His school bus driver loved him to death because every morning he got to that bus, he had her a flower. He leave? go to that bus? he had her a flower. Right now today? since he died? that flower died and never did come back. I had to go out and cut that flower down."

Thurnell Alston said: "The problem is that Rebecca wanted to blame.

"You know how a mother with a baby is, she wanted something to blame, but I wasn't even home when it happened. She really felt that if I was home that he wouldn't have gone out there. She came out and blamed me. She say it was my fault. See, he loved the twins more than anything in the world. And he was going to the store because he had some money; he was going to the store to buy them a surprise. So it was one of those things. What happened was the guys in the store went to talking to him, and I guess he wasn't paying too much attention when he got ready to cross the road. They were distracting him because he wouldn't buy the cookies over there, because I think they was two for twenty-five cents, and he goes to the store down the street, get him about four of the same cookies for twenty-five cents. And I believe that's what happened when he walked out in front of the car.

"And oh my God, it never gets out of my mind about him because he was—McIntosh County wasn't ready for him, that's the way I feel.

"It was a very bad time for me after Keith died. But I couldn't let my family see it, because I think it affected me more than it did Rebecca. I never let her know anything about it because I want to be the strong guy for the family, and they never knew how it was burning me up inside.

"He was something else. And I always think about him and knowing that there was no suffering—it was just bam! that was it. Maybe Rebecca thinking about from there to the hospital, I don't know. But I know it ended there. And maybe that's the difference.

"Not only that, but during that time, I feel more prejudice than I ever did in my life, because it was a white woman that killed him. She definitely was responsible, because there was no other cars coming down that road, no way in the world that she couldn't see a kid standing on the side of that road.

"But Rebecca wanted to blame somebody. So then we start having problems."

Rebecca Alston said: "That started trouble right then into my home. It happened like this: The night before Keith got killed, Reverend Grovner came by the house and Thurnell and Reverend Grovner were talking and Keith trying to ask Thurnell something, and Thurnell didn't have time to stop and see what the baby wanted, right? Thurnell told the child to hush and leave him alone, and my baby came back up there and sat on the chair and I said, 'Keith, don't cry,' and he said, 'I wish I was dead.' He said that that night and got killed next day.

"See, Thurnell don't want to admit it, but it's eating him too.

"I remember it so fresh," she said in early fall many years later, "because that time coming up now. I can feel it, that it coming up. It's very hard, you know. I'm living year to year with all that in my mind."

And Thurnell bottled up his grief. This was not an educated, middle-class family with access to psychologists or to support groups or to popular psychological wisdom. Keith was buried at a wailing church service during which Rebecca screamed and Thurnell stood bleakly like a statue, wiping away the occasional tear; and after the burial, the time for manly tears was over. The Alstons were not aware that marriages commonly self-destruct over the death of a child; they were not schooled to know that grief either had to spill out or wreak havoc. They didn't talk to each other. "It was a very bad time for me after Keith died. But I couldn't let my family see it. . . . I want to be the strong guy for the family," said Thurnell, an already-agitated man whose fuse had just gotten shorter.

2

Thurnell's life dropped off to loafing, Becca's to weeping. Both were exceptionally easy propositions in McIntosh County, where long hours of scant activity were possible. In midsummer one moved across the land as if underwater, the languorous movements of hot air like the pull of deep tides, the top-heavy swishing of the trees like a muffled noise of something waterlogged. The people in the county sat fatigued in the useless shade of their carports, on hot, rusty yard chairs, and sent barefoot children back into the houses for glasses of ice water or cold cans of Coke or beer, which the adults then pressed to their burning faces. The heat inside the houses was unspeakable. In an hour's time an adult might shift position once, to get up and go use the bathroom and holler at the children inside, sending them scampering back outdoors like little mice. In the long afternoons the hot black people dozed, heads thrown back, on their metal yard furniture, and the sunburned white people threw themselves across unmade beds under ceiling fans and snoozed, and the few people in Darien in business clothes working beside window air-conditioning units leaned way back in their chairs and chatted on the telephone for long nonsensical siesta hours, their chairs swiveled away from the white blaze of the windows. Only illicit businesses—drug deals and gambling and gunrunning—took place at civilized after-dark hours, in short-sleeve, light-colored polyester shirts, at far corner tables of mellow local bars. In a land of six-month summer, this was not a minor consideration in career decisions.

The county woke up in the evening. Bubbly lights advertising beers and liquors heated up inside the cheaply paneled juke joints, and in the cinder-block bungalows the young men and women showered and emerged with wet hair strangely curled and parted; rubbed tropical scents, lotions, and aftershaves on their damp skin; and donned clothes swirling with fluorescent summer colors. White beads, plastic earrings, and gold wristwatches stood out against the rich brown skin. The young people, dazzling in the hot, dim light of their own dens, where older people and children settled on the sofas to watch television, went off into the night laughing, their packed cars pitching gravel as they climbed the shoulder onto U.S. 17.

Among the teenagers, blacks and whites had begun mixing in the mid-1970s. Within an hour, the segregated carloads would be integrated, white girls leaning back on the arms of black boys they knew from classes in high school. Thurn had a white girlfriend and so, in time, would Van.

Thurnell Alston, after Keith's death, was drawn to the nightlife. Like the men half his age, he stood and preened, emerging from the bathroom in freshly pressed khaki slacks and a short-sleeve white shirt with two breast pockets and epaulets, African style, the spacious cleanliness of the shirt like the moon in the night sky. Becca, buried in twins, did not look at him or speak to him. She hated him for leaving the sweltering house, the TV, the heaps of laundry on the sofa needing to be folded, the unwashed dishes, the broken toys strewn through the rooms, the greasy smokiness. He was as remote as the moon, and as cold. It was as if *she* were the one ten years older and he were a bug-eyed youth itchy for fun, humming "Everybody loves Saturday night!" She stayed home, big and round in her tattered housedress, her weight on the sofa the room's anchor as she lifted a towel and folded it, lifted a shirt and folded it, and endless laugh-track TV shows rolled by. The twins climbed on her as on a piece of playground equipment. When Thurnell came back in the early morning, smelling of perfumed women, Becca lay awash in tears and sweat. If he touched her, she'd kill him; but he made no move to touch her. She believed he hadn't grieved, wasn't grieving for Keith, and if he hadn't ignored the child and told him to hush, the boy wouldn't have wished for his own death. And for Thurnell the little prince of the mansion was gone, and in his wake all was disarray, hatred, and pointlessness.

"I heard a lot of talk, but I'm a person I don't take hearsay," said Rebecca. "In twenty-five years of marriage I don't take no hearsay. I know Thurnell ain't here at night and I know he black, and they going to tell me, say 'Where he at?'

"I tell them, 'Where he *at?*'

"'Well, what he doing?'

"'Now you go find that out, that's your problem. You want to know what he doing, you go find that out. You want to find out something, buy you a newspaper.'"

In the nightlife, among the teenagers and twenty-year-olds, Thurnell's presence still meant something. Because he was some kind of leader and seen as lofty and puritanical, the ladies flirted with him and the men hesitated a half-second before passing him the bottle; and when he began to dissipate alongside them in the sultry night, to laugh louder than they laughed and to tell his own lewd stories, he seemed to them a strange catch. What he needed was to be let off the hook, to be forgiven: by Becca, for Keith's death, and by the county for being tired of serving, for abandoning the heroic persona they had elected.

What he could not bear was to be inside in the house with Rebecca. He *stayed* in the streets, as they say, drove his long car pointlessly up and down the county, made of any little thing a daylong activity. A letter to be mailed to Brunswick? He drove it there himself. A phone call to place? He drove to the man's house and waited to speak to him in person. He won't be back till after work? It's okay, I'll sit in my car, no problem. There was a big old oak tree at the edge of a vacant lot on U.S. 99 where unemployed men gathered. A few damp and mossy armchairs stood in the weeds and broken glass. Men assembled there to drink and kill time, and Alston became a regular. He was no stranger to drink. "Thurnell been drinking ever since I been knowing Thurnell," Nathaniel Grovner said. "I just thought it was something he would have to have always." And Sammie said, "People would say he's an alcoholic. I don't know whether you'd call it a drinking problem. He drank practically every day, but I have never seen him drunk."

Alston stood in the hot shade, sweating it out with the jobless and homeless, the toothless and shoeless, trying like them to get through the day. Everybody in the county drove past that corner sooner or later, and there stood the county commissioner swigging from a bottle in a paper sack, then passing it on. And when he finally returned home in the evening, he took one of his new drinking partners home with him to continue the conversation—such as it was—and the drinking, until long after Becca had cleared off the supper plates—the dishes angrily crashing together—and gone to bed. And people who stopped by his house as in the old days, on public business, on commission business, were compelled to address both red-eyed Alston and his drinking partner, usually a half-toothless younger man named Irvin Brennon, a convicted drug dealer who had returned home to McIntosh from prison.

Thurnell's Social Security disability case, long pending, was won on appeal, and the Alstons suddenly received nineteen thousand dollars in unpaid back benefits, with which they remodeled the house; although, without Keith, the jackpot had an acrid taste.

Either prayers were answered or they were not. But they made of the carport a large, plain, white-painted, carpeted den, and they added a bathroom and bought a glass-top breakfast table set. Alston's sudden wealth, coupled with his public idleness, raised eyebrows. There were only two or three ways idle men grew rich in McIntosh County, and none of them was legal.

"Thurnell kept saying, 'I'm going to get my money,' because he had an attorney," said Louise Rasheed. "And he got his award, and that's what Becky told me. That's how they remodeled the house. It was the Social Security money, because he told me, 'I got my money!'

"And I told him, 'I'm so glad you got your money.'

"And he said, 'Wouldn't you like to have a soda?' because we were down at the store.

"And I said, 'Oh, I'm not going to have a soda on you just because you got your money.'

"He said, 'Oh, let me buy you a soda.'

"I said, 'I'm trying to diet; I don't want anything.'

"And he said, 'What you want with a diet?'

"And I said, 'Nothing. But I'll tell you what, I'll be over one day and we'll have something then.'

"And he said, 'Okay, but I might be broke by that time, because you know I've already started remodeling the house.'

"And I said, 'Oh, that's going to be nice.'

"He told me people were saying they didn't know where he got the money. Said, 'They wondering where I got this money.' A lot of people didn't know he was fighting for his Social Security. And when he got it, he said that he was going to fix his house. He said, 'Because I couldn't do it when the children were small, so I'm going to fix my house up.'

"Thurnell likes nice things," said Louise. "Now Becky, I love Becky, but Becky, she like nice things, but she don't know how to handle it. She just don't know how to take care of it like he did. Because when Becky was in the hospital after the twins, he would keep everything in the house spotless. And I told her when we brought her home—I went with him to get her out of the hospital—I said, 'Becky, don't you come in here and mess up this house because Thurnell kept it.' He had kept those babies for three months and kept the place just all nice. The boys had to get in there and help keep everything straight.

"And we used to joke about it, and I said, 'Just put Becky out if she can't do these things!' You know, teasing him and stuff like that. And she's a sweet thing. I mean Becky is the sweetest child. I wouldn't take nothing for her. I used to tell her she was lazy. And I used to go over and clean up for her. I said, 'Get up, me and you going to clean up.'

"You see, their money was going downhill. They didn't have no business having any more kids. They *could* have left the fourth one off too. I told her, I said, 'Becky, you didn't have no business having those babies.' But you got to have your children, I guess."

Suddenly, in 1984, Thurnell Alston was indicted for malfeasance in office. His sudden windfall—Social Security or no—caused some in authority to scrutinize his affairs more closely, and a small crime immediately became evident.

The accusation was that in his capacity as a county commissioner, Alston had sent a county bulldozer to clear a woman's private property, and then he privately had charged her $150 for the labor and equipment.

David Walbert, now a rather celebrated attorney in private practice in Atlanta, flew down to rescue the man he'd helped to place in office.

"The most active member of the grand jury was a northern white woman who had just moved down and wanted to clean up the county," said Walbert. "The woman with the private property testified against Thurnell, but her goddamn story was practically incomprehensible. The evidence that came out of the witness was real loosey-goosey. If she'd testified five times, there would have been five different stories. There was nothing like evidence beyond a reasonable doubt. The local prosecutor recused himself [withdrew from the case], so there was a special prosecutor out of Atlanta, and they had a handwriting expert testify that it was Alston's handwriting on a receipt this woman had.

"It was, actually, probably beyond the woman's capacity to fake a receipt, and I could see that the jury was very concerned. The jurors were about 40 percent black, and I felt like the guys who wanted to acquit had looks of consternation on their faces. We argued that it just didn't happen. The evidence was so skimpy they had to acquit."

The prosecution folded. After the acquittal, Walbert, who began to accept a string of corruption cases involving black officials around the state, began to muse about the relationship between power and corruption. "First of all," he said, "in Thurnell's defense, I think the public perception of who's honest and who's crooked isn't worth much. Through the repetition of a story it starts taking on a veracity it may not intrinsically possess.

"But there are so many damn subtleties. Let's say there's a continuum from 0 to 100 for a public official, from being in such a vacuum that you don't have the slightest idea what's going on out there, to having your finger so much on the pulse of the community that you're accepting quid pro quo payments for your actions. There's no bright line."

From a distance, Michael Froman, former managing attorney of the GLSP office in Brunswick: "So Thurnell took a few bribes. That's not really so hard to figure out. You're talking about a man who learned everything he knew about political power in McIntosh County from Sheriff Tom Poppell."

Also from a distance, a psychologist on the faculty of Emory University, John Pani, said: "A lot of people who came up through the civil rights movement were rules-breakers; they had to be; if they'd have toed the line, they'd still be down on the plantation or wherever. But when do you stop breaking the rules? It's not always so easy to switch gears, to say, okay, this is it, I've made it. It's not easy to know when to change, and it's less easy to change."

Thurnell Alston said: "You just get really tired. A lot of people just really don't respect you when you're tired or vague or feel run to the extreme. I know God has helped through all these years, that all the trials and tribulations that I had, even when they indicted me for using county equipment or when my son died or when any other problem have risen up, I mean God have helped me through all those things, but you get really tired, you reaching for straws."

And David Walbert: "I now realize that I—that we—idealized the black civil rights people. They represented something we were looking for, but they were regular human beings. They were real people, and real people are imperfect. They just happened to be on the side of a political struggle we happened to believe in, but in a lot of ways it was just politics as usual. It was a mistake to put them all on a pedestal. We forgot they were gaining personal power as well.

"We were thinking: How do we make the system work fairly and democratically? *They* may have been thinking: How do I get my hands on the fucking power?

"What were they really like? Who the hell knows?"

3

Years dropped past Thurnell. He lost the 1984 county commission election following his trial and acquittal, and the idleness then was like death. He then had not so much as a letter to be mailed to draw him out of bed in the morning. There was no phone call to make. The ceiling fan churned the stuffy air of the bedroom like the blades of a washing machine chopping at soiled clothing; he kicked at the knot of sheets; the floor was littered with shoes and clothes; the plastic wrap stretched across the windows as insulation swelled and rattled in the hot morning wind. He was furious the moment he opened his eyes. He lay cursing as the stale air of the room heated up. The subtropical sun baked the cinder-block house and the gravel driveway as it steamed the nearby marsh; but the marsh drank in the heat with a million bright, slim green blades of grass—the heat over the marsh was like a golden shower of light—while the heat over Highway 17 blistered the tar and forced humans out of their houses, panting for air.

Rebecca came in, looked at him, got her things, went out; her look, her body, her existence a reproach to his idleness, his body, his existence. He was not naturally an indolent man. It was out of honesty rather than from indolence that he lay abed while people came and went in the outer rooms of his house. He could hear their voices muffled by his closed door. There was no reason to get up. It took all his bravery to lie there and see that. It was a *failure* of courage to rise and dress and exit the dead end of his slumberous room. Usually at noon or one o'clock when he finally got up, sweaty and unwashed, unshaved and parched, Irvin Brennon was at his kitchen table waiting for him, and together they put the day to bed. It took a long time, a long, long, hot, slow time, but they saw the day through to the expiration of its heat and light. They pushed a sweating bottle back and forth on the linoleum-topped kitchen table, leaving a beaded trail, and spoke in monosyllables.

Brennon had served time for selling ounces of marijuana, and was home now, unemployed, with no prospects and not much schooling. He had moved into a trailer with Thurnell's niece Vicki and her children. Brennon seemed to have gone overnight, without warning or preparation, from being a stocky ten-year-old of some promise, with his shoulders thrown back, to *this,* an irresolute small-time drug dealer. He actually had been a hero as a child, had pulled another child out of a river and saved him from drowning, and he'd had his picture in the *Darien News,* a little cropped-haired, shiny-wet black boy grinning from ear to ear. Now he was in his mid twenties, all his front teeth had rotted away, and his speech was unintelligible. Irvin had a child's hurt eyes and a child's smooth, plump skin. He exuded a sort of bewildered innocence despite his foul-talking swagger. Spending his days seated across the kitchen table from the silent gloomy old commissioner seemed, for a time, a quiet and safe place for Irvin Brennon to store himself.

When Thurnell raised his bloodshot eyes to events on the now-distant county commission, and in the county around him, it grieved him that his work was falling to nothing. He needed this rest, he told himself. But no one stepped forward as a new standard-bearer for the black community. The black county was again in deep slumber. He wanted a younger person to help him, to replace him, but there was not one old friend or colleague he trusted. He loved only half-toothless, slow-witted Irvin, having convinced himself he was exercising a benign and fatherly influence on the young man.

Was there no one to exercise political leadership in the black community beside himself? Thurnell ticked off the reasons why there was no one:

"Louise is a very intelligent person," he said of his old friend, "but her whole family is a part of Tom Poppell's programming. I mean the whole entire family was on Poppell's bandwagon. She was one of the main ones that really got the organization started in '71, '72. So we let her and some of those women cook for us and help us raise money. Her, Rebecca, Teretha, they wasn't really a part of the organization. We didn't even allow them at the meetings; we just had them if we planning a party or something like that—we have them get everything together.

"Now Sammie come down here from New York, and here come the big shot. But I was always skeptical of Sammie when Sammie came by from New York. You know, you just don't get that kind of money for working in New York as a cop. I'm still skeptical of him, because he always pretend he's more than what he really is. I mean, I don't know him, I don't really know him. Just like a person that just pop into my life and say, 'You know me all these many years.' I deal with him politically, on a political basis, but socially I prefer not to deal with him. Sammie was ambitious for glory.

"I been knowing Reverend Grovner all my life. I knew quite a bit of Reverend Grovner. I know that he's a talker, too. If anybody wanted something he had to give, all you had to do was strike up a good conversation with him and some of your business would be gone. So that's why we sort of duck by and be sort of skeptical about some of the things we said and did around him. Now the reverend, he had an idea of maybe, like Sammie, to improve his political career. When all the things got started, when Ed Finch got started, Sammie and Grovner was nowhere around."

Drinking and slanderously muttering about the lack of a decent replacement for himself, Thurnell Alston was prepared to let the election of 1986 go by without him as well.

"I lost one election," he said, "but that election I just didn't do anything. I just about give it up. I was trying to have a break, and somebody else just went on and put my name on the list. But I just wanted to get away from all of it. Even that election I didn't lose but by a few votes. If I had done anything at all, I could have won then."

He was reelected in 1986 and was disgusted rather than gratified by it. In his own mind he was increasingly alone, a taken-for-granted hero. The people no longer knocked themselves out for his campaign nor turned out in large numbers to elect him. He squeaked back into office. Nobody listened. They didn't even understand what he was trying to do for them, how he poured his whole soul into each problem, how he did nothing but good, good, good and got back nothing but ingratitude and evil.

"You've got to be totally sincere," he said. "You just can't be sincere of one thing and then when it comes to something else, you're lukewarm. Every issue that involve an individual is a very crucial thing, period. That's the way I feel about it. And I attack it the same way. The problems may be different, but you have to attack to let them know you trying to get results. You can't just sit here and think, 'Because you a *little* person, I'll take up with you next week.' That's the way Sammie and them work. I never did work like that. Maybe that's why I got so tired, because I was doing a lot of running. Every time somebody called, I'm there. My wife saying, 'You going out in those people house? You don't know those people!' I didn't care because they call me up, they had something they wanted to talk to me about."

"The people cared for him, now," said Becca, appraising her husband's public life and work. "The biggest of the people round here is on Social Security. That same station wagon you see sitting right there, he run back and forth taking them to Brunswick, to the lawyers' offices. For nothing. He was just that good. When they get ready to go to Atlanta on some commissioner thing, Thurnell the only one who put his name going. And he said, 'I will not use the taxpayers' money like that, just me one going.' All the other commissioners turned it down. You should see Sapelo Island now. It is beautiful. And he the one who did all that, running back and forth to Atlanta, and you watch and see who get all the credit. I'm proud of him because he's a person who will help somebody. A lot of them who was against him, he pulled them out of the bog. My mama said, 'All you do is wait; time will tell on itself.'"

He grew thin and irascible. There was no getting close to him for people who knew him, although he opened his heart and soul to citizens who had a complaint for the commission. "You *see?*" he would squeak. "That *exactly* what I been saying!" and he threw himself beside them—their knight—and got their sewage ditch dug or their water "cut on," then stared forlornly after them when, so easily satisfied, they returned to their homes and disappeared from his life. He burned with a revolutionary hatred now; his fervor could have leveled Darien. In his blood rode the black Union troops who had torched the town a century earlier; in his long hands, power trembled, and all his constituents asked of him was to get their water turned on.

He was like a New York City madman shouting on a streetcorner about the apocalypse. In the smirks and yawns of his fellow commissioners, he saw evil. Around him in McIntosh County, black and white families grew and thrived, cradled their children in their arms, sang in their crowded churches, appeared in stiff new clothes, played sandlot baseball, drank beer, swatted mosquitoes, and held hands. But he no longer remembered what all the hoo-ha was about; he no longer possessed the linchpin to all this evident enjoyment of life, and he didn't know when it had fallen out of his. He showed up looking ragged and unkempt at the fringes of their backyard barbecues and sounded—at anyone with the patience to listen—his one hoarse note: "What we *need* is . . . What the thing *about* it is . . . What we have to *do* is . . ." the coarse words swollen with his newfound hatred of whites. But the country people had had enough of *need* and *about* and *do* and wanted to be left alone to overfill their limp paper plates with ribs, corn, and slaw; and he felt himself staggering backwards from their gatherings, which had become indecipherable to him. The meaning of life was slipping from him, even the vision he'd once had of the county as a community of equals.

Blocking his sight and his sense and his memory was plump Rebecca, with her round, fat, busy self, with her gurgling laughter and her baby teeth, squeezing herself into what once had been *their* circles of friends, screaming with ludicrous laughter, pursuing false intimacy and false happiness, making him an outsider.

"I was tired," he said. "I needed some rest. Once they elect me, they drop me right then and there till the next election—unless a problem arise. Nobody questioned nothing. I was all alone. Nobody to back me up, for *nothing* that I come up with. I was tired."

Commission Chairman David Earl Lane saw a difference in Alston's performance. "I think he was serious in trying to help the people in his district until he came back on that last time. I don't think he was as dedicated to the job of being a commissioner at that time as he was in the years prior to that. He really didn't seem to be as aggressive or as interested."

"I was happy Thurnell had prevailed with the $150 situation," said Nathaniel Grovner. "But then I started to hear rumors that he was dealing in things, in drugs. I would sit and talk to him, come right out and ask him, 'Look man, you and I have always been close. I feel that if you heard anything out in the community about me you would come to me and talk to me and I will do the same. That's what I consider friendship.' He always denied it, so that's as far as I could go."

Sammie Pinkney said: "Thurnell still had the willpower, but he lost a lot of his tactics because of the association of people he was keeping, folks who weren't going anywhere or doing anything. Other folks seeing them would assume it was a drinking party. A lot of folks who have phoned for Thurnell many a time couldn't get him. If I didn't call him five times, I didn't call him once. Rumors began to get widespread in the county that he was corrupt. I went to him and told him, based on his association with Irvin Brennon, and his being a commissioner, and being with Irvin every day, when you do things like that, people form certain opinions. We never had any fights, never had any big arguments. I'm the type of person I don't like to have a lot of 'he say she say you say,' you know? Folks have gone out and *said* I've said this thing or that thing, but *I* talk to Thurnell like a man. I talk to him in private. I don't go out and say this or that. There's a lot of lies told about things I've said about Thurnell. But I'm still his friend. I'll always be his friend."

Becca said: "The day of Keith's death? All our happiness ended that day."

Thurnell appeared to have fallen as far down as a person could fall: wife hateful; friends cold; community distant; creditors hounding; commissioners sick of him; and precious, funny, bright, promising, happy little son dead and buried. But Thurnell wasn't near bottom yet. There was still daylight. He was in free-fall.

Sixteen

The Music Man

1

Into this commotion of the life of Thurnell Alston—where the hero himself was at great pains to retain the appearance of dignity—a new friend appeared one day. New in town, he introduced himself to Alston as J.R. on November 3, 1987, at the L&N Electronics store on U.S. 17 in Darien, a fine-looking black man with money to invest in McIntosh County. He was sultry voiced and hip, a tall, slender, sharply dressed man in his early thirties, with a handsome, thick, trim beard, pockmarked skin, and nicely curled hair. He wanted to open up some kind of club, he told Commissioner Alston, either a bar or a teenage night spot, and he wanted the black commissioner to shepherd his license application and zoning request through the county commission.

Thurnell was, as always, open, chatty, and wound up; he hastily set aside his own errand to assume, for the moment, the public trust. A teen club for the black youth would be a very welcome addition to the county, he said; he would be proud to introduce such a motion to the commission. He spoke to J.R. in the voice of his finer, public self, but J.R. answered in fast, low, vulgar slang. This man and the high-minded notion of a teen soda-pop dance-and-sporting club were an oxymoron.

"Look here," said J.R. "If I'm going to put some money around this town, I've got to know that I'm going to be able to deal with folk straight up, no bullshit, just like regular folks, man. If I can do anything for you, *you* know, I don't care what it is, if I'm going to put money in this town I need to know who's on the team. Not today, but sometime in the future, whatever you need in the next couple of weeks, yeah, I can handle it. The only thing I'm going to do is get my business going and be left alone, either way, whether it's alcohol or a teenage club."

Alston helpfully named the county inspector responsible for making zoning recommendations to the commission.

"What I'm *saying* man," said J.R., in his inflected street talk, "you, you not *hearing* me."

"I hear you," said Thurnell.

"I just need to *know*."

"You talking about somebody to help you get started, period," said Thurnell, "to cause you no kind of difficulties, maybe like those things that I can perform, or somebody." But that was not what J.R. was saying.

"What's it going to *cost* me?" asked J.R. again.

And here Alston did a double take, began to say one thing, then switched and said another, having suddenly sensed that the conversation was on a different track than he'd realized: "I mean . . . for *me*?"

"Who, I, whoever, I don't care," said J.R. "I'm not obviously going to get out here and give somebody something if they can't do anything for me, but if I see where it's going to benefit me and I can get out here and get my thing going and be left alone, man, *you* know, it's worth it. It's worth it to know that I'm going to have somebody right there that can let me know what's happening on the inside. That's all I ask; I don't ask for anybody to stick their nose into any of my personal business."

"One thing about me, I never do that," interjected Alston, trying to keep up. "Your business will be your business, you know, period."

"Well, that's what I'm looking for," said J.R. "You can deal with your folk; but like I say, I want that to remain between you and I. I don't want *you* know fifty folks."

"Right here," said Alston.

"There you go."

"And that's it, right?"

"That's all I want."

"Okay."

"And I just, you know, like I say, I hate to be blunt, man, but you know we going to have to play hardball. If I need something, if we decide to stick a liquor license in there, obviously I'm going to need your cooperation. I'm sure word will get around, 'Hey, here's this guy, he's not from around here and he's running the club,' and other folks going to say, 'Maybe we need to look at him a little harder,' and you going to have to handle things. So that's what I need. And whatever it's going to cost me, *you* know I'm willing, but I've got to have something to start kicking around in my head."

"Okay."

"If you want something on a monthly basis, on a weekly basis, or you want to, you know, one-time thing and we call it even, whatever you want to do, you know, at least something for me to start kicking around in my head, *you* know."

Thurnell, grasping that he was being offered a bribe, said flatly, in recognition: "*Oh* boy."

"There's just no other way I can put it man, *you* know."

"Oh, I would never interfere in your business down there though, no bullshit," said Alston, responding to an earlier question while getting his bearings.

"I would *like* to be in business," said J.R.

"It's going to be kind of difficult for me to come up with something like that."

"Yeah. Well, it's basically left up to you. Whatever you feel comfortable with, I'll work from there. It might be too much for me, but I'm willing to listen."

Thurnell stammered in response.

"Ten thousand a week is too much," said J.R.

"Oh yeah, I understand."

"You know, that's too much."

"No no no no, it won't be worth ten thousand dollars a week," said Alston. "How about twelve? I got a deal going now, fifteen."

"You got a deal now going about fifteen? You want twelve every what?"

"Every two weeks."

"Twelve hundred every two weeks? All right."

"I'm not, I'm not a greedy man."

"Oh, I might be able to live with that, twelve hundred."

"I'm not greedy; right now, with white guys I'm going that much a week."

"Okay, that's not a bad figure, and if things go right, then obviously there'll be a little more in it for you. Throw a little something my way and, you know, I'll throw a little something your way over and above what we agree to. And I'll tell you what I'm going to do, just to let you know I'm about business: I'll be back first part of next week and I'll give you that up front, let you know I'm not trying to put you in a trick bag. But like I say, it's between us."

"Confidential, period."

"Yeah, I have no business putting my business in the street, you know."

"What we talking about, it'll stay confidential," said Alston, and they shook hands.

J.R. burst into their lives like the Music Man. Within a month he was showing up at the Alstons' house every day to talk about the teen club. He was attentive to Thurn and Anthony and Van, and he kindled their enthusiasm for the project. The Alston boys frequently drove to Brunswick to play basketball on a court in a black area, and when J.R. proposed a neighborhood state-of-the-art court with lights for night play, and a snack bar in which to relax and meet their friends afterward, the boys were ecstatic. J.R. got out a pen and paper and appointed each of them to a future position within the club: Thurn will coach basketball, he promised, writing it down, Anthony will coach girls' basketball, Van will coach softball. To Becca, J.R. promised the teen club snack bar; so she and Vicki, Irvin Brennon's girlfriend, sat down together and drew up a future menu and prices. Thurnell drove around the county looking for a building and found a vacant nightclub, an abandoned cinder-block building formerly called the Hid-A-Way Club on Smith Road, near Louise Rasheed's brick ranch house and fenced-in yard. Becca and the boys and their friends cleared and raked the yard, washed and painted the building.

It was a cheerful and hopeful time; the Alstons possessed a family project again, Thurnell had something to give the black county again, and the immediate future seemed full of novelty and progress. Louise watched the busy family out her side window as they raked and painted: "I saw the kids over there cleaning the yard, clearing up around there. I went over there and said, 'What y'all doing?' and they said, 'We going to open up the club over here!' and 'We'll be over here close to you!' Becky was, 'Oh child! I'm going to be down there by you! I know you coming over there when I get there!' I thought it was good. I said, 'Well, my brother will be over there and everybody else.'"

Who was this tall, bearded, handsome black man; this self-confident, smooth, money-flashing individual with no local connections, who could talk the local talk and walk the local walk? Accepted quicker than overnight by Thurnell Alston—accepted inside of twenty minutes by Thurnell Alston as his best friend, his confidante, his drinking partner, his sole employer; better to him, more to him than Pinkney, Grovner, Louise, or Rebecca—J.R. was scrutinized more closely by everyone else except Irvin Brennon, who followed Thurnell's lead.

Thurnell glided like an old bateau onto the stream of J.R.'s words and let himself be lulled into the promise of a safe harbor. J.R. became like the father of the family and Thurnell just another son, burbling with excitement whenever J.R. said "teen club" or "basketball." But J.R. had a secret agenda, and Thurnell should have known better.

Thurnell Alston ought to have known, as the commissioner of a poor coastal county, that outsiders opened nightclubs in isolated, untraversed McIntosh for only one reason: drug dealing.

In fact, in the fall and winter of 1987 when Thurnell Alston spent his afternoons cruising around with J.R. and his nights drinking with Irvin Brennon, he was officially, in his capacity as a commissioner, the leader of his county's fight against drugs. He took an antidrug campaign to the county schools in September, and in October he made a motion that the county commission request federal assistance to combat drugs. Over his signature, the commission sent a letter to the U.S. District Court in Brunswick asking for federal law enforcement to intervene in the county's crack business. Thurnell became the chief contact person between the county commission and the Savannah-based Drug Enforcement Agency.

McIntosh, a coastal county with dozens of private harbors, fleets of underused shrimp boats, numerous out-of-work crews, few local sources of income other than the failing fishing industry, a long history of officially sanctioned gunrunning, drug smuggling, game-machine distribution, and other illegal activities, and a reputation as a sanctuary for unscrupulous types, was fast becoming a prominent American drug capital. The backwoods hamlets were seething with drugs and all the associated evils: school failure;

early, unwanted pregnancies, high infant mortality, neglected and abused children, and escalating rates of robbery, theft, and shootings. Savannah-based GBI agent Harry Coursey, observing the predominantly black face of drug use in McIntosh, lamented, "They are more slaves to crack cocaine than they ever were to whites."

The storefronts, so to speak, of the drug trade were the numerous roadside juke joints, the cinder-block nightclubs that had become the local drug users' "crack houses." Cocaine in powder form was being imported into the county at the rate of one to two kilos a week and was cooked into crack in Crescent. The crack was sold out of several nightclubs: the Georgia Soul Finger Nightclub in Darien, the Club Omega in Eulonia, the Paradise Club on Highway 99. These clubs were owned by Irvin Brennon and his brothers.

In November 1987—the day *after* he met J.R.—Alston drove to Richmond Hill, north of Darien, with two other county officials to meet with FBI and DEA agents and outline for them the serious drug situation in the county.

This was the immediate background to J.R.'s approaching Alston about opening a "club" in the county. It was the reason why Thurnell was not surprised that an unknown, slick-talking businessman approached him with large sums of money to finesse simple zoning and liquor-license applications. The opening of a new nightclub in McIntosh should immediately have been suspect, since the shabby little nightclubs had become, almost without exception, cover operations for hugely profitable drug businesses. Yet he wordlessly pocketed the fat, soft rolls of bills that J.R. delivered to him promptly every other week.

Because of the drug situation in the county, the other commissioners were less enthusiastic about J.R.'s proposed teen club than Alston was. "The community was probably more fired up about drugs at that time than they are right now," said David Earl Lane, chairman of the county commission. "And we just weren't giving out liquor licenses right and left like we had done in the past. We asked for a sheriff's report on anybody that tried to get a license. When Thurnell took J.R. over to the sheriff's office, the sheriff had some things on the computer showing the man had a marijuana conviction or something. Later that day, Sheriff Echols told me, 'I don't know who that SOB is, but there's something fishy about him.' He said, 'I don't know what it is or who he is, but there's something damn sure fishy about him, and we need to see if we can find out who he is before we welcome *him* to the community.'

"Next day," said Lane, "Thurnell brought him in here. So I was really on my guard that there was something fishy anyway. I said, 'Very nice to meet you. The best thing for you to do is get approval from the sheriff, because the way the community is right now, I don't think we're going to give anybody a license if the sheriff doesn't think you should have it.' I told him I didn't have anything against nightclubs or bars or establishments like that; sometimes I go in them myself; but if he couldn't get the sheriff to give him a clean bill of health, then he probably wasn't going to get a liquor license."

Rebecca Alston didn't like him either. "He stay to dinner," said Becca. "He give Vicki a fifty-dollar bill for me and Vicki to take to the store, get enough shrimp for everybody. We eat the food, and then J.R. began to talk about the club and J.R. say, 'Well, I want to get this club because we need a club.'

"I say, 'We need a teenage club *bad,* so young people can get over there from the older people, that'll draw some of these younger people away from this dope. I'll get in the kitchen and work my butt off to help buy equipment to help with the basketball and baseball.' Because he say he going to set up a basketball court with the lights on the outside. He going to set up a tennis court. And say Irvin will be over the girls' softball game. We talked about *all* of that. I say, 'All you got to do is give us the kitchen.

We'll have the kitchen, and the money we make out the kitchen, that'll be the money to help buy the stuff for the sports.'

"And honey? we carry on that conversation for a long time. I'm talking about for *months*."

2

Between themselves, in midwinter, J.R. and Thurnell no longer spoke of a teen club. Between them, the understanding grew that J.R. really wanted to open an ordinary nightclub, and he now began to hint that a lucrative drug business could be conducted out the back door. In conversations held in J.R.'s parked car or in motel bars in Savannah and Brunswick in the early months of 1988, talk was of Thurnell looking out for J.R.'s "interests"; about whom else in the county J.R. might pay off; and about how to get the county commission to approve J.R.'s liquor license. J.R. had turned in an application for a liquor license only partially completed; it lacked, among other details, his name, his address, and his Social Security number.

"I need to probably get this in early in the morning," said Alston one afternoon, "because we having a hearing on it next week." Thurnell planned to speak on behalf of J.R.'s liquor-license application at the commission, but the paperwork needed to be in order before that time.

"Well, look here," said J.R., "you mind if I use your address as a mailing address?"

"No, I don't mind," said Alston.

"I'll have to call you back and give you my Social Security number. I couldn't find my darn wallet."

"Okay."

"What else do I need to do with this?"

"I don't think you need anything else."

"Now let me ask you, what about—now I didn't use my real name on that contract [to lease the building]."

"Uh huh."

"Now *that's* my real name, okay? That's what my driver's license and everything else is in."

"Okay, okay."

"Now what are you going to do? They going to go ahead and try to check my record?"

"Check the record out, okay?"

"So when they try to check my record, it's going to show some stuff on there now. You pretty sure you can handle that?"

There was a pause. Then Thurnell said, "Do we have something bad on there, with this name here?"

"Yeah, that's me."

"But as far as McIntosh County, there's nothing?"

"Not in McIntosh County, no."

"Okay."

"But I got some stuff in Georgia."

"Uh huh. Okay. But that's none of their business, in Georgia. We're only interested in McIntosh County, you know."

"Don't they check it statewide?"

"No, them guys, they just do a little thin check, you know."

"Well, see, when they stick my name in that computer, it's going to light up some lights up."

"Let me, let me, let me see what I can find out," said Thurnell, stammering.

"I'll call you in the morning and give you my Social Security number, okay?"

"Okay."

"See," said J.R., "what I'm really concerned about is make sure I can *get* the thing, *you* know."

"Okay."

"And *you* know if I have to spread a little money around, just you let me know."

"Okay, I'll do that."

J.R. learned that Alston was the county commission's contact person with the federal law enforcement agencies bringing the war against drugs into the county. At first taken aback, J.R. quickly saw how it might be useful. "That's all right man," said J.R. "So you're going to be up on that all the time, so there's not going to be any in-between. Somebody said something, you'll know directly."

"I'll know directly," agreed Alston.

"I'm not going to lie to you and tell you, you know, I don't handle the package of cocaine and stuff," said J.R. "I'm not going to lie to you." Then he questioned Thurnell closely about the federal agents with whom he'd met in Richmond Hill in his capacity as the leading antidrug commissioner.

"What the guy look like you met with? White guy, black guy?"

"White guy."

"Long hair or short hair?"

"Short hair, neatly dressed and all that."

"Dark or blonde?"

"Dark hair."

"Dark. Want to know who to look out for. All right man, just keep me up on all this."

At times their conversations were so cool, so understated, so closely adhering to the drug dealer's law not to name names or places, that it isn't clear whether *either* J.R. or Alston knew at any given moment precisely what the other was talking about. They sat for long hours in the air-conditioned twilight of interstate motel bars, their staccato talk interrupted by waitresses delivering drinks: Corona to J.R., Black Velvet to Alston.

"What I'm going to do is proceed with caution, *you* know, just like a caution light," said J.R.

"Yeah," said Alston.

"I just couldn't stand the heat, couldn't stand the heat."

By mid-April, Sheriff Lamar Echols was in possession of J.R.'s liquor-license application, birth certificate, Social Security number, and criminal record of marijuana convictions. Echols appraised J.R. as a typical midlevel drug dealer attempting to put down roots in McIntosh. Holding J.R.'s license application before him—with its obvious misstatements and with Thurnell Alston's address given as J.R.'s mailing address—the sheriff told J.R. he would not recommend approval of the liquor license to the county commissioners.

J.R. drove from the sheriff's office to the Alstons' with the bad news. Thurnell was momentarily taken aback, but suddenly wondered what *else* there was to know about J.R.: "You ain't got no record, nothing, in McIntosh County?"

"Unh unh, I ain't got nothing anywhere 'round here."

"You're not, you're not wanted, you're not wanted for murder?"

"Huh?"

"Could happen."

But J.R. reassured him: "I ain't wanted for none of that."

So Thurnell voiced his anger and disappointment with Sheriff Echols's office. "Now they don't worry about them crackers now. Them crackers bring the dope in the front door and then sell it *out* the front door. Big and bold. Don't worry about them crackers. They don't want, they don't want the black boys here to make no money . . ."

Since the final decision on licensing rested with the county commission—which could override the sheriff's recommendation if it saw fit—Thurnell coached J.R. on how to present himself to the commission. He dissuaded J.R. from trying to bribe outright any other commissioners. "The guy that applies for the license, commissioners will have to talk to him. You don't have to give them *nothing.* What kind of business you have in mind about operating—you can bring food in the front door, carry drugs out the back door—don't you say a damn thing about what you got in your mind of doing. You are running a drug-free business."

J.R.: "Huh?"

Alston: "That's all you're interested in, right?"

J.R.: "Yeah."

Alston: "'Cause man, they mess around, man. That's why I didn't come up with that idea about giving them nothing, okay? You start doing that, they say you bribing."

J.R.: "No, no—I wouldn't do that, *you* know, up front like that anyway."

Alston: "You don't need to be watched. You need to run a carefree business. I'll tell the cops, 'Anytime you come by there, I want you to do a periodical check on the grounds outside.' Let them know you're willing to work with the cops. Deep down within you ain't goddamn willing worth a damn, and they ain't going to do shit for you no way."

J.R.: "Oh. Okay."

Alston: "But don't let *them* know you know that shit. You tell them, 'I'm willing to work with the cops!'"

As the plot to obtain a liquor license reached its climax, so too did J.R.'s negotiations with Brennon over the purchase of a large quantity of cocaine. By March 1988, J.R. had entered into a buyer/supplier relationship with Irvin Brennon. He negotiated drug deals with him at the Alstons' kitchen table and relayed phone messages to him through Thurnell: "Tell Brennon I'm ready for those twins [two ounces]," said J.R., and Thurnell said, "Yeah. Okay."

At the asking price of $33,000 a kilo, J.R. ordered three kilos from Brennon. Brennon responded that one was all he could do. J.R. pressed him for three.

The Alston clan loved Brennon and felt protective of him. He was a man who, in virtually every public adult endeavor, found himself in over his head.

Brennon was not connected to a major drug distributor, although he enjoyed posturing as though he were; no one in the county besides J.R. believed him. Brennon, in fact, did not know how to procure such quantities of drugs as he had promised J.R.

J.R.: "Yeah man, my folk come down and I been with them trying, *you* know, to get the green straightened out."

Brennon: "Son of a bitch, I *told* him again yesterday. He said the only thing he could handle was one right now; he said he's stocking up, and he said he could let you have one."

J.R.: "Well, I thought three, *you* know."

J.R. promised Brennon he would return one Friday with the cash to purchase three kilos of cocaine. He persisted in believing that if Brennon reported to his people all the cash J.R. had in hand, he might wrangle two more kilos out of them.

On Friday, April 22, 1988, as promised, J.R. showed up at the Alstons' house. "Hey man," he said to Brennon, "I got something I want to show you while I was down here. It's good I caught you over here, man." He invited Alston and Brennon to take a ride with him.

At 2:30 P.M. he drove the two men to the Best Western at the I-95 exit and parked at the back of the lot, next to a parked car in which a new man waited. J.R. got out, spoke to the man, and was handed the keys to the trunk. He opened it and grandly displayed to Brennon and Alston $100,000 cash. "That's what I been doing all day, counting money," he said. "Yeah, you can look at it man, *you* know, make sure it's, *you* know, soup; $2,500 in each one of them, forty of them."

And for Thurnell, it was as if he suddenly woke up to find himself a county commissioner standing in a motel parking lot looking at drug money. His mute appearance in the presence of $100,000 in the trunk of a car effectively implicated him in a major drug conspiracy, and he suddenly sensed as much. Thurnell Alston viewed the money in silence and fright, and in silence and fright returned to J.R.'s car and got into the backseat.

"Irvin and I were sitting at the house, and J.R. came out and said, 'What's going on man?'" said Alston. "And I could sense there was something, I didn't know exactly what it was. I said, 'We are going to lunch.' He said, 'Yeah, we'll get lunch.' So we went out to the Best Western and he pulled around, made a circle, came around and there was a car parked. He said, 'Get out, get out.' So I hesitated for a while to get out. He got out first, got the keys from the guy in the car, and he came back and started to open the trunk. I was standing at the back of his car. In the trunk he zipped open a bag and said, 'See man, I got the money!' I was really stunned to see that money.

"I was just standing there, because I know for a fact they makes more busts out at the Best Western in that area with drugs than they do just about anywhere else. Because every now and then you find out they bust somebody in a room with the drugs, and here I am a commissioner, with a friend of mine, that says he's my friend, and he takes me out there to the Best Western for that kind of junk. And I just got in the car and I just sat there. It really stunned me.

"After he pulled off that, what I told him, I said, 'If this is the kind of business partner you are, we need to dissolve our business relationship because I don't go for taking me out to the Best Western in broad daylight. This looks like you're trying to set me up."

J.R. and Brennon, still negotiating over one kilo or three kilos, agreed to perform their drug transaction at the end of April.

On Thursday, April 28, J.R. drove to fetch Alston and Brennon again. He roamed through the county in search of them and located first one, then the other, by sighting their parked cars.

"I had stopped in Briarpatch," said Alston, "and was talking to guys there and I said, 'Well, I better go.' When I got ready to go, J.R. popped out there in front, say, 'I need to see you man, see what phase we in on the license.'

"I said, 'Well, the sheriff hasn't approved it. You *know* what phase we in with the license.'

"He say, 'Where you heading?'

"I say, 'Well, I'll go back to the house, and I'll talk to you.'

"I got in my car, drive back to my house, park it, got in the car with him, we rode back down the road. Sure enough, we come back down into Irvin. Irvin got in the car, and they talking about something."

J.R. told Brennon he had a "package" for him. Brennon said *his* package was due in town that evening. Another man, a stranger, sat in J.R.'s passenger seat, and Alston was already sitting in the back, so Brennon climbed into the backseat, too.

Alston said: "J.R. say, 'I'm going to get me a soda because I want some liquor.'

"I say, 'Well, I don't want no liquor.'

"He stop at the store—'Go get me a soda, you know.'

J.R. pulled into a Jiffy Mart on U.S. 17 to buy a soda. He and the other man got out of the car. Brennon and Alston decided to go buy a couple of sodas too; but when they attempted to get out, they found the back doors were childproof, locked from the outside. Annoyed, they struggled with the door handles. Suddenly, black and white men with guns ran out of the Jiffy Mart and surrounded the car. J.R. jerked open Thurnell's door and said, "Get down on your face, get down on your face, you're under arrest!" and the man from the passenger seat began a rapid-fire reading of Thurnell's Miranda rights. To hear suddenly the invocation of the Miranda warning from a man who, moments earlier, had appeared to be J.R.'s coconspirator took Thurnell's breath away.

"Getting Mirandized is the most depressing thing that can happen to an American citizen," said Don Samuel, then a criminal defense attorney in Atlanta. "They used to say, 'Cuff him,' or 'Spread 'em,' or 'Hands on the roof of the car.' Now they say, 'Sir? You have the right to remain silent . . .'"

"I was shocked to death," said Thurnell Alston.

"He stop at the store and got out the car. Irvin and I in the back. When I go to get out, J.R. come back and unlock my door, let me get out and say, 'Get down on your face!'

"I say, 'For what?'

"'Get down on your face! Get down on your face! You under arrest!'

"I say, 'I'm not getting down, not going nowhere.' So he got on my back. I say, 'You hurt my back any damn more, you damn sure pay for it, you hear?'

"So he goes, 'Don't put him down, don't put him down.'

"So I stood there the whole time; they put Irvin on the ground. And I say, 'Well, ain't that something new?' Then they holler out, 'Big bust!' A bust for what?"

Alston and Brennon were driven to the U.S. marshal's office in Brunswick, where they were fingerprinted, photographed, and incarcerated. Alston was held without bond. On May 3, 1988, he was indicted by the grand jury in the Southern District of Georgia on one charge of extortion [accepting bribes], one charge of conspiracy to distribute cocaine, two counts of possession and distribution of cocaine, and two counts of using a telephone to facilitate drug sales.

Thurnell said: "In the paper next day, they had, 'A Big Bust!' A big bust for what? There was no drugs involved, no nothing involved. And, they *could* have come to my *house* and said, 'Thurnell you under arrest.' Right? They didn't do that. They could have come down to Crescent where I was and say, 'You under arrest.' But they came all down through the community.

"I had told J.R. point-blank, 'Something we don't need no more of in McIntosh County, we don't need no more drugs, we don't need no more prostitutes. Those things we don't need in McIntosh County.' I told him point-blank, 'Now you want the club for teenagers, I'll do everything I can to help you. But I'm not going to jeopardize my life, my job, and my family for nothing that not legit. Period.'"

"He was set up," said Sammie Pinkney. "He was set up so pretty that it's unbelievable. But you don't go all sorts of funny places to accept money if it's legit. At some point Thurnell had to gather that something was going wrong. Hey, a man is just not going to constantly keep giving you that kind of money without looking for something. If a man says, 'I want you to do something and I'm going to pay you a thousand dollars a week,' and you *know* it's not worth a thousand dollars a week, you're going to start saying, 'Wait a minute, why *is* he paying me this kind of money?'

"He got caught into a situation he couldn't get out of. He was set up, he know he was set up, and him being a elected official."

J.R.'s real name was William R. "Billy" Carter. An Atlanta native, from a stable, middle-class background, he had completed three years of college before attending and graduating from the Atlanta Police Academy and the Georgia Bureau of Investigation (GBI) Academy. He began police work as a patrolman, became a detective and investigator, then received additional training in narcotics and undercover work. In other words, Billy Carter, alias J.R., was in McIntosh County in the fall and spring of 1987 and 1988 as an undercover agent for the GBI, developing a sting operation that had as its target McIntosh County Commissioner Thurnell Alston.

In a routine drug bust in the summer of 1987, a low-level dealer in the county had offered Alston's name as part of a plea-bargain agreement, saying Thurnell was a local official who could be bought. The FBI office in Savannah was given the file, and Billy Carter of the GBI was brought in to handle the joint FBI and GBI undercover investigation. Carter never spoke with Alston in person or over the phone that he didn't tape the conversation by tapping the phone or wearing a bugging device. His cash payments to Thurnell frequently were done within view of an unmarked van in which another agent operated a hidden video-camera.

When the microcassette tapes were played in court in Brunswick, the other voice—the natural voice—of Billy Carter was heard: a smooth, deep, distinguished, quiet, well-modulated voice, neither black nor white: "Special Agent W. R. Carter," spoke the unruffled, uninflected voice, "Tuesday, January 19, 1988, 4:25 P.M., contacting Thurnell Alston at his residence." The phone rang. Thurnell said, "Okay." Then the voice of J.R., loud, slurred, insinuating: "'Ay man, wha's up?"

"Nothing at all, man."

"Watcha been doing, man?"

"Oh, around here being busy."

"I hear you, I hear you."

"Yeah man, how you making it?"

"Oh shit, it's just, ah, you know, one thing after another, man."

"It is?"

"Yeah, yeah, man; I've been trying to do a couple of things, *you* know."

"I wasn't really streetwise—I didn't have that kind of upbringing," said Carter in Atlanta in 1989, then a private investigator, a security consultant, and a small-plane flight instructor.

"I had a middle-class upbringing. I could talk about business, current events, real estate. My sergeant took me under his wing to teach me about drugs. Today, I still can't play poker. I'm not good at gambling or 'skin,' a gambling card game. Sheriff Echols in McIntosh told me later: 'Man, I knew something was wrong; I didn't know if you were a real gangster—you were too smooth.' I took it to mean that whatever he wanted, I was just happy to go along with the project. He wanted a birth certificate and I produced it. Sometimes you need to be difficult.

"When people ask me, 'Aren't you a cop?'

"'Yeah, I'm a cop. I look like one don't I?'

"'Come on, man, come on, man, tell me the truth.'

"'That's the truth. I'm a cop.

"'Man you are not.'

"It looks glamourous, you know; people see me riding around in a nice car. They're not out at three in the morning on a dirt road, only help is a hundred miles away.

"I can't remember any investigation of any substance that I've lost—maybe a small marijuana case, two joints. I usually get guilty verdicts. But I always leave people a way out. At some point I'll create a little tension—'Hey look, you don't have to do this.' I might get mad and just leave—'Let's not do this, it isn't right.' Or, 'You just call me when you get ready.' It'll be a clear part on the tapes. U.S. Attorneys stress that in a federal case: 'Let's make sure it's something *he* wants to do.' With Alston, now, I used restraint. I could have implicated his wife as well, and I left her alone. I could have hooked in those boys.

"I had a guy who wanted to make a little bit of money—'Let me know when you want me to come do your big one.' I tell him, 'You don't really need to go with me, I can handle it.' 'No, I want to go!' His kids are sitting there, wife sitting there. He wasn't a drug dealer, just wanted to be present with the dope, with the big man. He knew all these people were making all that money, and he wanted just a little piece of it. I said, 'No man, I'm going.'

I knew we were going to take them down that night. 'Let me put my kid in! I'm with you,' he says. I remember the little kid in the window waving like this, opening and closing his little hand, saying, 'Bye-bye, Daddy.' It was a while before he saw his daddy again. We had to take him in, and the big dealer got convicted too—he'd been sitting down the road in his car like he had nothing to do with it. When we asked the big man to step out of his car, he said: 'I don't know anything about any cocaine.' He got ten years for those words—most costly seven words I ever heard. None of us had said a thing to him about cocaine."

"I hated the fact that it was a black commissioner," said Billy Carter. "But we had heard about Thurnell, if you were paying him, he'd do whatever. My conscience is clean as far as Thurnell. Thurnell Alston is not a bad person, he's a nice guy, good family life; he just happened to be doing something wrong. A lot of dopers are like that."

"Our confidential informant on Thurnell Alston was involved in some other drug transactions. Agents approached him: 'This is what we have on you.'

"'Okay, I want to help. I know this drug dealer, I know that drug dealer.' He became our main informant. I was introduced to him, worked with him, didn't like him. He whines all the time. One of the Brennons cut him up. I wouldn't trust him as far as my own safety was concerned.

"As our confidential source, he told us Thurnell Alston was involved with drugs. When a source tells you something, you ask, Well how do you know? Generally what happens during the course of an investigation, you hear something or see something and it goes into a confidential memo. People tell me things all the time. I say, 'Unh huh. How do you know?' If it's a public official, I'll put something in a confidential intelligence report. Any time a public official is bad and he turns up in your case, you write a confidential memo. Eventually someone will see it and ask, 'Who put this in there?' If something else comes up that is substantive, they'll review it: 'All these people are saying the same thing about this official. Do they know each other? No?'

"When our source said Thurnell is involved with drugs—how do you know? Just like when he told me the assistant police chief of McIntosh was trafficking, I didn't believe him. I didn't like him, didn't care for him. His information was accurate, but at first I was reluctant to believe him. Then the assistant police chief approached *me* one day asking how about this, how about that?

"When I first asked Thurnell how much and he said $1,200 every two weeks—well, that's the going rate, he didn't even respond ignorantly. He met with the DEA as a county commissioner concerned about drugs in the county—he made no effort to tell *them* about *me,* but he told *me* about *them.* He described them to me. He put DEA Agent Keller in a dangerous position if I'd been a real drug dealer.

"I wouldn't say the sting operation against Thurnell was racially motivated—no, they wouldn't have picked me, they would have brought someone in from the outside; it would have been hush-hush. I don't want to say the GBI is a racist organization, but it has its share; big-time has its share. I will say, though, that I think we could have expanded the investigation a little further. I think there were some other folks, some white officials, we could have looked at. I told my supervisor. But it comes out of Washington that you can run an investigation a certain number of weeks or months. With the white official, I got: 'Let's wait and see what he has to say.' From my point of view we were already in it; here's somebody we know; there's been enough people sitting there saying things. At my office, they heard exactly what I was saying, but didn't let me go ahead the way I needed to.

"I'll say it's run through my head that there were racial considerations at work, letting me pursue the two blacks, Alston and the black assistant police chief, and tying the purse strings when it came to the white, but I can't justify an affirmative answer on that.

"But my conscience is clean as far as Thurnell is concerned. I've told my boss this, will tell everybody he's a nice guy. He's a nice guy. But I always come back to Thurnell saying, "I've got a deal going now for fifteen."

"If he'd said $5,000 or $200 it might be a little questionable, but '$1,200 every two weeks.' I can tell something by looking at the expression on his face—looking up, kind of smiling, 'Hmmmm, make it *X* amount.'

"I don't think to this day that Thurnell used cocaine, but he always used to tell me, 'Hey man, these people around here use cocaine,' he'd hold up his Black Velvet, 'This my cocaine!' I used to pour mine out when I sat drinking with him. Those plants are probably drunk. I'd walk outside and water the plants. But there were days when he didn't drink, just as straight as he could be.

"He used county dump trucks to help private citizens. One guy said how Thurnell let him use the city landfill to pick up dirt. These people need money—they sell the dirt—but they didn't sell any dope, so are you going to prosecute these people for selling dirt? I don't think the county has lost a whole lot in Thurnell. I think they have plenty of good people to run for office.

"Is everyone ultimately corruptible? Thurnell took me to one of the other commissioners—Steve Jesup, white man, worked at the hardware store. He wouldn't have anything to do with me. Back at my office, they said, 'Go talk to him again.' I went back. He came right out and said, 'I don't like the sheriff, but I'm not going to go against him.' I told them at the office, 'He told me straight out that he's not going to budge.'

"But as I say, the county didn't lose much in Alston."

3

Thurnell maintained an attitude of shocked, appalled innocence throughout his arrest, indictment, and trial. He protested steadfastly that he had only wanted to see a teen center built in the county. "J.R. didn't never tell me anything about drugs. It was always about his license. It was never anything about his drugs!" he protested.

"Now when him and Irvin was getting together, he was giving Irvin money to hunt drugs for him. See, I didn't know that. I didn't know that. I mean, how could I know? I wasn't worried about it because Irvin had no money for no drugs. When Irvin *was* selling drugs, they cut him off. Nobody will sell Irvin no drugs."

Thurnell Alston never understood why this laissez-faire attitude on the part of an elected official irritated the jury and outraged the judge. Nor did Alston ever accept his lawyer's advice and instructions, which would have required him to acknowledge his guilt.

His attorney was Don Samuel, an old friend, a former paralegal in the GLSP office in Brunswick, and a former federal law clerk for U.S. District Judge Harold Murphy. Samuel was now a partner in a well-known Atlanta criminal defense law firm, the Garland Firm (later to become Garland & Samuel), where the senior partner was the charismatic Edward T. M. Garland, one of the South's most famous criminal defense lawyers and son of the flamboyant trial attorney Reuben Garland. The firm agreed to let Samuel handle Alston's case for a fraction of his usual fee.

Samuel hoped to argue entrapment: that the undercover agent virtually had forced Thurnell Alston into crimes he had not intended to commit. In order to use this defense, the defendant must introduce some evidence that he or she was not predisposed to commit the offense in the first place, and that the government agent used either trickery or undue coercion on him or her. The entrapment defense relies, from a practical standpoint, on a defendant's admitting that he or she committed the crime. This Thurnell refused to do.

Thurnell denied everything, declined to accept responsibility for his actions. The judge refused to allow the defense to argue entrapment because Alston failed to introduce sufficient evidence of undue persuasion. He had taken the bait too fast. Ten minutes into the tape of the first conversation with J.R.—"You mean . . . for *me?*"—Alston had expressed a willingness to accept money in exchange for political favors.

Thurnell pleaded his innocence from the stand. He testified eloquently but foolishly. Certainly he *felt* innocent, wished in his heart to be innocent, perhaps appeared before God as innocent; but to the judge and jury he appeared to be simply another corrupt black official.

Thurnell's defense on the bribery charge was that J.R. had told him they were business partners. J.R. had told him they might name the nightclub "Alston's." There is nothing illegal about accepting money from your business partner. But the vast majority of the tapes contradicted this theory. Clearly, J.R. was interested in purchasing Thurnell's vote and his influence, not his labor or business savvy.

To his family and friends at the trial, Alston appeared haggard, ill, shell-shocked. He raised the ethic of "it's none of my business" to a new eminence:

"Irvin said he sold him about two ounces first, sold him four ounces next," he testified. "I didn't know nothing about that. Period. I mean I figured if Irvin did it, he had to have a reason for doing it, but I didn't have no part of it. If Irvin do it, that's Irvin. I didn't have nothing to do with it."

Coming from a long-standing member of the board of commissioners, from the antidrug commissioner, and from a man who had represented so much to his community, this defense was paltry. Alston stood bravely on the stand in his old frilly outfit and stoically maintained his innocence. Into his voice entered that old hysterical, cracking, high-pitched note, the note of truth and of violation that had made people follow him. Rebecca and a couple of Thurnell's brothers and her sisters milled around in the linoleum foyer outside the tall, wooden doors of the freezing courtroom and leaned with indifference against a federal display of the Constitution of the type found in high school hallways. They drank Diet Cokes and tolerated the noisy high jinks of Becca's youngest sister, Joey. Inside the courtroom the voices of the men were swallowed up by the frosty, almost-tinny air and the roar of the air-conditioning blowers in the huge, somber room. Thurnell on the stand, dressed in white satin, appeared to be arguing into the abyss. He was cross-examined by Assistant U.S. Attorney for the Southern District of Georgia, William H. McAbee II.

McAbee: "Agent Carter told you he was messing with drugs on November 5th when he told you, 'I'm not going to lie to you, I'm going to deal packages of cocaine.'"

Alston: "That's when I got uninterested."

McAbee: "Uninterested in what?"

Alston: "Uninterested in helping him."

McAbee: "Good gracious, Mr. Alston! Isn't it true after that meeting, right after that, you took him to see Mr. Lane promoting his liquor application?"

Alston: "Yes."

McAbee: "You took him to see Mr. Jesup promoting his liquor application?"

Alston: "I did."

McAbee: "And you were losing interest?"

Alston: "What I was doing, he told me that and the sheriff also told me that he had an extensive record. So I said, 'Well, I have to play my part. Number one, he was paying me, so I took him to see Steve Jesup and David Earl Lane."

McAbee: "Do you recall the sheriff saying that you were promoting the application and he felt that he was being pressured by you?"

Alston: "That was the sheriff's opinion."

McAbee: "It was after you had lost interest you went out and made the arrangements for Mr. Mitchell to meet with him?"

Alston: "Because Mr. Mitchell said he could work a deal for the rental of the building."

McAbee: "But it was after you lost interest you did that?"

Alston: "Sure."

McAbee: "After you lost interest that's when you allowed him to use your address on the application?"

Alston: "He was still paying me."

McAbee: "It was after you lost interest you talked to him about how to conceal his record, and not put it on the application?"

Alston: "I never told him to conceal his record . . ."

McAbee: "The bottom line on this is if you had lost interest in the license all it would have taken was a phone call to the sheriff telling him this fellow's got a record for drugs, he ought not get a license?"

Alston: "No I wasn't going to do that because I promised him I would help him get a license."

Thurnell Alston was acquitted on the two charges alleging that he possessed, with intent to distribute, cocaine. But he was convicted of *conspiring* to possess, with intent to distribute, cocaine; and of two counts of using a telephone to facilitate a cocaine transaction—"Tell Brennon I'm ready for those twins"; and of one count of extortion, for violation of the Hobbes Act, which outlaws a public official from accepting bribes.

Under the new federal sentencing guidelines, enacted one day before J.R. had begun his sting operation, Alston's sentence was based on the amount of drugs involved in the conspiracy—

three kilograms, the amount negotiated between J.R. and Brennon. Oddly enough, when Brennon pleaded guilty in a different courtroom, his judge found that the conspiracy involved only one kilo of cocaine, and Brennon was sentenced on that lesser amount.

Thurnell Alston was sentenced to seventy-eight months in a federal prison camp, first in Montgomery, Alabama, and later thirty miles west of McIntosh in Jesup, Georgia. He should be released in late 1993.

The conviction was appealed to the U.S. Court of Appeals for the Eleventh Circuit. The appellate court rejected Alston's arguments about the unfairness of the jury selection process—that he was tried by eleven whites and one black—and the refusal of the trial judge to submit the issue of entrapment to the jury. It upheld the conviction.

"Thurnell by nature was a person who wanted to please," said Don Samuel. "The government argued that Thurnell was acting as a double agent, a "fox in the henhouse"; that he went to Richmond Hill to meet with the DEA so that he could warn the drug dealers in McIntosh of impending busts. The fact of the matter, though, is that Thurnell Alston just acted on a day-by-day basis. He did want to be a good county commissioner; he did want to lead the fight against drugs in the community; but the next day, literally, when a drug dealer came and asked for his help, he was equally accommodating.

"As in all sting operations, when you listen to the tapes and study them for hours and hours, you discover all kinds of incriminating 'unh hunh's' and incriminating silences; but you can't tell what a person was actually hearing or thinking at the time, how closely he was paying attention, how distracted he was, how drunk he was.

"When a person in a conversation repeatedly says, 'unh hunh,

unh hunh,' it usually means he's not paying the slightest bit of attention, not that he agrees with everything the other person is saying. But when a jury takes transcripts out, and they read: 'J.R.: "Let's sell cocaine." Thurnell: "Unh hunh,"' it makes a very different impression. It's a two-dimensional reduction of reality.

"Thurnell wanted to be a team player, and it simply didn't make a huge difference to him at that point who was giving orders. And I believe the money became truly alluring.

"But I also have problems," said Samuel, "with the allocation of federal resources that says let's go out and create a drug dealer and then arrest him. You'd think there was enough crime all around us to keep law enforcement agents busy, without their searching for a so-called weak link and pressuring him to transgress."

4

"When Thurnell went to jail, we all went to jail," wailed a woman from Sapelo Island, and her neighbors hummed their agreement.

"It just took a whole lot out of us," said Nathaniel Grovner. "The arrest took me totally by surprise. I was really shocked. It was just something, I guess, that he got caught up in. Life is rough. Life is rough."

Fanny Palmer, in great old age, from her bed to which she was confined, croaked, "My boy Thurnell okay? He doing okay?"

"I think he was entrapped," said David Earl Lane, commission chairman. "But he was also guilty."

"I think if you go throughout the county and took a sampling of public opinion, man-on-the-street type of thing, you would find shock and outrage to be the primary thread of feeling," said Buddy Sullivan, editor of the *Darien News*. "Here was a public official indicted for alleged misuse of office and that sort of thing and people were furious. Thurnell strikes me as being not a natural type of person to be a bad person or to do bad things; I believe he was a vulnerable type of person."

Vic Waters said, "When Thurnell got involved with Irvin Brennon and those guys got busted for the cocaine thing, it might have surprised his mama, but it didn't surprise me. Because too many times I've driven by the park out there and seen all those dudes leaning up against a truck, sitting there drinking that ninety head and, you know, talking that thing. He'd be out there. There's a big old oak tree out in Crescent, and all the black guys hang out around there when they're not working, and you'd see four homeless guys and Thurnell. When that deal came out, that didn't surprise nobody. Everybody said, 'Hey, THUR-nell got busted—I was wondering when that was going to happen, wasn't you?' That was the consensus in this neighborhood."

Chester Devillers, the black principal and city councilman, said, "People have ways of getting around you if you're not there. I still feel that, oh, people have meetings after you go to bed, they make plans when you're not there. It's not as bad as it used to be. We have voices now; we have young people who have come up, Thurnell Alston, for instance. This is why they struck him down. I don't say it was anyone's fault but his own, but he was an outspoken person, he didn't take no for the answer unless you proved to him it *was* no; he stood up. He didn't care anything about color, and people loved that about him. I'm proud of him, just sorry he made the mistake."

"I don't know what happened to Thurnell," said Gay Jacobs. "I really don't. It seemed as though power, or lust for power, or something changed him. And it's a very heady thing, and it happens to everybody. It's not anything to do with the races. That sort of thing has no regard for race. But it's embarrassing to pick up the newspaper and find your representative arrested. To pick up the Atlanta newspaper and there your county commissioner is on the front page makes us all look bad."

"Becky called me when she heard that he was arrested," said Louise Rasheed, "and she asked me had I seen Thurnell. And I said no, but she said, 'Did you see a certain car?'—I forget the color. She was trying to describe it to me. I said, 'Well, I was outside, because you know I'm usually outside when it's time to rake, but I made up my mind that I am not going to rake until this March.' So she said, 'You didn't see him? Well, let me tell you something. I have heard that they have arrested Thurnell.'

"I said, 'Arrested?'

"She said, 'Yes, but I don't know. I'm going to call the jail house.'

"I said, 'For what?'

"She said, "I don't know. Somebody just told me they arrest Thurnell down by the store.'

"So I said, 'If you hear anything call me, because I can't go out there because I have my grandkids.' And I think my children were sleeping at the time. But I said, 'My goodness, what is that?' I didn't know what it was about. Then when it came out in the paper, I couldn't get through to Becky. She called me back and told me they took him down to Kingsland [the Camden County jail], but she didn't know anything yet. When he did get out, I went over there with this paper and asked him different things, I asked him, and he said no, none of this was true."

Seventeen

"Head in the Lion's Mouth, Got to Ease It Out"

1

Becca abruptly was left with four children at home, a house being seized by the government as the locus of drug deals, and her only income, Thurnell's disability payments, terminated. She was crushed by shock and fear, sorrow and poverty. The warm community suddenly dropped away from her; she traveled to church alone with her stout, first-grade, pigtailed twins and sat alone in her pew, clutching their hands, and came home with scarcely a greeting or a kiss from anyone. Thurnell's people, in the cabins and trailers all around, didn't call or stop by or help with groceries or child care, and she grew more and more bitter and cocky. She relied on her own people. She took a job as a maid at Days Inn, where two of her sisters worked, out by I-95. The government seized her house as the locale of drug transactions, but Donald Samuel interceded with the judge and arranged for Becca to keep the house—which the Alstons had owned outright—and commence house payments to the government.

Margo and Michelle badgered her endlessly: "Where my daddy? My daddy ain't home yet?" They woke from nightmares about him, sobbing. He'd always been the one to check their schoolwork, so they stopped doing their schoolwork. "First time I took the girls down to see Thurnell in jail, they cried the whole time," said Becca. "Thurnell, the girls—don't know whose nose was running the most; they cried the whole time. I just stood looking out of the glass to keep myself from crying. When I took them the next time, Margo hold up pretty good, but Michelle didn't, so I thought each time I take them they get better and better. It is sad, honey, it is *sad.* Margo and Chelle so used to kissing him goodnight and hugging him goodnight. If you could see them on their knees praying, it'll break your heart. I tell them, don't forget to say your prayers, pray for your daddy. You listen at them say their prayers for their daddy, it'll break your heart: 'God, please send my daddy home,' and how much they love him, and they miss him, and they don't have a daddy no more to come home to, and asking the Lord please to send their daddy back home. Margo pray different from Chelle. Margo pray low. But Michelle she praying *out.* She have a loud voice. You can stand down the hall and hear that child praying. She pray different from any child I ever heard pray—six years old. They be saying their prayers ever since two years old. Then they get up in the bed. Chelle be between sleep and awake, she say, 'Good night, Mama!' then she say, 'Good night, Daddy, I love you!' See, I can't stay put then, have to start walking then. All you have to do is mention his name, and the water start rolling. Sometime I try not to mention his name, but they ask about him."

At school, children taunted the twins: "'Chelle and 'Go's daddy in *jail!*" They came home to report, "Titia say my daddy in jail, that's why I slapped her." Their clapping games, those intricate, singsong, face-to-face, patty-cake games played by little girls on the coast since slave times, reflected a new consciousness in their childish verses:

"Mama in the kitchen, burning rice
Brother on the corner, shooting dice.
Daddy in jail, raising bail.
Sister on the corner playing fruit cocktail.
Rocka Robin, tweet tweedle-dee-dee,

> *Rocka Robin, tweet tweedle-dee-dee.*
> *Daddy say you a doggone liar*
> *Mamma say you the FBI.*
> *Rocka Robin, tweet tweedle-dee-dee."*

"There is nothing for us anymore," said Becca coldly, speaking of her jailed husband a year after his prison time began. "I mean, I feel sad for him to be where he at, but there is nothing there for us anymore. I'm just sorry he had to get where he at to find out he love me. It's been five years since I feel close to him. It hurt me to see him in the position he in. Like I say, I love him, but it's not the love like I used to love him. I'm going to always have feelings for him on account I have kids from him. I told him I want to divorce him, but he goes to crying. Every time I mention Margo and Chelle's name, he go to crying. There's no feeling, no nothing for me. I been up there a few times, and every time I go up there I try to check my own self, I try to test myself, but it's very hard. There's nothing there for us. There's not going to be any more happiness in this marriage. The only thing in common is the kids. I told him, I say, 'Right now I prefer us being the way we are.' And he will not believe that the house is the federal government's. He's better off than I am, got a roof over his head, eating healthy food. I'm the one catching all the devil at this end. The main thing that worry me now is I'm not happy. It don't feel like I have any happiness in my life.

"But, you know, head in the lion's mouth, got to *ease* it out"—meaning she'll save herself and her children, but it will take time.

At the federal prison on the grounds of Maxwell Air Force Base in Montgomery, Alabama, Thurnell Alston rested for the first time in years and grew a beard, trimmed his hair short, and looked muscular, physically jaunty, serious, and sober. The moment he was taken into custody, he began to grieve for his lost son, Keith, and he mourned Keith and cried for Keith for the first time in the Camden County jail in Kingsland. His trial came and went, his reputation publicly was challenged and destroyed, his family was distraught; but he returned to his cell at night and sobbed for Keith. And for six months after he was incarcerated in federal prison, he continued to cry for Keith; then he was finished.

"I've lived with it and prayed about it and alone by myself now I cry about it, but it didn't happen until after I got here," he said. "That's when it really came out, when I got here. It seem like I worried more about my son when I came here than I did about Rebecca and the girls. And I never could understand that. But I was just definitely tired. I slept more in Camden County than I did for a long time. I was trying to keep everything together, I just didn't have time. Then after I got locked up, all of that—whoosh!—comes to you all at once. But I worked it out, and I got rid of it, and that was about it.

"I think of it as God took one but He gave me two, because Margo and Chelle, they were small. And when he got killed, they were really small. And I really didn't know what they was going to be like, because they was just babies. But I'm thankful for them, because something could have happened to both them *and* Keith. And I just thank the good Lord that he saw fit to take one and leave the others. I'm thankful for that. I learned by being more religious, you learn these things are going to happen in life. And everything that is done in life is done for a purpose. I believe I'm here for a purpose, that God couldn't get me straightened out back home and needed to just remove me from all that for a time."

2

Deep in the black county, off the road and far from corruption, the people have their own way of taking in and understanding events. Deep in the county, the hand of God is perceived behind the ups and downs in the lives of individuals. Already the story of the rise and fall of Thurnell Alston has begun to be told in a parablelike rhythm. "We got to lean on the Lord," said Florine Pinkney. "You just got to give Him the sense of your heart, let Him know you need Him to do something for you and He'll take care of it."

The story of Thurnell Alston resembles, to the wise old people, a story that Deacon Curry used to tell. It was his finest story, the story it took his whole lifetime to perfect. Deacon Curry's story expresses the belief that human beings control their own fate, but that they do so within a world imbued by God with meaning, direction, and goodness.

The frail, rheumy-eyed gentleman near the end of his long life, in his chair by the front window, said in his fine, clear, deep voice:

"The Bible say, 'Be not deceived. God is not mocked. Whatsoever man sow, that shall he reap. The bread that cast upon the water, after many days it return.'

"In 1905, when I was quite a kid, there was an old man with an ox, he went down to the riverfront. The bank was steep then, around ten or twelve feet. The old man take and tie his ox and leave his cart there, and went on his boat on into the river. Me and my first cousin went down there and looked, didn't see nobody, and take that man's wagon and dump it right down that steep hill.

"In 1971, I was shrimp fishing in a bateau, a fifty-horsepower motor on the boat, twenty-five gallons of gas, my nets, my tools, and all. The weather was calm. I went down one evening and anchored out there. Later that evening, after I'd gone home, a friend saw white mens bending over where my bateau was, and when he come 'round the bend, they run back up the hill. So when I went down there next morning, I saw they'd taken that bateau and turned it upside down in the river.

"I went and got my friend. I say, 'You know how come this bateau is over here?' He say, 'The white mens?' I say, 'Tommy, I throwed a old man's wagon down a hill sixty-six years ago, and it come back to me now plain to think how I did it.'

"The next one: One day I went down a road and there was a house there. A preacher lived there who used to make nets for the shrimp boats. So I come in there and I stop. There was a wind blowing from the southeast, and I see something down there like that, and I look, and it was a hundred-dollar bill. I take that bill and put it in my pocket. I walk up to that house and say, 'Hey, Reverend, you miss anything?'

"He say, 'No, no, not to my knowing.' He run his hand in his pocket. He say, 'Wait a minute.' He walk in the house, come back, say, 'No, I ain't lost nothing.'

"I say, 'Here, I pick that up right here, just now.'

"He say, 'Yeah, yeah, I remember now, that is mine. And I thank you for it.'

"The next year I come through here to sell some shrimp to a restaurant down here. I bring some of mine in a truck and some for a friend of mine. The man paid me for mine, but I tell him, 'Don't pay me Jesse's money. Give me a slip for the amount of it; he come on Sunday to get his money.' I was late getting back, so I say I'll give the receipt to him at the landing the next morning. I was at the landing four o'clock the next morning. Jesse come to my truck, I turn the light on, take out my billfold, all right, get him the slip, his receipt.

"About twelve o'clock we were about fifty miles from the landing. I seen a man coming to me, say, 'All right, Cap'n, how you feel?'

"I say, 'I feel all right, how you feel?'

"He say, 'I feel all right,' say, 'I got something for you.' I ask him what he had, and he run his hand in his pocket. He come back out, he say, 'That the billfold you left on Jesse truck this morning.' And I had $335 in it.

"So the same way I did that man with his'n, it come back to me. Now he could have kept that; I wouldn't have known. I would have said I dropped that billfold in the river. The good that you do for someone, that good will come back to you. And the evil that you do will return.

"The next one was in 1916. I was a grown man then, got married. I was on my way to Savannah to pick up a load of freight, and my mother give me a basket of eggs to carry and sell. Most of them was duck eggs. I get to Thunderbolt dock, before Savannah, and I went in the shop there because I didn't want to carry the eggs into town or get on the street to sell the eggs. I thought I'd stop and sell them there. The man was Sam Byrd. I say, 'Mr. Byrd, do you want to buy some eggs?'

"He say, 'No, but let's look at them.' So I handed him the basket. He say, 'Ooooh! What lovely eggs! These duck eggs, ain't they?'

"Well, that the quickest lie I ever tell. 'No sir,' I say, 'them chicken eggs.'

"He say, 'Where you get a chicken lay such eggs as that?'

"I say, 'I got them eggs from the captain on Catherine Island.'

"He say to his wife, 'Honey, let's buy these eggs and *get* that breed of chicken. I'll look after them, and we'll get a *extra* breed of chicken.'

"She say, 'All right.'

"I say, 'Thank God I don't live *here.* When them eggs hatch they going to be looking for a extra breed of chicken and they all going to be ducks. And I'll be gone—about sixty-three miles back this way.'

"So we come on back. That was 1916. In 1928, twelve years later, I come out of the river, and there was a man there from Gainesville, Georgia. Says to me, 'Uncle, you want to buy some trees?'

"I say, 'What kind of tree it is?'

"He say, 'Plum.'

"I say, 'What kind of plum?'

"He say, 'Japanese plum.'

"I say, 'Yeah, how you sell them?'

"He say, 'Them tallest ones is twenty-five cent apiece. If you buy the three large ones, I'll give you the small one.'

"I say, 'All right.' So I paid the price. And I say, 'Now listen, I sold a man some duck eggs once for some chicken eggs. This ain't the same thing is it?'

"He say, 'Oh no!' and he went in the car and got a pamphlet and come back and show me the picture. I said, 'I just wanted to tell you what I did.'

"When I got home I told the wife and she said, 'Let's look after them.' She say, 'You ain't got no Japanese plum!'

"I say, 'Yeah it is.'

"She say, 'No you ain't.'

"I say, 'He show me the picture of it.'

"She say, 'That nothing. You ain't got no Japanese plum.'

"I say, 'I got a good mind to set it out and we'll tell.'

"The third year they bear. Them little hog plums. Will cut your throat, so sour when you go to eat it. See? The same way I sell that man a duck egg for chicken egg, he sell me hog plum for Japanese plum. That just what the Bible say. Reap just what you sow. So many things I've did come back indirectly, but these come back directly, just like how I did it."

In like manner, the life of Thurnell Alston is at this moment being transformed and suffused with meaning, stitched into the quilt of the county's age-old oral history, the stories reaching back into slave times. This quilt is pulled out and shaken and reworked while the black people saw the trees, haul in the fish nets, peel the shrimps, sit side by side in the cinder-block juke joints, and circle the smoky grills of backyard barbecue pits, balancing babies and full paper plates.

3

In September 1989 an election for the post of superintendent of education was held in McIntosh County. Two candidates ran, a white woman, Carol Clayart, and a black woman, Evella Brown, and an at-large election was held.

"I voted for Evella Brown," said Vic Waters. "I voted for her because of her qualifications. I've got friends, one of my very best friends voted for Carol Clayart for the very simple reason that she was white: 'I ain't voting for Evella Brown, you can believe that!'

"And I said, 'Why, man? She's the only one qualified to run.'

"And he said, 'Are you crazy? You want a nigger running the *school system?*'

"And I said, 'Man, first thing you got to do is understand that 'nigger' is not a color, it's a state of mind. I know plenty of white people I wouldn't let come in my house. If you can learn that, you know . . .'

"But he can't learn that because his daddy told him different, and his daddy before him told him different, and his daddy before that."

Chester Devillers, the retired mayor pro tem, said, "There are still too many bigots and racists among both black and white. It has gotten somewhat better, but we still haven't arrived. We have a long way to go. Some people feel we should never have integrated, that we should have worked on making things equal. We were separate, but we never would have been equal. There are people here today who are not totally pleased with integration, and I guess they never will be. But if they can just leave the young children alone, integration will do some good. My philosophy has been in order for me to get the same food, I have to sit at the same table."

Evella Brown won the election.

And a black man replaced Thurnell Alston on the county commission for the Crescent district. And another black man displaced a longtime white county commissioner in a racially mixed voting district; a black woman runs the tourism office; a black woman teller works in the Darien bank. Van Alston graduated from his integrated high school with honors, joined the military, and served in Saudi Arabia. Fanny Palmer's grandson, educated in New York, runs the presses at the *Darien News.*

Of course, it is not enough, but it is a beginning. The descendants of the Scottish settlers start to view the descendants of the African slaves not as aliens in their midst, and not as servants, but as neighbors, colleagues, partners, fellow Americans, and increasingly, as leaders, as a rich human community without whom McIntosh County—financially, among the poorest counties in Georgia—would be halved, bereft, and truly poorer than any chart could document.

Meanwhile, it is peaceful again in McIntosh County and very quiet, except in the hummingbird season.

Acknowledgments

Thank you to the McIntosh County citizens who shared their time and their stories with me, especially Thurnell and Rebecca Alston, Nathaniel Grovner, and Sammie Pinkney; to the law enforcement agents who were generous with their records, photographs, and recollections, especially Police Chief Bill Kicklighter; and to my former colleagues in Georgia Legal Services Program, especially Mark Gorman, David Walbert, and Thomas Affleck. Many thanks to David Black of David Black Literary Agency, whose high-pitched voice, full of news, always was a joy to hear on the answering machine, not to mention in real life. Thank you to Heather Lantz and Marty Hagen, who helped transcribe the tapes and who offered telling insights. Thank you to Martha Moutray, former senior editor at Addison-Wesley, who responded with enthusiasm to the proposal for this book and who gently led me and an eight-hundred-page manuscript into the world of editorial cuts. And thanks to Jane Isay, editorial director, who closed the door of her executive office and sat with me and a set of pruning shears, cutting and taping and laying out chapters across the carpet in the best kind of old-fashioned editing. Thank you to my husband, Don Samuel, my classmate in college, my colleague in GLSP, and my equally enchanted partner in raising our three children. He produced files, court documents, anecdotes, and legal theories, and offered a score of helpful suggestions on the book, which meant a lot, coming from a man whose idea of leisure reading is *West's Federal Case News*. Thank you, thank you, thank you, Molly, Seth, and Lee Samuel! And thanks finally to the good friends and relations who wished me well.